DAVID MORALES
RHODE ISLAND STATE REPRESENTATIVE D7
A Kid From Soledad Making History

Edited By

Tomás Alberto Ávila

Milenio Publishing
Providence, Rhode Island

© 2021 Tomás Alberto Ávila. All Rights Reserved. All rights reserved.

This book or any portion thereof may not be reproduced or used in any manner whatsoever without the express written permission of the publisher except for the use of brief quotations in a book review or scholarly journal.

First Printing September 2022

Published by
Milenio Latino Institute, Inc.
Providence, Rhode Island
tavila@mileniolatinoinstitute.org

ISBN 978-1-928810-43-8

Library of Congress Catalog Card Number: Pending

Printed in the United Stated of America.

Table of Content

Table of Content 3

Meet David Morales 13

Protecting And Expanding Healthcare 15
Fighting Against Cuts to Medicare 15
Lowering Prescription Drug Cost 16

Representative David Morales Bio 23

Member, House Innovation, Internet and Technology Committee 23

Member, House Municipal Government and Housing Committee 23

Today, I officially declared! 24

Today, I officially voted for myself 26

Yesterday, over 500 of our neighbors showed up to vote because they believe in systemic change. 28

This is really thrilling! David won this race with his incredible work ethic. 29

Almost six years ago you walked through the doors of my classroom. 30

The future of RI politics? A more-diverse General Assembly 31

Youngest elected Black & Brown Candidates 41

Soledad native wins State Representative seat in Rhode Island 42

Guided by grassroots advocacy, David Morales MPA'19 will now enter R.I. State House 44
Inspired by Sen. Bernie Sanders (I-VT) 45
Advocacy and the push to run for office 46
The campaign trail 46
Issues and policy ideas 47

There is a political revolution happening in our State .. 50

3

Rhode Island Progressives Won Big in 2020 With Help From Youth Activists _____ 52

Rep. Morales sworn in as General Assembly convenes __ 55

Caucus Vote Abstention _____ 56

There's a lot revolving around Rhode Island's air space today. _____ 57

That's my friend and (now) State Representative in the Rhode Island General Assembly, David Morales! _____ 59

This past week has been an emotional one. On Tuesday, I was officially sworn to the RI House of Representatives. _____ 61

Former Soledad resident takes office as state representative in Rhode Island _____ 65

RIMEO Elected Officials _____ 68

Monterey County to Honor 50th Anniversary of Local Landmark Case That Ended Use of Discriminatory IQ Tests Against Latino Children in California! _____ 69

Just a kid from Soledad making history. David Morales _ 72
    What motivated you to go to college? _____ 74
    What motivated you to run for state assembly? _____ 74
    U.S. Rep. Alexandria Ocasio-Cortez, is a breakout young elected official who has become a national celebrity. What do you think of her and her rise _____ 74
    Why did you stay in Rhode Island instead of coming back home to Soledad? _____ 75
    What would you like to say to teenagers and young adults from Soledad _____ 75

Very important town hall that David Morales and Sam Bell are hosting 👀 💯 _____ 76

Sunday Funday _____ 77

Fortunate to have friends and acquaintances _____ 80

Morales introduces bills to address prescription drug costs _____ 81

Please to see Newly Elected Black & Brown Legislators drafting Community based Legislation, as opposed to the typical Funders & Special Interest legislation. _____ 83

Sen. Bell, Rep. Morales raise concerns about SMART clinics in Providence Schools _____ 84

Morales to serve on committees on Municipal Government and Housing; Innovation, Internet and Technology _____ 86

HB #5151 which would limit out-of-pocket expenses for Insulin at $25 for a 30-day supply. _____ 87

Morales bill would prohibit utility shutoffs during declared emergencies _____ 88

THIS young man gives me hope for the future! _____ 92

House Bill #5442 _____ 93

Outside the Lillian Feinstein Senior Center with David Morales _____ 95

Mexicanos en Rhode Island, unidos, jamás serán vencidos. _____ 96

The Rhode Island Legislative Black & Latino Caucus Book _____ 97

The Need Behind H-5781 Establishing An Elected And Appointed Minority Officials Commission _____ 98

Thank You very much For sponsoring bill H-5781 _____ 100

The freshman House Reps dropping an album soon what should we name it? _____ 102

Tomás Ávila Legislative Testimony _____ 103

A Flippable Rhode Island 2022 Budget _____ 104

Morales and Cano bill would ensure all children have health care coverage regardless of status _____ 105

Capitol Spotlight: Representative David Morales with Margie O'Brien _____ 111

March 17, 2021 _____ 111

Eight Months After Posting 115

Ray-ality TV Episode 10: State Representative David Morales (D-Dist. 7) 116

MEDIA ADVISORY: Legislators to participate in Third Annual RI Multilingual Education Advocacy Day tomorrow, March 23 143

Vaccines are now available for ALL 18+ Providence 144

Rhode Island's Act on Climate bill passes House, 53-22 .. 145
    2021 -- H 5445 SUBSTITUTE A 149
    2021 -- H 5151 149
    2021 -- H 5218 149

The Progressives have won the Democratic Ideological Battle 167

In leftward move, RI Democrats hire progressive strategist to modernize the party 168

USHCC Virtual Legislative Summit on March 30-31, 2021 171

PCTA 172

Morales and DiMario file bill to prohibit insurers from imposing cost-sharing for COVID services during emergency 178

Rhode Island's youngest state legislator: An advocate for the working class 184

    So who is the man behind the mask? 186

    "Our goal was always to make our mom proud," Morales said. 186

    Community Service 190

3 years ago, I was running for City Council and David was one of my amazing volunteers. Today, I'm Mayor and he is the elected State Rep in Rhode Island! 195

Call Speaker Joseph Shekarchi (401) 222-2447 and tell him we are sick of paying taxes for colleges and now high schools???? 197

Rhode Island Interfaith Coalition to Reduce Poverty ___ 198

Rhode Island 2030 _____ 204

"vale la pena _____ 207

Neighbors, this has been a heavy week of emotions in our City of Providence as we experienced multiple shootings and a scandal in our Providence Public Schools_____ 211

2021-H 5130A, 2021-S 0001aa Raising the Minimum Wage to $15.00 _____ 212

Overdose" Prevention Site" display model yesterday. ___ 216

It is so important that our community take pride in the neighborhood we live in! _____ 219

RI State Representative David Morales and Sen. Sandra Cano will be joined by community advocates at a State House even _____ 221

RI State Representative David Morales is sponsoring legislation to protect Rhode Islanders from workplace bullying and harassment. _____ 222

Media Advisory: Event slated Thursday to push for 'Cover All Kids' bill to expand Medicaid to all children, regardless of immigration status _____ 238

2021-H 5714 _____ 239

It was great to be back on the House Floor yesterday! Looking forward to the rest of the session! _____ 243

Flanked by advocates, Morales and Cano call for passage of bill to expand Medicaid to 'Cover All Kids' _____ 244

A few months ago when session first started, Senator Sandra Cano and I introduced legislation (Cover all Kids) to expand healthcare coverage to ALL low-income children in our State, regardless of immigration status. _____ 247

What an honor to be surrounded by amazing leaders! _249

Last week, we unanimously passed HB #5196 to limit monthly out-of-pocket expenses for Insulin at $40 — one of the lowest rates in the entire country! _____ 253

Legislation to ensure that all low-income children, ____ 254

Introduced and passed a resolution thanking our Senior Centers _____ 257

Thank you again to all our community members who came together to clean our Valley neighborhood! _____ 260

Fue un fin de semana de mucha ayuda voluntaria y inversión comunitaria en nuestras comunidades de Providence. _____ 263

House passes bill prohibiting insurers from charging copays for COVID services and vaccines _____ 264

House passes bill prohibiting insurers from charging copays for COVID services, vaccines _____ 266

As we continue to recover from COVID-19 _____ 269

RI State Rep Wants Less Money in Budget for New State Police Barracks, More for Children's Health _____ 273

Hi neighbors, tomorrow (6/24) our State Legislature will be voting on the State Budget for this year. _____ 275

   June 23, 2021 _____ 275
      I. Medicaid: _____ 275
      II. Affordable Housing: _____ 275
      III. Public Education: _____ 276
      IV. Social Services and Programs: _____ 276
      V. An Overview of Taxes: _____ 277
      VI. Funding for Providence via PILOT Program: _____ 277

House approves 2022 state budget bill _____ 279

   June 24, 2021 _____ 279

General Assembly OKs bill prohibiting insurers from charging copays for COVID treatments _____ 285

   June 25, 2021 _____ 285

Black & Brown Leadership 2020-2040 _____ 298

Black & Brown Leadership 2020-2040 The Future of Rhode Island Political Transformation _____ 298

Liderazgo & Negro y Latino 2020-2040 _____ *302*

Liderazgo latino 2020: honrando nuestro pasado, nuestro presente y liderando nuestro futuro _____ 302

About Tomás Alberto Ávila _____ *321*

Dear Rep Morales'

Congratulations on a successful 2020 election season, and a very successful and productive 2021 Legislative se.

Although I have not had the pleasure of meeting you personally, I've been a fan of yours and your eventual 2020 campaign since I heard about you in 2018 by a former D7 candidate who described you as very smart, and very smart and ready to legislate if you decided to seek elected office, and sure enough you prove it right/

I

State Representative David Morales

David Morales

RI State Representative for District 7 (Mt. Pleasant, Valley, Elmhurst).

www.DavidMoralesRI.com

- Studied at **Brown University**
- Studied at **University of California, Irvine**
- Lives in **Providence, Rhode Island**

Meet David Morales

I was raised by a single mother in poverty and I understand the struggles working families experience.

I know how hard you have to work to get ahead because at a young age I quickly realized how stacked the deck is against regular people. At 16, I started doing farm labor to help support my family. In high school I took college courses at night, graduated from college at 19, and got my Masters in Public Policy from Brown University at age 20. For many this would be the "American Dream," but I still struggle to pay my bills, much less, invest and save for a future.

For too long, the wealthy and well-connected in Rhode Island have gotten their way with state policy, winning tax-cuts and special favors. Meanwhile, far too many families in our neighborhood are struggling due to low wages, the rising costs of living, and the impact of COVID-19.

We need to end corporate welfare and put people first in our policies.

We can't continue neglecting our roads, schools, public health, and affordable housing stock.

I am prepared to work hard and help our community recover from COVID-19 together.

We need bold action that includes: Hazard Pay, Small Business Relief, and a Moratorium
on Evictions.

I'm incredibly proud to not accept any donations from: Corporate PACs, Corporate Lobbyists, the Fossil Fuel Industry, and other special interests that have corrupted our government. Instead, I'm focused on empowering working people and ensuring that we are the ones being represented at the State House.

Take care, I look forward to meeting you!

¡DAVID MORALES!
STATE REPRESENTATIVE DISTRICT 7

I was raised by a single mother in poverty and I understand the struggles working families experience. I know how hard you have to work to get ahead because at a young age I quickly realized how stacked the deck is against regular people. At 16, I started doing farm labor to help support my family. In high school I took college courses at night, graduated from college at 19, and got my Masters in Public Policy from Brown University at age 20. For many this would be the "American Dream," but I still struggle to pay my bills, much less, invest and save for a future.

For too long, the wealthy and well-connected in Rhode Island have gotten their way with state policy, winning tax-cuts and special favors. Meanwhile, far too many families in our neighborhood are struggling due to low wages, the rising costs of living, and the impact of COVID-19.
We need to end corporate welfare and put people first in our policies.
We can't continue neglecting our roads, schools, public health, and affordable housing stock.

I am prepared to work hard and help our community recover from COVID-19 together. We need bold action that includes: Hazard Pay, Small Business Relief, and a Moratorium on Evictions.

I'm incredibly proud to not accept any donations from: Corporate PACs, Corporate Lobbyists, the Fossil Fuel Industry, and other special interests that have corrupted our government. Instead, I'm focused on empowering working people and ensuring that we are the ones being represented at the State House.

Please contact me if you ever need any assistance or if you have any questions/ideas on how we can improve our neighborhood and state.
Take care, I look forward to meeting you!

As our State Representative, I'm focused on improving the standard of living in our neighborhood.

Mt. Pleasant, Valley, and Elmhurst are diverse communities and it is important all our neighbors receive the representation they deserve. From working families to our aging seniors, we will not leave anyone behind!

Protecting And Expanding Healthcare

No one in our community should have to worry about whether or not they can afford to visit the doctor. Unfortunately, I have spoken with hundreds of our neighbors who have shared personal stories about their medical debt or inability to visit their primary care provider because of how expensive healthcare is.

I believe healthcare is a human right and I am going to fight so all our neighbors can receive the treatment they deserve, regardless of their economic background.

As your State Representative, I will unapologetically advocate for:

Fighting Against Cuts to Medicare

Over the last few years, Rhode Island has continued to cut Medicaid from the state budget (in 2016 alone, we cut more than $70 million from the program). This has led to the closure of state hospitals, nursing homes, and other primary care providers. At the same time, co-pays for Medicaid recipients continue to increase.

It does not have to be this way. Instead of spending tax-dollars on "management consultants" and the privatization of government services; we can stop cutting Medicaid and further expand access to the program. **When I am at the State House, I will vote against any budget cuts to Medicaid and advocate for further expansion.**

Lowering Prescription Drug Cost

Each year, prescription drug prices continue to increase, forcing working families and our senior citizens to choose between paying for their medication, rent, or groceries. This is not an exaggeration as I have spoken with dozens of senior citizens who tell me they have either reduced their fillings or stopped taking their medications completely because of how expensive it is.

Our state government has the ability to address the greed of the pharmaceutical industry and it is an urgent issue we have to act on. **When I am at the State House, I am going to fight for:**
- Limiting Monthly Co-Pays on Prescription Drugs
- Establishing a "Prescription Drug Affordability Board" -- an independent body with the authority to negotiate with drug companies and establish fair drug costs

A FAIR ECONOMY FOR EVERYONE

We deserve a fair economy that allows everyone to earn a living wage, achieve economic mobility, and live with dignity. For too long, wealthy people and large institutions have gotten their way with state policy, winning tax-cuts and special favors. Meanwhile, our middle-class families, working families, and low-income communities are struggling due to the rising costs of living and stagnant wages.

As your State Representative, I will unapologetically advocate for:

Fighting Against Cuts to Medicaid

Over the last few years, Rhode Island has continued to cut Medicaid from the state budget (in 2016 alone, we cut more than $70 million from the program). This has led to the closure of state hospitals, nursing homes, and other primary care providers. At the same time, co-pays for Medicaid recipients continue to increase.

It does not have to be this way. Instead of spending tax-dollars on "management consultants" and the privatization of government services; we can stop cutting Medicaid and further expand access to the program. **When I am at the State House, I will vote against any budget cuts to Medicaid and advocate for further expansion.**

f 🐦

Lowering Prescription Drug Costs

Each year, prescription drug prices continue to increase, forcing working families and our senior citizens to choose between paying for their medication, rent, or groceries. This is not an exaggeration as I have spoken with dozens of senior citizens who tell me they have either reduced their fillings or stopped taking their medications completely because of how expensive it is.

Our state government has the ability to address the greed of the pharmaceutical industry and it is an urgent issue we have to act on. **When I am at the State House, I am going to fight for:**

- Limiting Monthly Co-Pays on Prescription Drugs
- Establishing a "Prescription Drug Affordability Board" -- **an independent body with the authority to negotiate with drug companies and establish fair drug costs**

f 🐦

Supporting our Nursing Homes

Our nursing homes are suffering from staff shortages, a lack of personal protective equipment, and inadequate support. As a result, Rhode Island has the lowest average number of 'care hours' in all of the New England Region. Our seniors deserve to be cared for with dignity and respect! That is why I fully support the efforts of "Raise the Bar on Resident Care" (a coalition of nursing home caregivers, clergy members, community partners, nursing home residents and family members working to end the staffing crisis in Rhode Island nursing homes). **When I am at the State House, I am going to fight for:**

residents and family members working to end the staffing crisis in Rhode Island nursing homes). **When I am at the State House, I am going to fight for:**

- Safe Staffing Regulations
- A state budget that provides nursing homes with an adequate funding stream strictly for resident care and staffing purposes
- A minimum standard of 4.5 hours of resident care per day (slightly above the federal recommendation for quality care)
- Higher wages for caregivers and healthcare workers (no caregiver and/or healthcare worker should have to work multiple jobs to make ends meet)

f 🐦

Achieving Universal Healthcare

Even if you have health insurance this does not necessarily mean you have access to affordable healthcare. There are thousands of neighbors in our community, who have health insurance from their employer or a private provider, but still do not receive the care they need because of how expensive it is. In between health insurance premiums, co-pays, and deductibles -- it is no wonder why so many of our neighbors are "underinsured".

We need a more efficient healthcare system that will guarantee coverage to everyone and will be more cost-effective for our local businesses. **When I am at the State House, I am going to fight for a universal healthcare system that:**

- Removes the burden of healthcare on employers
- Reduces government spending on administrative costs and shifts these dollars to the actual provision of healthcare
- Eliminates out-of-pocket healthcare expenses for working and middle-class residents
- Provides comprehensive healthcare to ALL Rhode Islanders

f 🐦

A FAIR ECONOMY FOR EVERYONE

We deserve a fair economy that allows everyone to earn a living wage, achieve economic mobility, and live with dignity. For too long, wealthy people and large institutions have gotten their way with state policy, winning tax-cuts and special favors. Meanwhile, our middle-class families, working families, and low-income communities are struggling due to the rising costs of living and stagnant wages.

As your State Representative, I will unapologetically advocate for:

ADVOCACY EFFORTS

Since being elected in September of 2020, I have used my platform as a State Representative to advocate for the changes our neighborhood deserves and help elevate important issues happening across our state.

On this page you will find some of the issues I've been advocating for.

As always, please contact me if you have ideas about any issues and/or areas that I should be focusing on.

Thank you for being engaged!

Opposed State Budget Cuts that would hurt Providence

David spoke at a press conference to publicly oppose Governor Raimondo's proposal to cut state funding for "distressed communities" (Providence, Pawtucket, Cranston, and others).

Advocated against National Grid Rate Hikes during COVID-19

David wrote a letter to the Public Utilities Commission demanding that they reject National Grid's proposal to raise utility rates during the COVID-19 pandemic. These rate hikes would increase utility bills by nearly $11 a month.

Opposed State Budget Cuts that would hurt Providence

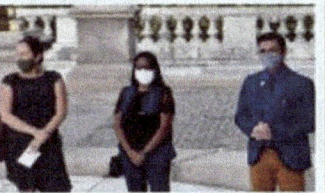

David spoke at a press conference to publicly oppose Governor Raimondo's proposal to cut state funding for "distressed communities" (Providence, Pawtucket, Cranston, and others).

Advocated against National Grid Rate Hikes during COVID-19

David wrote a letter to the Public Utilities Commission demanding that they reject National Grid's proposal to raise utility rates during the COVID-19 pandemic. These rate hikes would increase utility bills by nearly $11 a month.

Opposed State Budget Cuts that would hurt Providence

Advocated against National Grid Rate Hikes during COVID-19

David wrote a letter to the Public Utilities Commission

Opposed State Budget Cuts that would hurt Providence

David spoke at a press conference to publicly oppose Governor Raimondo's proposal to cut state funding for "distressed communities" (Providence, Pawtucket, Cranston, and others).

Advocated against National Grid Rate Hikes during COVID-19

David wrote a letter to the Public Utilities Commission demanding that they reject National Grid's proposal to raise utility rates during the COVID-19 pandemic. These rate hikes would increase utility bills by nearly $11 a month.

Advocated for Hazard Pay for All Lifespan Healthcare Workers

David wrote a letter to Lifespan Health urging that they provide immediate Hazard Pay to all their frontline healthcare workers.

Opposed the State's Proposal to Break up Kennedy Plaza

David protested and spoke out against the RI Department of Transportation's proposal to remove buses from their central location (Kennedy Plaza) using voter-approved bond money.

Fought Against CCRI and RIC Layoffs Affecting More than 70 Workers

David joined other legislators to demand that the Community College of RI (CCRI) and Rhode Island

Called for Action in Response to COVID Outbreak at ACI Facilities

David joined a coalition of advocates and other legislators to demand that the Governor, the

¡DAVID MORALES!
STATE REPRESENTATIVE DISTRICT 7

CONSTITUENT SERVICES & RESOURCES

As our State Representative, I'm committed to serving our community and helping our neighbors however I can. From unemployment claims to enrolling in health insurance.

Please contact me with any questions, comments, ideas, or requests you may have.

I hope you find the following resources useful.

COVID-19 RESOURCES

MUTUAL AID

AMOR Mutual Aid
AMOR, a local non-profit, has organized a COVID-19 Response Team to help those in need of groceries, transportation, cleaning supplies, home cooked meals, and/or housing support.
Please complete this linked form if you or someone you know requires aid.

Rhode Island Community Food Bank
The RI Community Food Bank has organized a comprehensive list with all active food pantries and meal sites in the city.
Please visit this linked page to view food assistance programs.

MENTAL HEALTH SUPPORT

BH Link
If you would benefit from mental health support or substance use counseling, please call the following 24/7 Hotline:
401-414-5465

If you are under 18, please call the following 24/7 Hotline:
855-543-5465

VOTING RESOURCES

Register to Vote

View your Polling Place here

Apply for a Mail Ballot

FINANCIAL ASSISTANCE FOR RI WORKERS & SMALL BUSINESSES

Unemployment Insurance
If you:
1. Are quarantined and unable to work or your workplace has been temporarily closed; OR
2. Are out of work and are not being compensated

Please review the following information about assistance available through State programs here.

Assistance for Small Businesses
If you own a small business and need assistance due to COVID-19, please do the following:
1. Visit the RI Commerce website: https://commerceri.com/covid-19/
2. Call the Small Business Hotline at (401) 521-HELP from 9am-5pm

Assistance for Small Businesses
If you own a small business and need assistance due to COVID-19, please do the following:
1. Visit the RI Commerce website
2. Call the Small Business Hotline at (401) 521-HELP from 9am-5pm

Paid Sick Leave
Most part-time, full-time, seasonal, temporary or other employees who work in Rhode Island are eligible for paid sick leave.
Find out more here.

Representative David Morales Bio

Member, House Innovation, Internet and Technology Committee

Member, House Municipal Government and Housing Committee

David Morales was elected on Nov. 3, 2020, to serve the people of District 7 in Providence's Mount Pleasant, Valley and Elmhurst neighborhoods. Representative Morales is a member of the House Innovation, Internet and Technology Committee and the House Municipal Government and Housing Committee.

Born September 16, 1998, he was raised by a single immigrant mother in the rural town of Soledad, CA alongside his older sister. He graduated from Soledad High School in 2016 and two years later he graduated from the University of California Irvine with a bachelor's in urban studies. In 2019, at age 20, he became the youngest graduate in the history of the Brown University Public Affairs master's program.

Representative Morales is a member of the National Association of Latino Elected Officials (NALEO) and is also one of the only Democratic Socialists of America (DSA) members elected to public office. Inspired by his socioeconomic background and lived experience, he is a passionate advocate for public education, affordable housing, and healthcare accessibility.

Representative Morales works at Year Up Rhode Island as an internship and employment specialist. He resides in the Mount Pleasant neighborhood.

Today, I officially declared!

June 20, 2020

7 months ago, I announced my candidacy for State Representative in District 7 (Mt. Pleasant & Elmhurst).

Since then, I have received support from countless neighbors because we are the campaign advocating for our working families, youth & elderly.

Today, I officially declared!

I'm grateful for the support we have earned and I'm excited to continue this hard work as we head to our election in September. #ChangeStartsWithUs

Today, I officially voted for myself

September 5, 2020

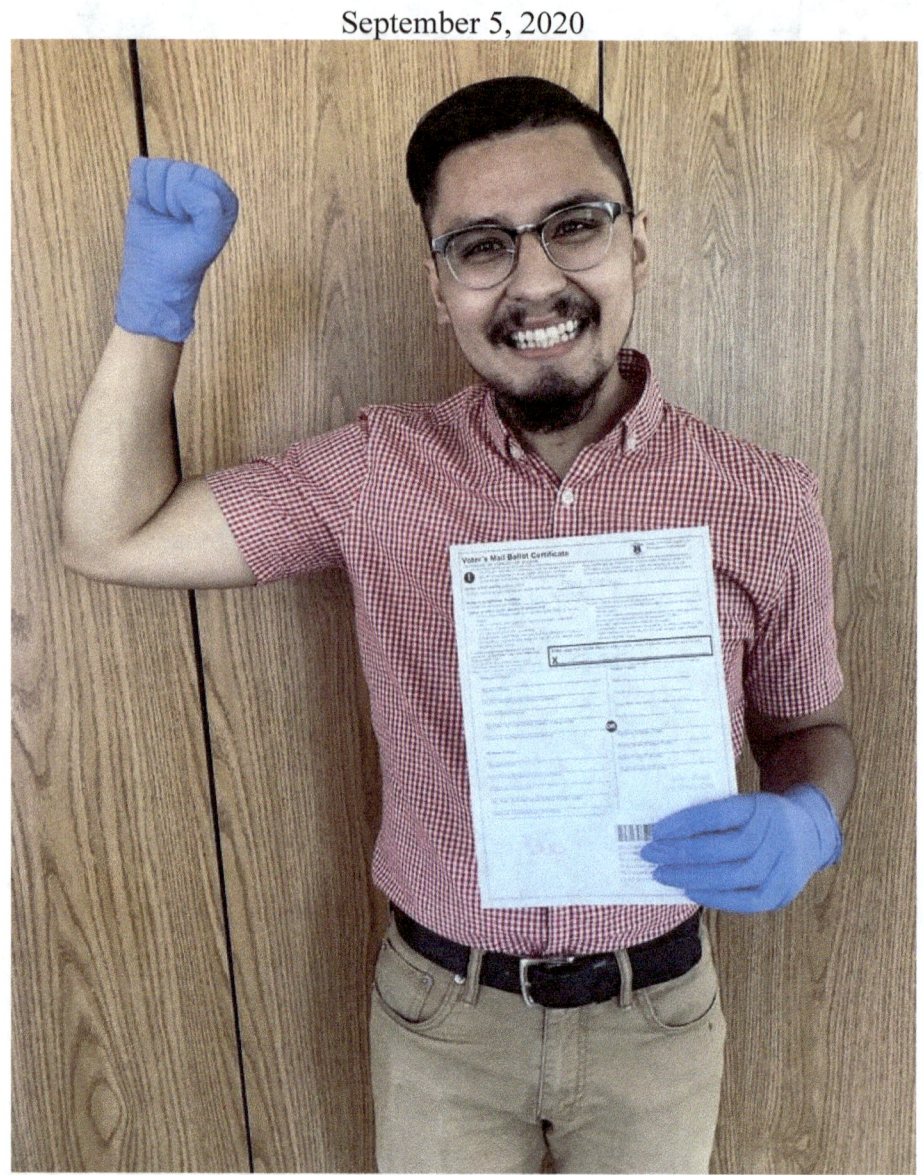

10 months ago, alongside a small team, we launched a grassroots campaign for State Representative. Today, I officially voted for myself. Throughout this entire journey, however, it has never been about me. This campaign is not about 'David Morales'.

I decided to run for office because I firmly believe working people deserve a lot better. I believe everyone deserves to make a living wage ($15-plus) that allows them to make ends meet. I believe everyone should be able to visit the doctor without going into debt.

Alongside personal experiences, these last several months have constantly reminded me of the socioeconomic struggle our people are going through. Today, I had perhaps the most emotional conversation with a neighbor who hasn't paid for her utilities or medication in months. She is literally on the brink of homelessness. This is further proof that politics isn't a game. The lives of working people literally depends on the decisions from our government. I'm confident that come Tuesday we will be victorious but most importantly, I know that we will have started a small movement of working people who recognize that they deserve a lot better from their government. #ChangeStartsWithUs @ Providence, Rhode Island

Yesterday, over 500 of our neighbors showed up to vote because they believe in systemic change.

September 9, 2020

Yesterday, over 500 of our neighbors showed up to vote because they believe in systemic change.

While these results are not yet final, I'm incredibly proud of our grassroots campaign! For 10 months, we tirelessly organized and helped empower our neighbors into the electoral process.

Higher wages, healthcare expansion, affordable housing, and public education investments — these are the values we advocated for. When all is finalized tomorrow, I look forward to working directly with our community on these legislative efforts! #ChangeStartsWithUs

2020 Statewide Primary

Representative in General Assembly District 7

View votes by precinct

Unofficial results: Updated September 08, 2020 08:34 PM
2 of 2 precincts (100%) reporting for this race

Representative in General Assembly District 7

Candidate	David Morales (DEM)
Total votes	522
Pct	47.1%
Candidate	Daniel P. McKiernan (DEM)
Total votes	294
Pct	26.5%
Candidate	Angel Subervi* (DEM)
Total votes	292
Pct	26.4%

This is really thrilling! David won this race with his incredible work ethic.

Sally Jane Wilson
September 9, 2020

This is really thrilling! David won this race with his incredible work ethic. While visiting the homes in his district, he was always respectful ("What can I do to help you?) and socially distanced during his canvassing. He's strong and true on all progressive issues, and he has the intelligence and experience to understand all the nuances of every issue, and you know he will be working especially hard to help all of his constituents, and everyone else in the State of Rhode Island. He is in a great position to fight the stupidity and corruption of the house leadership, as he will never compromise his values to 'get along'. All my best wishes for you in this new adventure! <3

2020 Statewide Primary

Representative in General Assembly District 7

View votes by precinct

Unofficial results: Updated September 08, 2020 08:34 PM
2 of 2 precincts (100%) reporting for this race

Representative in General Assembly District 7

Candidate	David Morales (DEM)
Total votes	522
Pct	47.1%
Candidate	Daniel P. McKiernan (DEM)
Total votes	294
Pct	26.5%
Candidate	Angel Subervi* (DEM)
Total votes	292
Pct	26.4%

Almost six years ago you walked through the doors of my classroom.

Grant Allen
September 10, 2020

Almost six years ago you walked through the doors of my classroom. The first student I met on my first day as a teacher. A senior who was eager, bright eyed, and passionate. You cannot imagine the joy and pride I felt when I learned tonight that the results had been certified, you had won, and that I now get to call you Representative-Elect David Morales.

In a year full of challenges, you continue to remind me of the limitless potential of our students & young people. That a better, more empathetic country is possible. And how deeply fortunate I am that I get to be a public school teacher.

Well done, David. A+ work if you ask me. And a tremendous congratulations from your old high school speech & debate teacher.

The future of RI politics? A more-diverse General Assembly

'What we are witnessing is the mainstreaming of Black and brown communities across this country,' one activist says

By Edward Fitzpatrick Globe Staff, Updated
October 30, 2020, 6:00 a.m.

Collection of photographs of elected leaders and candidates of color in Rhode Island

Collection of photographs of elected leaders and candidates of color in Rhode Island COURTESY OF TOMÁS ÁVILA

PROVIDENCE — Tuesday's elections could produce the most diverse General Assembly in Rhode Island history.

When he began tracking the number of elected leaders of color in Rhode Island 25 years ago, Latino activist Tomás Ávila counted just one Latina state legislator and a dozen Black legislators, accounting for 9 percent of the General Assembly, which then had 150 seats.

On Tuesday, the number of legislators of color could jump from 15 to 20, which would represent 18 percent of a General Assembly that now has 113 seats.

Ávila said that would give Black and Latino lawmakers more political power than they've ever had in Rhode Island.

"What we will see next week is what I consider the future of Rhode Island politics – a future that is more diverse," he said. "What we are witnessing is the mainstreaming of Black and brown communities across this country."

Though it would be a significant step forward, a General Assembly with 18 percent people of color still does not completely reflect the diversity of the state, where 29 percent of residents are people of color. According to U.S. census Bureau figures, 16.3 percent of Rhode Island residents identify as Latino or Hispanic, 8.5 percent as Black or African-American, 3.7 percent as Asian, and 1.1 percent as American Indian.

"We have made a lot of progress in electing officials," Ávila said. "But we still haven't reached parity in the demographic groups."

Tomás Ávila, Latino activist and author of books on the rise of Latinos in Rhode Island politics COURTESY OF TOMÁS ÁVILA

As president of the Milenio Latino Institute, a nonprofit research organization, Ávila has written two books documenting the rise of Latino political power in Rhode Island. He said he is looking forward to Election Day, when the number of state senators of color could increase from three to five, and the number of state representatives of color could jump from 12 to 15.

As president of the Milenio Latino Institute, a nonprofit research organization, Ávila has written two books documenting the rise of Latino political power in Rhode Island. He said he is looking forward to Election Day, when the number of state senators of color could increase from three to five, and the number of state representatives of color could jump from 12 to 15.

Ávila said the change reflects the renewed national focus on racial equity.

"It's part of an awakening," he said. "It's an awakening to the reality that the only way a lot of the systemic racism is going to be changed is through running for office, getting elected, and becoming part of the decision making and law making of the country."

Increasing the number of legislators of color in the Rhode Island House and Senate will "actually have true influence in the legislature," Ávila said – power that will give them the ability to shape key policy areas such as policing, poverty, and economic development, he said.

Ávila said Tuesday's victors are likely to include young candidates of color who are emphasizing a "general agenda" – as opposed to issues identified with a particular racial or ethnic group – reflecting the mainstreaming of Black and Latino elected officials.

When Ávila first started keeping track 25 years ago, he said the only Latina legislator was Representative Anastasia P. Williams, a Providence Democrat born in Panama who identifies as both Latina and Black.

Representative Anastasia P. Williams, a Providence Democrat COURTESY OF REPRESENTATIVE ANASTASIA P. WILLIAMS

"It was very lonely," Williams said Thursday, recalling the early days of her 28-year career. She said she is glad to see "fresh eyes and fresh minds" joining her on Smith Hill.

"It's their time," Williams said. "One statement you hear is 'This will be their future.' No, honey, this is their present – right now. They are saying they are not being heard, so now they are here, and they are claiming it."

With greater numbers, legislators of color will be able to do more than raise questions – they will be able to get results, Williams said.

She noted the death of George Floyd, a Black man who was killed in May when a white Minneapolis police officer knelt on his neck for nearly nine minutes, focused national attention on police brutality and criminal justice.
Since then, Williams has called for overhauling the Law Enforcement Officers Bill of Rights to increase accountability for police misconduct. "While justice is blind, that scale has been tipped on their side for far too long," she said.

She has called for greater diversity among state judges, pressing Governor Gina M. Raimondo to appoint the first person of color to the Rhode Island Supreme Court and the first Latina judge to the Family Court.

And Williams has sponsored the legislation that sets up Tuesday's referendum on changing the state's official name from The State of Rhode Island and Providence Plantations to simply "The State of Rhode Island."

In 2010, voters resoundingly rejected a ballot question to change the state name, with 78 percent voting against the idea and only 22 percent in favor. Historians say that in the 17th century, "plantations" referred to colonies or settlements with agricultural economies, not slavery.

But Williams said many more people now recognize that Rhode Island played a big role in the slave trade and that the word "plantations" is inexorably linked to the enslavement of Black people. She thinks the name change stands a "very good chance" of passing this time around.

While she applauds the increasing number of candidates of color, there is still room for more diversity in the General Assembly, Williams said, adding that she knows of no Asian, Southeast Asian, or Native American legislators. "Rhode Island is a melting pot overflowing with many different cultures," she said.

When Williams was first elected, David Morales had not yet been born. But Morales, a 22-year-old Providence Democrat, will soon join her in the House.

After knocking off Deputy Majority Leader Daniel McKiernan in a three-way primary, Morales has no opponent in Tuesday's general election, and he said he will become the youngest Latino legislator in any state legislature in the country.

David Morales, Democratic candidate for state House of Representatives District 7 in ProvidenceCOURTESY OF DAVID MORALES

"The importance of having a diverse government body in the legislature is our lived experience," Morales said. "A lot of us from communities of color grew up in low- and medium-income households."

So he and others are focusing on issues such as income inequality, housing, and public education. He has called for Rhode Island to invest in affordable housing on an annual basis, rather than with occasional bond items, and for changing the state education formula to better serve English language learners.

Morales said he expects the legislature to grow more diverse in the years ahead.

"I think 2022 is going to be a year where a lot of young, diverse candidates might feel inspired by the 2020 election and will step up to challenge incumbents that are not supporting policies that help improve the quality of life for our communities," he said.

The progressive Rhode Island Political Cooperative formed last year, and one of the group's goals was to increase the diversity of the General Assembly, said co-founder Jeanine Calkin, a Warwick Democrat who will return to the Senate this year after winning a primary and facing no general election opponent.

"It's good for the people of Rhode Island to see people who look like them in these legislative positions," Calkin said. "Going forward into 2022, we are going to be looking for more people of color, more women of color, to run for office."

This year, for example, the Rhode Island Political Cooperative supported three candidates of color who are on track to join the Senate: Jonathon Acosta, of Central Falls; Cynthia Mendes, of East Providence, and Tiara Mack, of Providence.

Mack defeated Senate president pro tempore Harold M. Metts, the only Black senator, in a Democratic primary. At age 72, Metts has served in the Senate for 15 years and in the House for 13 years, emerging as a leading opponent of same-sex marriage and abortion rights. At age 26, Mack is a self-described Black, queer woman and Planned Parenthood youth organizer who has fought for abortion rights.

The Rhode Island Political Cooperative also backed House candidate Brianna E. Henries, who is of Native American, African-American, and Cape Verdean descent. She faces no general election opponent.

As young candidates of color step forward, they will be following the path first blazed by the Rev. Mahlon Van Horne, who was elected in 1885 as the first Black member of the General Assembly.

The Rev. Mahlon Van Horne, of Newport, who was the first Black person elected to the Rhode Island General Assembly.COURTESY OF KEITH STOKES

Keith Stokes – the vice president of the 1696 Heritage Group of Newport, who speaks around the country on early African heritage and history – said Van Horne, who is one of his ancestors, led passage of the state's first civil rights legislation.

Stokes noted that in the late 1880s and early 1900s Black people accounted for the majority of non-white Rhode Islanders. These days, the state's population – and the country's – includes a growing number of Latinos and members of other ethnic groups.

The racial and ethnic categories of the US census often fail to capture the complexity of this increasingly diverse population, he said. But many different groups share "African heritage" – a broader category that includes multi-racial families, people from the West Indies and Cape Verde, those who just arrived from African nations and eighth-generation Rhode Island families such as his own, he said.

In the General Assembly and elsewhere, political power is all about numbers, Stokes said. "And if we can unify the people of color with African heritage in this state, that's a pretty powerful political force," he said. "Now, our voices can be heard."

Edward Fitzpatrick can be reached at edward.fitzpatrick@globe.com. Follow him on Twitter @FitzProv.

Youngest elected Black & Brown Candidates

Tomás Ávila
November 6, 2020

Youngest elected Black & Brown Candidates: Generation Z: Providence State Representative Elec David Morales, and Central Falls City Councilor Elect Adamaris Villar.

 Tomas Avila is with **Ed Fitzpatrick** and **22 others** in **Rhode Island**.
Nov 6, 2020 ·

Youngest elected Black & Brown Candidates: Generation Z: Providence State Representative Elec David Morales, and Central Falls City Councillor Elect Adamaris Villar.

Soledad native wins State Representative seat in Rhode Island

Avery Johnson
December 2, 2020

David Morales

RI State Representative-Elect David Morales PROVIDENCE, R.I. (KION) David Morales is about to become the youngest state legislator in the country, and he got his start on the Central Coast, according to Supervisor Luis Alejo.

Alejo said 22-year-old Morales, who just won a Rhode Island State Representative seat, is a Soledad native who was raised in public housing and Soledad High School grad.

Morales says on his website that he was raised by a single mother and started working in farm labor at 16 to help support his family. During high school, he said he took college courses at night and was able to graduate with a Bachelor's degree from UC Irvine at 19. By the time he was 20, he graduated with a Master's in Public Policy from Brown University.

"Proud of our inspiring young leaders from Monterey County who are representing us well in other parts of our nation!! WE ARE PROUD OF YOU, BROTHER!" Alejo said in a social media post.

Morales is set to be sworn in on Jan. 5.

Luis Alejo
@SupervisorAlejo

CONGRATULATIONS! I want to personally congratulate @DavidMoralesRI, a young progressive City of #Soledad native, who won a Rhode Island State Representative seat! At 22, he will be the youngest state legislator in the country when he gets sworn in on January 5, 2021! #FELICIDADES

3:01 PM · Dec 2, 2020 from Salinas, CA

Guided by grassroots advocacy, David Morales MPA'19 will now enter R.I. State House

State Representative-Elect Morales to push for affordable health care, housing, Green New Deal legislation as youngest Latino state legislator nationwide

By KARLOS BAUTISTA
SENIOR STAFF WRITER

Friday, November 20, 2020

Man in a suit wearing a red mask that reads 'Power to the Workers'
VICTORIA YIN / HERALD

State Representative-elect David Morales MPA '19 plans to push for affordable healthcare, housing and Green New Deal legislation in the RI state house.

Just under one year ago, David Morales MPA'19 was in the midst of organizing a protest for climate justice with Sunrise Rhode Island.

Now, he's the District 7 state representative-elect, and he has no plans to stop advocating for progressive causes.

Within the first several weeks of arriving in Rhode Island for his Master of Public Affairs at the Watson Institute for International and Public Affairs, Morales was already a presence in the Rhode Island State House. He worked with local advocacy groups to lobby representatives to enact a Percentage of Income Payment Plan and testified on behalf of the Reproductive Health Act.

Morales is the youngest graduate of the University's MPA program at 20 years old. Now, at the age of 22, he will become the youngest Latino legislator in any state legislature in the country, he said.

"I realized that there's a lot of potential to create systemic change here, given the scale and (Rhode Island's) size," Morales said. "If you believe very strongly about a particular issue, you can have an advocacy group of just five people … and really make a lot of noise at the State House."

Inspired by Sen. Bernie Sanders (I-VT)

Morales grew up living in public housing in Soledad, California. He was raised by a single mother who immigrated from Mexico, worked 2–3 minimum wage jobs and worried that her son would become a victim of the school-to-prison pipeline and end up incarcerated.

Morales, while in high school, took college courses at night and over the summers and joined extracurriculars like speech and debate. Near the end of his time in high school, Morales said he was inspired by Sen. Bernie Sanders' (I-VT) 2016 presidential bid.

"I realized what I wanted to do, and that was some form of political advocacy," he said. "I wanted to be involved at the table where the decisions are being made on whether or not we increase the minimum wage, whether or not we decide to invest in affordable housing."

Morales would go on to receive his bachelor's degree in urban studies by the time he was 19 at the University of California at Irvine, before arriving at the University to pursue his MPA.

Advocacy and the push to run for office

While at Brown, Morales worked with various local advocacy groups, such as the Providence Democratic Socialists of America, Sunrise RI and immigrant rights organization Never Again Action Rhode Island. After graduation, he continued to work with those groups, which eventually encouraged him to run for the State House.

Together, Morales and other activists saw running for office as a way to address what they viewed as "complacency" among current State House leadership.

During his time living in Mount Pleasant — a neighborhood located within District 7 — Morales said he felt a lack of engagement from Deputy Majority Leader and Rep. Daniel McKiernan, the incumbent for District 7 whom Morales would unseat in the Sept. 8 primary election.

While campaigning, Morales said he "was often told by people who lived in the neighborhood for over 10 years that I was the first candidate to ever come to their door."
"I realized that if I … had a grassroots message centered around a $15 minimum wage, universal health care, public school investments and affordable housing, that I could be successful (and) that our campaign would be able to change the culture of local politics in our neighborhood," Morales said.

The campaign trail

To get an early start on fundraising, Morales started his campaign against McKiernan in December 2019, 10 months before the statewide Democratic primary. According to Morales, over the course of the campaign, he raised $23,000 — none of which came from any corporate political action committees or special interest groups.

Morales spent time canvassing in the district's neighborhoods, which consist of Mount Pleasant, Valley and Elmhurst, from February until the pandemic hit in March. As Rhode Island went into a state of emergency in response to COVID-19, he and his team pivoted to phone banking and working to connect neighbors with resources for free food delivery. Morales also wrote letters to neighbors he had visited before the pandemic and distributed homemade face masks.

In June, Morales and his team went back to canvassing in person with public health guidelines in mind. The primary would ultimately be a three-way race between Morales, McKiernan and Angel Subervi, director of small business development for the City of Providence.

On Sept. 8, despite not receiving the local Democratic committee's endorsement, which went to Subervi, Morales won the primary with 49.4 percent of the vote, effectively securing the seat with no Republican contenders in the Nov. 3 general election.

Issues and policy ideas

In his first year in office, Morales wants to get a lot done.

"We have a lot more people here at the State House now than ever in any time in history, I would argue, that recognize the importance of policies such as the Green New Deal and investment in affordable housing," Morales added.

His first priority, he said, will be to address the state's finances. "We will not allow for a state budget that cuts social services while using COVID as an excuse for the reduction of spending," Morales said.

Throughout his first year, Morales plans to focus on the state's health care, affordable housing, minimum wage, hazard pay and utilities costs.
To tackle the Ocean State's recurring fiscal woes, Morales wants to address what he calls the state's "unfair" tax code and pass legislation that would allow cities and towns to tax wealthy nonprofit institutions like the University, Rhode Island School of Design and Johnson and Wales University.

As a nonprofit institution, the University is largely exempt from paying property taxes to Providence, but has an agreement to make voluntary payments in lieu of taxes, or PILOT payments. For fiscal year 2020, the University has paid $6.2 million in PILOT payments, up from $4.38 million in fiscal year 2018. According to an estimate from 2012, the University would owe the city about $38 million per year if it paid commercial real estate taxes on its properties.

Taxation of wealthy nonprofits like the University "would open us up to pursue a lot of these different policy ideas … such as affordable housing, quality public education, making investments toward renewable energy and other initiatives that are part of a Green New Deal," Morales said.

While campaigning and canvassing, Morales said that access to affordable health care was an issue for every constituent he met. He plans to "start raising the conversation about what a universal health care system would look like here in Rhode Island."

According to Clinical Assistant Professor of Family Medicine Dannie Ritchie MPH'03, a rise in health care costs, along with reductions on spending for services like Medicaid, has limited access to affordable care in the Ocean State.

In 2018, the Rhode Island Department of Health found that 32.5 percent of the state's adults were either uninsured, did not have a doctor or could not afford insurance.

With Morales and other progressives in office, Ritchie said that she is "more hopeful that we will have legislative changes that actually change the conditions for the better, for those that are marginalized or pushed out and pushed down."

Morales also intends to work with housing advocacy groups, such as Brown student group Housing Opportunities for People Everywhere, which Morales volunteered with during his time at the University. One of his first orders of business will be to add a housing line item on the state's budget.

HOPE plans to also work with Morales on legislation to ban source-of-income discrimination in housing, in addition to a program that would grant those facing eviction the right to free legal assistance, HOPE Co-Director Dhruv Gaur '21 said.

Former HOPE Co-Director Nathaniel Pettit '20, who had Morales as a teaching assistant for URBN 1260: "Housing in America," said that Morales "sets a pretty great example for Brown affiliates in the potential of what you can do to … commit yourself to understanding and advocating for the issues that are most important to folks throughout Providence, throughout Rhode Island."

"I believe systemic change will only happen through grassroots advocacy. It won't simply happen through the push of a button at the State House," Morales added. Instead, "it's going to happen if we mobilize working people in our communities of color to advocate for laws and policies that will improve their standard of living."

Topics: politics, Rhode island, state representative

There is a political revolution happening in our State

December 30, 2020

☰ **teen**VOGUE SUBSCRIBE

David Morales, 22, first-time candidate and Representative-elect of Rhode Island's District Seven

"Coming from a low-income community, I thought it was normal for people to work long hours just to make ends meet. For too long, Rhode Island's state government has refused to help working people. Unlike our neighboring states, we do not have a path

There is a political revolution happening in our State and I'm glad a national outlet like Teen Vogue highlighted how important it is *everyday working people with lived experience* have the

50

opportunity to advocate for the needs of our communities as legislators.

It was an absolute honor to be featured in this piece and I'm proud of all the work us advocates were able to accomplish together this year.

I'm excited to be sworn in next week as I am prepared to fight for the needs of our working people alongside our neighborhood, grassroots organizations, and activists. To keep up with this work please like our political page: RI State Representative-Elect David Morales

Thank you as always for the support family and I hope to make us all proud!
https://www.teenvogue.com/story/rhode-island-progressive-democrats-statehouse

Rhode Island Progressives Won Big in 2020 With Help From Youth Activists

Progressive Democrats in Rhode Island won victories that could transform the state's politics.

BY MARA DOLAN
DECEMBER 29, 2020

Several thousand people angered by the death of George Floyd held a rally at Burnside Park in Downtown Providence RI on...
BOSTON GLOBE

One of the biggest and most overlooked election stories may have come out of the country's smallest state.

Rhode Island, only 1,200 square miles and home to a little more than 1 million people, is rarely the subject of national political interest. With a majority-Democratic legislature, Democratic governor, and an all-Democratic congressional delegation, the state's politics might seem sleepy to outsiders. Hiding beneath the surface is a much deeper story.

Much of Rhode Island's Democratic leadership is, put simply, quite conservative. The long-standing (and now outgoing) Democratic Speaker of the House, one of the state's most powerful elected officials, voted down abortion rights legislation, and has an A rating from the National Rifle Association. Democrats in the state House voted in 2010 to cut taxes for the rich, and in 2011, a majority of Democrats voted for repressive voter I.D. laws. The Rhode Island Democratic State Committee stripped the Women's Caucus of privileges after the group lobbied for a reproductive rights bill. As a Republican official once told NPR, "[Rhode Island has] a lot of Democrats who we know are Republican but run as a Democrat — basically so they can win."

In this year's elections, progressive Democrats mounted their most organized challenge to date, and earned victories that could transform the state's politics.

Over the past year, progressives across Rhode Island mobilized to lay the groundwork for this crucial moment. Activist movements and progressive campaign veterans built an infrastructure to back insurgent candidates ready to challenge more conservative incumbents. Their preparation paid off in a huge way.

These wins were made possible thanks to the Rhode Island Political Cooperative, an initiative launched in 2019 to recruit, train, and financially support progressive candidates. All candidates endorsed a shared progressive slate of policy positions, creating a unified front of candidates fighting for a Green New Deal, single-payer health care, and a $15 minimum wage. Joined by additional candidates backed by Providence Democratic Socialists of America (ProvDSA), Reclaim I (a group of former volunteers for Senator Bernie Sanders's presidential campaign), and the Rhode Island Working Families Party, almost two dozen progressives mounted challenges from the left for state House and Senate seats. In partnership with movements like Sunrise Rhode Island, a youth-led climate justice group, candidates had full-time organizers dedicated to mobilizing voters. More than half of the progressive challengers won their races.

The first-time candidates that emerged victorious included Tiara Mack, a 26-year-old Black, queer reproductive justice advocate who challenged an anti-abortion Democratic incumbent who had held his seat for 35 years. Mack beat him in the primary and won her seat resoundingly, with nearly 90% of the vote. David Morales, a 22-year-old activist who will become one of the youngest Latino candidates elected to any state legislature, also defied expectations when he won. When the local Democratic committee endorsed his opponent, Morales found support and a volunteer army through partnerships with local progressive groups like ProvDSA. Mack and Morales were joined by 13 other progressive challengers who ousted more conservative Democrats or Republican incumbents.

Pundits like The Hill's Krystal Ball argued this state-wide progressive takeover in Rhode Island could offer lessons to the rest of the country. "A little-noticed local movement of left activists appears to have just successfully executed a massive overhaul of the Rhode Island legislature, in a model that could easily be replicated in states all across the country," said Ball. To understand how this statewide progressive strategy came to be and what it can teach us, Teen Vogue caught up with a few of Rhode Island's young leaders — including two new elected officials and two movement leaders who mobilized to create real change in their state.

Editor's note: These responses were condensed and lightly edited for clarity.

Rep. Morales sworn in as General Assembly convenes

January 5, 2021

STATE HOUSE — Rep. David Morales was formally sworn into office Tuesday, Jan. 5, as the 2021-22 session of the Rhode Island General Assembly convened.

Representative Morales (D-Dist. 7, Providence) was one of 14 new members of the House of Representatives who took the oath of office, which was administered to all 75 House members by Rhode Island Secretary of State Nellie Gorbea.

The House of Representatives began its legislative year today meeting at Veterans Memorial Auditorium in Providence to provide greater social distance than is possible at the State House, which is closed to the public during the pandemic. The session also included the election of Rep. K. Joseph Shekarchi (D-Dist. 23, Warwick) as the speaker of the House.

Representative Morales, whose district includes Providence's Mount Pleasant, Valley and Elmhurst neighborhoods, works at Year Up Rhode Island as an internship and employment specialist. Born Sept. 16, 1998, he was raised by a single immigrant mother in the rural town of Soledad, Calif., alongside his older sister. He graduated from Soledad High School in 2016 and two years later graduated from the University of California Irvine with a bachelor's in urban studies. In 2019, at age 20, he became the youngest graduate in the history of the Brown University Public Affairs master's program. Representative Morales is a member of the National Association of Latino Elected Officials (NALEO) and is also one of the only Democratic Socialists of America (DSA) members elected to public office.

Caucus Vote Abstention

Sally Jayne Wilson
January 5, 2021

 Sally Jane Wilson
Jan 5 ·

I have had 2 different people from David Morales' District (also mine) call me and beg that I talk with David about abstaining. I told them that Rep. Morales had actually called me, and some other constituents to explain why he was abstaining at the caucus vote. And, wouldn't you know it, I received another call today, where Rep. Morales explained that he had spoken to a number of his constituents and come to the decision after listening to us all. I told him that he didn't even have to call, because I know he's completely aligned with me on all political matters. He has my support and absolute trust. <3

Now...this guy? Not so much.

UPRISERI.COM
Sunrise RI: Statement on Rhode Island Senate and House leadership vote – Uprise RI

There's a lot revolving around Rhode Island's air space today.

Jordan Goyette
January 5, 2021

There's a lot revolving around Rhode Island's air space today. I know many are anxious about the EC certification tomorrow, and the elections today in Georgia that could finally topple Mitch McConnell. But above all I want to send the warmest love and congratulations to my new and returning friends to the general assembly here at home, who will be sworn in today and make their first vote for the new speaker of the house & Senate President. Like many, I'm not happy with how the process has unfolded, and like many others, wish that it could be someone different, someone more progressive. But the fact that so many progressive priorities (taxing the rich, a living wage, improving affordable housing, legalized cannabis, etc.) are even being talked about in ways they wouldn't have been last year shows the fact that we are winning the battle of ideas and have an opportunity to unite the divided factions of the party towards a shared direction that achieves more progressive priorities than ever before. I know some of you plan to abstain, and I respect that. I too would personally abstain if I was in your position. I don't fault any of you who will make a different decision, as the vote today isn't a vote to pledge your undying loyalty to a leader, and I know where you all stand on progressive priorities. I want to give special congratulations to some friends, many of whom I was privileged to help win on the campaign trail:

Brianna Escelia Henries, my unmoderated comrade from EP who took on an establishment conservative Democrat and knocked it out of the park 62-38%. Tiara Mack, who finally ended the tenure of one of the most bigoted members of the State Senate. Sam Bell, the perpetual thorn in leadership's side who weathered all the conservative establishment had to throw at him and still came out on top 70-30%. Kendra Anderson, who I was pleased to help beat one of RI's worst Trump acolytes throughout the general election campaign here in Warwick. She ran in a purple seat and her progressive platform won the day. Jonathon Acosta, who mobilized the people of Centrals Falls to believe they deserved better than what the establishment had been offering. Cynthia Mendes, a single mom who wouldn't accept half-handed late to the game representatives anymore, and showed that using your political clout to advance your own personal status comes at a cost. Meghan Kallman, who I waited to support until after the Pawtucket City Council's vote on ratifying the new police union's contract, and who I immediately donated to after she was the only dissenting vote. Jeanine Calkin, the cofounder of the RI Co-Op, and the fighter the establishment just couldn't keep down. Thanks to her and Kendra's people powered campaigns 2/3 State Senate seats in Warwick are now held by progressive members. Alana DiMario, who I later found out I was the first person she got a donation from during this cycle. Even in a competitive 3-way open seat contest, she still won with a majority of the vote. David Morales, who will be the only member of the PVDDSA in the State House of Representatives. Brandon Potter, who I know will stand up for the progressive issues he beat a truly awful conservative Democrat by campaigning on. Leonela Felix, a resident of my old home in Pawtucket also, and who beat a 10 year establishment incumbent by a 2-1 margin in September. Michelle McGaw for RI State Representative District 71, who made an undying supporter of Speaker Mattiello opt for retirement rather than face her. This is a truly awesome moment for you all. You will face a mountain of challenges no one should have to have laid before them. But i am extremely optimistic and confident you all will celebrate major achievements over the next two years. There will be stumbles and roadblocks along the way, but I am more hopeful than ever that Rhode Island is poised for great things because of your elections.

That's my friend and (now) State Representative in the Rhode Island General Assembly, David Morales!

Apriln Yee
January 6, 2021

Biography
Representative David Morales
Member, House Innovation, Internet and Technology Committee
Member, House Municipal Government and Housing Committee

David Morales was elected on Nov. 3, 2020, to serve the people of District 7 in Providence's Mount Pleasant, Valley and Elmhurst neighborhoods. Representative Morales is a member of the House Innovation, Internet and Technology Committee and the House Municipal Government and Housing Committee.

Born September 16, 1998, he was raised by a single immigrant mother in the rural town of Soledad, CA alongside his older sister. He graduated from Soledad High School in 2016 and two years later he graduated from the University of California Irvine with a bachelor's in urban studies. In 2019, at age 20, he became the youngest graduate in the history of the Brown University Public Affairs master's program.

Representative Morales is a member of the National Association of Latino Elected Officials (NALEO) and is also one of the only Democratic Socialists of America (DSA) members elected to public office. Inspired by his socioeconomic background and lived experience, he is a passionate advocate for public education, affordable housing, and healthcare accessibility.

Representative Morales works at Year Up Rhode Island as an internship and employment specialist. He resides in the Mount Pleasant neighborhood.

CONTACT INFORMATION:
16 Academy Avenue
Providence, RI 02908
(401) 480-1322

This past week has been an emotional one. On Tuesday, I was officially sworn to the RI House of Representatives.

January 8, 2021

Growing up in a small rural town (Soledad) to a single immigrant mother who worked multiple jobs just to make ends meet and support my sister and me — I never thought I'd be here.

As I reflect now, however, I know that my lived experience of coming from a low-income household and a tight-knitted community, has prepared me in this fight for justice.

It was at 16 that I started to become conscious and understand the inequalities that exist in our communities. I realized that poverty, homelessness, and a lack of healthcare were the results of policy decisions by 'people in power' who do not understand the challenges that working people experience and would rather suppress them than help. In other words, I became aware with how broken our systems are and the sad reality that it is mostly done by design.

Since then, I've grown to be an activist. I've grown to be an outspoken advocate who is not afraid to fight for the needs of working people, from classrooms to meetings to protests to now — the State House.

As one of the youngest Latinos ever elected to any State Legislature, I take great pride in this and recognize the responsibilities that come with it.

It's with honor, that I'm committed to the working people of Mt. Pleasant, Valley, and Elmhurst because I'll always be here to advocate for us. Most importantly, I'm determined to change the culture of local politics and ensure that everyone, regardless of their socioeconomic background, is a part of the legislative process.

Thank you again for being with me on this journey over the last several years family, we are now just beginning!

New member of the RI House, Providence Rep. David P. Morales (Dist 7) listens as House members nominate Rep. K. Joseph Shekarchi for House speaker.
THE PROVIDENCE JOURNAL

Rep. David Morales, D-Providence, is ing for action, "That's going to provide ediate relief to small business owners king class individuals, to essential ers, to teachers, and to our nursing es."

New Rep. David Morales, D-Providence, is looking for action, "That's going to provide immediate relief to small business owners, to working class individuals, to essential workers, to teachers, and to our nursing homes."

Former Soledad resident takes office as state representative in Rhode Island

David Morales' local origins lead to political office

By Sean Roney -
January 12, 2021 617

David Morales, who was elected as a state representative in Rhode Island, grew up in Soledad, where he attended high school and took early college courses. (Contributed Photo)

RHODE ISLAND — Former Soledad resident David Morales began his duties as a member of the Rhode Island House of Representatives last week after being voted in during the November 2020 general election.

The 22-year-old is among the youngest leaders to have been elected to state office in the United States, after having secured 49.4% of the votes in a three-candidate primary against incumbent Daniel McKiernan and challenger Angel Subervi in September, and receiving 96% of the general election vote.

Morales, who took office Jan. 5, came to the East Coast from Soledad and still has family who lives in the Salinas Valley town.

"I see this as an exciting opportunity to be able to advocate for working people in our communities of color who oftentimes are overlooked," Morales said. "It is important that we have individuals with lived experience who can attest to why affordable housing is important, to why we need to increase the minimum wage, and why we have to have a health care system that guarantees coverage for everyone."

Morales called the journey difficult, but credited grassroots campaigning with helping in his election.

"Door knocking and making phone calls clearly paid off, as I'm preparing to be the youngest Latino to ever serve in a state legislature," Morales said.

Morales grew up in public housing in Soledad, raised by a single mother who cared for himself and his sister. He said his parents separated due to his father suffering from drug and alcohol addiction, which led to him not having seen his father since he was 8 years old.

"My mom had a lot of responsibility to take care of myself and my sister and make sure we were able to pay the rent and have groceries," Morales said. "I recognize I had a lot of responsibility at a young age, and that to me meant I had to invest in my education to the best of my ability."

Morales said he joined the Upward Bound TRIO program when he entered Soledad High School, a program that helps first-generation high school students who come from a low-income background to take early college courses. He took summer courses during his freshman and sophomore years, then added night classes with Hartnell College when he started his junior year at SHS.

Earning college credit early allowed him to begin his junior year at UC Irvine upon graduating from high school.

Morales earned his bachelor's degree in urban studies in a year and a half before going to Brown University to work on his Master's of Public Affairs program in 2018. That took him to the Rhode Island capital of Providence. He said he gained an interest in political involvement while at UC Irvine.

"It was definitely a lot of long nights, a lot of studying in between, and a lot of grassroots organizing," Morales said about his experience.

He said Providence differs from the Central Coast in that it has more multi-family homes, which led to a culture shock when he first moved. He said one similarity is the number of people working minimum-wage jobs, which force them to take multiple jobs in order to pay bills.

Morales encouraged youth in the Salinas Valley to recognize how special places like Soledad are because of their tight-knit communities, something not found in large cities. He also offered them advice.

"Our potential is limitless and it is ultimately about the investments you're willing to make for yourself, knowing you have the support of your family, your friends and ultimately your community," Morales said.

While recognizing the importance of community, Morales recommended against trying to leave the area.

"The goal shouldn't always be to get out of the 831," he said, adding that there is value in making large social impact in rural towns with predominantly farmworker and Latino populations.

In the end, Morales said it is important to "create the best outcomes for the people that live there," no matter where one lives.

RIMEO Elected Officials

Tomás Ávila
January 16, 2021

Monterey County to Honor 50th Anniversary of Local Landmark Case That Ended Use of Discriminatory IQ Tests Against Latino Children in California!

Luis Alejo
Monterey County Supervisor
January 21, 2021

🚨 Monterey County to Honor 50th Anniversary of Local Landmark Case That Ended Use of Discriminatory IQ Tests Against Latino Children in California!

Supervisor Chris Lopez & I will honor the courage of #Soledad children, parents & local advocates to end this insidious practice! https://monterey.legistar.com/View.ashx?M=F&ID=9081240&GUID=66DC0C4C-5D18-4F95-8771-153F122EE0AB

🚨 ¡El condado de Monterey honrará el 50 aniversario del caso emblemático local que puso fin al uso de pruebas de coeficiente intelectual discriminatorias contra niños Latinos en California!

¡El supervisor Chris Lopez y yo honraremos la valentia de los niños, padres y abogados locales de #Soledad para poner fin a esta práctica insidiosa!
https://monterey.legistar.com/View.ashx?M=F&ID=9081240&GUID=66DC0C4C-5D18-4F95-8771-153F122EE0AB

Press Advisory
January 22, 2021

Contact:
Supervisor Luis Alejo (831) 726-6032

MONTEREY COUNTY TO HONOR 50TH ANNIVERSARY OF LOCAL LANDMARK CASE THAT ENDED USE OF DISCRIMINATORY IQ TESTS AGAINST LATINO CHILDREN IN CALIFORNIA
IQ Tests Were Once Used to Place Thousands of Limited English Proficient Latino Children Into "Educable Mentally Retarded" Classes in California

SALINAS- The Monterey County Board of Supervisors will be considering a resolution next Tuesday to honor the 50th Anniversary of a landmark civil rights case in Monterey County that ended the use of discriminatory IQ tests to place limited English proficient Latino children into "Educable Mentally Retarded" (EMR) classes in California.

In 1969, *Diana v. California State Board of Education* (CA 70 RFT (N.D. Cal. 1970)) originated when a group of Spanish-Speaking students from Soledad, California, were inappropriately assigned to EMR ("Educable Mentally Retarded") classes based on an assessment by an unqualified assessor. The case arose because a monolingual psychologist at Soledad Elementary School tested Spanish speaking children in English, made determinations of intellectual disability, and used his data to wrongly place students in special education classes. At the start, two Soledad parents had the courage to complain to the late California Rural Legal Assistance (CRLA) Community Worker Hector De La Rosa, also a resident of Soledad, who eventually worked closely with the families throughout all the legal preparation and proceedings.

The landmark case was the first effort to outlaw the insidious IQ testing practices that unjustly led to thousands of Mexican-American Limited English Proficient children being placed in special education classes. The tests heavily depended on verbal responses and the questions that were culturally biased. At the time, African-American and Mexican-American students made up 21.5 percent of the state population, but were 48 percent of special education program pupils.

Salinas CRLA attorneys Marty Glick and Mo Jourdane initially took on the case on behalf of nine Soledad migrant children, Diana, Arturo, María, Manuel, Rachel, Ramón, Armando, Margarita and Ernesto, ages 6 to 13, who were kept in the same classroom all day long, coloring, cutting out pictures and occupying themselves with other activities the children described as "baby stuff." The class action lawsuit was filed on January 7, 1970, on behalf of the 13,000 Mexican American children already placed in EMR classes and another 100,000 at risk of being placed in these classes.

The case later inspired another subsequent landmark case of *Larry P. v. Riles* (495 F. Supp. 926 (ND Cal. 1979) to ban culturally biased IQ test against African American children. The book "Soledad Children: The Fight to End Discriminatory IQ Tests" documents the history and impact of this case and all those involved.

"This landmark case exemplifies the courageous efforts by Monterey County students, parents and advocates to champion for the education and civil rights of children of color in California," said **Supervisor Luis Alejo, who is authoring the resolution with Supervisor Chris Lopez**. "This case is largely unknown today, but it changed the lives of thousands of children in California for the better. These valiant efforts must be remembered and honored."

Just a kid from Soledad making history. David Morales

Ricardo silva
January 23, 2021

 **Ricardo Silva**
Jan 23

Just a kid from Soledad making history. David Morales

MONTEREYCOUNTYWEEKLY.COM
Soledad native David Morales is the youngest Latino state lawmaker in the country. He has so...

Soledad native David Morales is the youngest Latino state lawmaker in the country. He has some advice for youth back home.

Celia Jiménez Jan 21, 2021 0
Power Player

Growing up in Soledad, David Morales says he didn't think of running for public office, but pursuing change as an activist: "I always thought of myself as being someone who would support the movement through activism and advocacy."
c/o David Morales

David Morales, a 22-year-old from Soledad, became the youngest Latino state legislator in the nation this year when he was sworn in on Jan. 5. Morales comes from humble roots; he was raised by his mother who worked multiple jobs to provide for him and his sister. He finished his undergraduate degree at age 19 at UC Irvine. By the age of 20, he became the youngest student to complete a masters of public administration at Brown University. Two years later, he won an election for State Assembly and is now representing the 7th District in Rhode Island.

The issues he campaigned on and now plans to advocate for – well paying jobs, affordable housing, health care and access to clean water

– are issues that he got involved in via the Sunrise Movement and Democratic Socialists of America, after being inspired by Sen. Bernie Sanders' 2016 presidential run.

Morales spoke to the Weekly about his rise to power, connections to his hometown and his advice to young people back home.
Weekly:

What motivated you to go to college?

Morales: My mom inspired me more than anything else. I know how hard my mom was working, and it was my goal to make her, and my sister, as proud as possible and show my mom that si, vale la pena, it was worth all of the efforts that you put yourself through in order to ensure that myself and my sister had the resources to attend a four-year university, have a degree and be able to have a self-sustaining job.

What motivated you to run for state assembly?

My lived experience. Living in public housing. Growing up with a single mother who had to work multiple jobs with a minimum wage job that paid below $12 and recognizing that that is a common experience. And for too long, in Rhode Island specifically, we have not had enough officials who understand the struggles of what poor people, working people have to experience on a daily basis.

You are the youngest Latino in a state legislature anywhere in the U.S. What does it mean for you? What do you want to accomplish?

I take it as a very significant responsibility. I see this as an opportunity to advocate for the issues that are most important to young people and to also send an example to all the older officials to recognize that our generation is engaged.

U.S. Rep. Alexandria Ocasio-Cortez, is a breakout young elected official who has become a national celebrity. What do you think of her and her rise?
She is an inspiration of what more public officials should strive to do. Despite her own socioeconomic background, working as a bartender,

she understood that she had a voice, and that by coming together with her different neighbors she could build a movement that would be able to provide it and create the change that working people desperately need. I think we got AOC as an inspiration on how to mobilize, how to organize within your community, and ultimately how to use your voice and demand change.

Why did you stay in Rhode Island instead of coming back home to Soledad?

I think I got my home in Rhode Island. I found a community that I felt embraced by. I live in the Mount Pleasant neighborhood in Providence, which is 40-percent Latino, predominantly working-class and it reminds me a lot of home. While I do think there is some good work happening in Monterey County, specifically the work of MILPA, an advocacy group in Salinas, I did not think that my skills and my approach to create change was going to be most effective there than where I am right now.

What would you like to say to teenagers and young adults from Soledad?

My advice for all young adults in Soledad is to remember that there is a bigger world that exists outside of the 831, and to recognize that how you invest your time is really going to make a difference in terms of the change that you will be able to create. I don't believe that the goal should always be to escape, or to get out of the 'hood.' I think the idea is we take the lessons we've learned from Soledad and we try to apply them out in the bigger world knowing that we always have the responsibility to pay it forward.

Very important town hall that David Morales and Sam Bell are hosting 🙌 💯

Enrique Sanchez
January 26, 2021

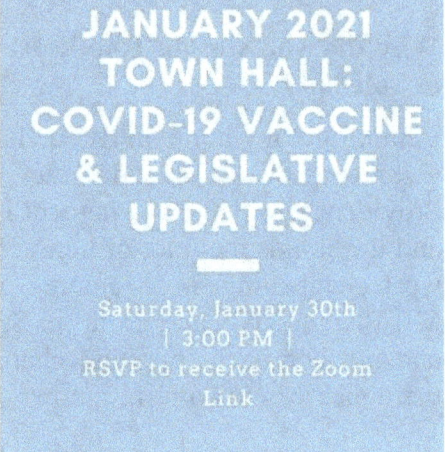

SATURDAY, JANUARY 30, 2021 AT 3 PM EST
January Town Hall: COVID-19 Vaccine Distribution & Legislative Updates

Sunday Funday

January 24, 201

Sunday Funday: A peaceful walk with Mochi as we visit our local small businesses while our neighbors look at us in amusement.

Who said you can't take your cat on a walk?

Fortunate to have friends and acquaintances

Clara Amanda
January 26, 2021

I consider myself fortunate to have friends and acquaintances who are politicians. I am especially thankful that they take public service seriously, including making themselves accessible to help their constituents in need.

That being said, I want to publicly thank Senator Sam Bell and Representative David Morales for helping my client who is disabled and mostly bedridden, by buying her boxes and helping me to find volunteers to help her pack her stuff so that she can have a successful move this weekend! Thank you for not only your work on the macro-level, but remembering that small deeds to help others are also important!

Morales introduces bills to address prescription drug costs

January 28, 2021

STATE HOUSE – Rep. David Morales has introduced two bills to limit the out-of-pocket expenses of prescription drugs for insured people.

The bills would limit the total cost of insulin to $25 per 30-day supply and set a limit of $100 for a 30-day supply of any other prescription drug, including specialty drugs.

Representative Morales (D-Dist. 7, Providence) said introducing these bills was important to the communities he represents because alongside the impact the COVID-19 pandemic has had on Rhode Island's public health, high prescription drug costs continue to be an unacceptable barrier that endangers the lives of working people and further threatens their public health.

"Long before COVID-19, prescription drug costs were unaffordable for many middle-class Rhode Islanders, let alone the working-class and poor. Prescription drugs are a necessity because without them the lives of people are literally at risk, yet so many of our neighbors are forced to skip doses or ration their prescriptions because they simply cannot afford them. With so many people out of work, underemployed, or experiencing other financial barriers due to the pandemic, there are now more people who are concerned with how they will afford their prescription drugs," said Representative Morales. "Just like COVID, high prescription drug costs are a raging public health crisis that requires immediate action. If maintaining your health by taking prescribed drugs is unaffordable for many, especially during these times, then it is clear that our health care system is failing. Therefore, it is the responsibility of our government to address this."

Many specialty drugs — drugs that fight chronic conditions and treat serious diseases like cancer and AIDS — costs tens of thousands of dollars per year, and the costs have been rising sharply each year. The result is often high cost-sharing for patients.

The cost of insulin, in particular, has risen sharply in the last several years, and the cost is much higher in the United States than in other countries. Millions of Americans depend on insulin for the management of diabetes, and rationing insulin to save money can have dire consequences. In Rhode Island, over 80,000 adults, nearly 10 percent of the state's adult population, have been diagnosed with diabetes.

The bill limiting insulin costs to $25 per 30-day supply has been cosponsored by more than a dozen representatives, including Rep. Michelle McGaw (D-Dist. 71, Portsmouth, Tiverton, Little Compton) Rep. Joseph McNamara (D-Dist. 19, Warwick, Cranston), Rep. Karen Alzate (D-Dist. 60, Pawtucket), and Deputy Majority Whip Mia A. Ackerman (D-Dist. 45, Cumberland, Lincoln).

Both bills were introduced this week and have received support from the Rhode Island Nurses Association. The insulin bill (2021-H 5151) has been sent to the House Health, Education and Welfare Committee. The $100 limit bill (2021-H 5146) has been transmitted to the House Corporations Committee.

Please to see Newly Elected Black & Brown Legislators drafting Community based Legislation, as opposed to the typical Funders & Special Interest legislation.

Tomás Ávila
January 29, 2021

Tomas Avila is with **Adán Tanán** and **38 others**.
Jan 29 · 🌐

Please to see Newly Elected Black & Brown Legislators drafting Community based Lesgislation, as opposed to the typical Funders & Special Interest legislation.

Sen. Bell, Rep. Morales raise concerns about SMART clinics in Providence Schools

February 2, 2021

STATE HOUSE – Sen. Samuel Bell and Rep. David Morales wrote to state and Providence education leaders today expressing deep concern about SMART clinics opened in recent weeks at Mount Pleasant High School and Roger Williams Middle School.

The legislators listed numerous concerns, including lack of transparency shrouding the program, apparent release of students' personal and health information without proper consent, reports of the program billing students' families' insurance for services usually performed by school nurse teachers, the dismissal of the school nurse teachers at the schools, and more.

"These clinics appear to be a commercial intrusion into public schools, one that opportunistically lures students into using fee-for-service health care, possibly without obtaining proper consent, including in situations where a language barrier might prevent students and their parents from being able to learn that they will be billed. These clinics appear to be privatizing the valuable services that are provided for free at all other public schools by school nurse teachers, at students' families' expense," said Senator Bell (D-Dist. 5, Providence).

Said Representative Morales (D-Dist. 7, Providence), "While these are being touted as community health clinics, they are charging students for services that are supposed to be provided by a school nurse teacher free of charge. What is most concerning is the lack of transparency around these clinics when it comes to privacy and obtaining the consent of students and their families. From the experiences I've heard of, there are students and families who have no idea what they are signing when provided with forms from the clinic. Instead, all our public school students deserve a full-time school nurse teacher they can approach with comfort, not a fee-for-service health care system."

The letter, sent to state Education Commissioner Angélica Infante-Green, members of the state Council on Elementary and Secondary Education and Providence Schools Superintendent Harrison Peters today, is below.

Morales to serve on committees on Municipal Government and Housing; Innovation, Internet and Technology

February 5, 2021

STATE HOUSE – Rep. David Morales has been appointed to the House Committee on Municipal Government and Housing and its Committee on Innovation, Internet and Technology, House Speaker K. Joseph Shekarchi has announced.

The Committee on Municipal Government and Housing represents a change for the House. Formerly the Committee on Municipal Government, the committee's duties have been expanded to reflect the importance of housing issues to the state.

The Committee on Innovation, Internet and Technology is a new committee created by the House this year to address issues relating to cybersecurity, data and internet privacy, and emerging technology, including technological innovation in state government.

Representative Morales (D-Dist. 7, Providence) is serving his first term in the House of Representatives.

HB #5151 which would limit out-of-pocket expenses for Insulin at $25 for a 30-day supply.

February 7, 2021

Hi Friends, this Tuesday (2/9), the House Committee on Health and Human Services will hear a bill I introduced, HB #5151 which would limit out-of-pocket expenses for Insulin at $25 for a 30-day supply.

This would be the most affordable rate in the nation if passed and we need YOU to help by providing testimony in support of HB #5151. Below is a guide that will provide you with instructions on how to sign up to testify and a template to draft your testimony!

Review HB 5151 which would limit monthly out-of-pocket expenses for Insulin at $25 here
Below are the 2 ways you can provide testimony (the next page will guide you on how to draft your testimony):

Verbal Testimony:
Giving verbal testimony is the best way to have your voice heard. For verbal testimony, prepare to talk for 1-2 minutes on why you support HB #5151.
You can always read off a script or speak from your heart.

If you would like to provide verbal testimony, please send an email to HouseHealthandHumanServices@rilegislature.gov with the following information:
- Bill you are testifying on (HB #5151)
- State that your support it
- Your Name and Phone Number

What to expect: Once you have signed up, you will receive a call on Tuesday evening during the Committee Hearing (around 6pm to 8pm) to provide your testimony.

The deadline to request verbal testimony is Tuesday, February 23, 2021 at 11AM

DOCS.GOOGLE.COM
Supporting HB 5151: Guidance for Providing Testimony

Morales bill would prohibit utility shutoffs during declared emergencies

February 12, 2021

STATE HOUSE – Rep. David Morales has introduced legislation to prohibit electric, gas and water utilities from terminating service to Rhode Islanders for nonpayment during and after the COVID-19 emergency declaration or any future declared emergency.

The legislation ([2021-H 5442](#)) would institute a moratorium on service shutoffs for failure to pay during all declared emergencies.

During public health emergencies, it would also require the Public Utilities Commission (PUC) to issue orders suspending payment requirements during the emergency and for 90 days afterward, and canceling all late fees accrued during that time. The order would also prohibit utilities from allowing any nonpayment during that time to affect any customer's credit rating, and would require utilities to restore service to anyone whose services they terminated from the start of the declared emergency.

"Rhode Islanders are facing tremendous challenges as this pandemic nears the year mark. Some have been unable to work for months due to illness, job loss or lack of child care. Many people who were already living on the edge of poverty have been pushed over, and they don't have options in the middle of the pandemic," said Representative Morales (D-Dist. 7, Providence). "Shutting off their essential utilities would add a second public health crisis to the first, leaving families in dangerous, unhealthy living situations. For the sake of both human rights and public health, no one should lose their electricity, water or heat during an emergency like the pandemic we are experiencing now."

Currently, qualified low-income customers are protected from termination of electric and gas utilities for nonpayment due to the annual winter moratorium, which runs from Nov. 1 through April 15.

While the PUC had instituted wider emergency protections before the winter moratorium began, nothing is currently in place past April 15.

2021 -- H 5442

LC001366

STATE OF RHODE ISLAND

IN GENERAL ASSEMBLY

JANUARY SESSION, A.D. 2021

AN ACT

RELATING TO PUBLIC UTILITIES AND CARRIERS -- TERMINATION OF SERVICE DURING PERIODS OF DECLARED EMERGENCIES

Introduced By: Representatives Morales, Vella-Wilkinson, Barros, Giraldo, Ackerman, Caldwell, McEntee, Henries, Alzate, and Amore
Date Introduced: February 10, 2021

Referred To: House Corporations

It is enacted by the General Assembly as follows:

1 SECTION 1. Title 39 of the General Laws entitled "PUBLIC UTILITIES AND
2 CARRIERS" is hereby amended by adding thereto the following chapter:
3 CHAPTER 1.3
4 TERMINATION OF SERVICE DURING PERIODS OF DECLARED EMERGENCIES
5 39-1.3-1. Moratorium on termination of service during periods of declared
6 emergencies.
7 (a) No public utility which distributes electricity or supplies natural or manufactured gas,
8 electric or water service shall terminate service to any household for failure to pay an outstanding
9 indebtedness for service during a period of any declared emergency issued by the governor pursuant
10 to the provisions of chapter 15 of title 30.
11 39-1.3-2. Declared health emergencies.
12 (a) During declared health emergencies related to epidemics, including the statewide
13 Covid-19 emergency, the commission shall issue the following orders:
14 (1) Suspension of any requirement to make payment for utility service statewide during the
15 duration of the emergency and for a period of ninety (90) days following the end of the emergency;
16 (2) Cancellation of late fees accrued from the date of the emergency declaration and for a
17 period of ninety (90) days following the end of the emergency;
18 (3) Prohibiting utility companies from adversely affecting the customer's credit rating for

any non-payment for utility service during the period of the emergency and for the period of ninety (90) days after the end of the emergency;

(4) Requiring utility companies to resume services for anyone whose services were terminated from the date of the declared emergency and for a period of (90) days following the end of the emergency; and

(5) Any orders the commission deems appropriate in order to protect the health and welfare of the public during a declared health emergency.

39-1.3-3. Rules and regulations.

The commission shall promulgate appropriate orders, rules and regulations for the implementation of the provisions of this chapter.

SECTION 2. This act shall take effect upon passage.

LC001366

EXPLANATION

BY THE LEGISLATIVE COUNCIL

OF

A N   A C T

RELATING TO PUBLIC UTILITIES AND CARRIERS -- TERMINATION OF SERVICE
DURING PERIODS OF DECLARED EMERGENCIES

***

1   This act would impose a moratorium on the termination of utility services throughout a
2   limited period of any emergency declared by the governor, with special provisions related to
3   emergencies related to health epidemics.
4   This act would take effect upon passage.

LC001366

THIS young man gives me hope for the future!

Sally Jane Wilson
February 16, 2021

THIS young man gives me hope for the future! So proud to call David Morales my good friend! Congratulations on your new job, RI Representative-Elect David Morales! Here we are in my backyard, on my 65th birthday. Love this kid! <3

House Bill #5442

February 21, 2021

Tomorrow (2/21), House Bill #5442 which would prohibit utility shut-offs throughout the COVID-19 pandemic, will receive a committee hearing.

We need your support to pass this bill so please sign up to testify! Below is a guide to help you sign up and draft your testimony:
https://docs.google.com/document/d/1c90qPUebVktuxdf9yO0eh6C8MjSew5DYx5Ig72HgBWY/edit

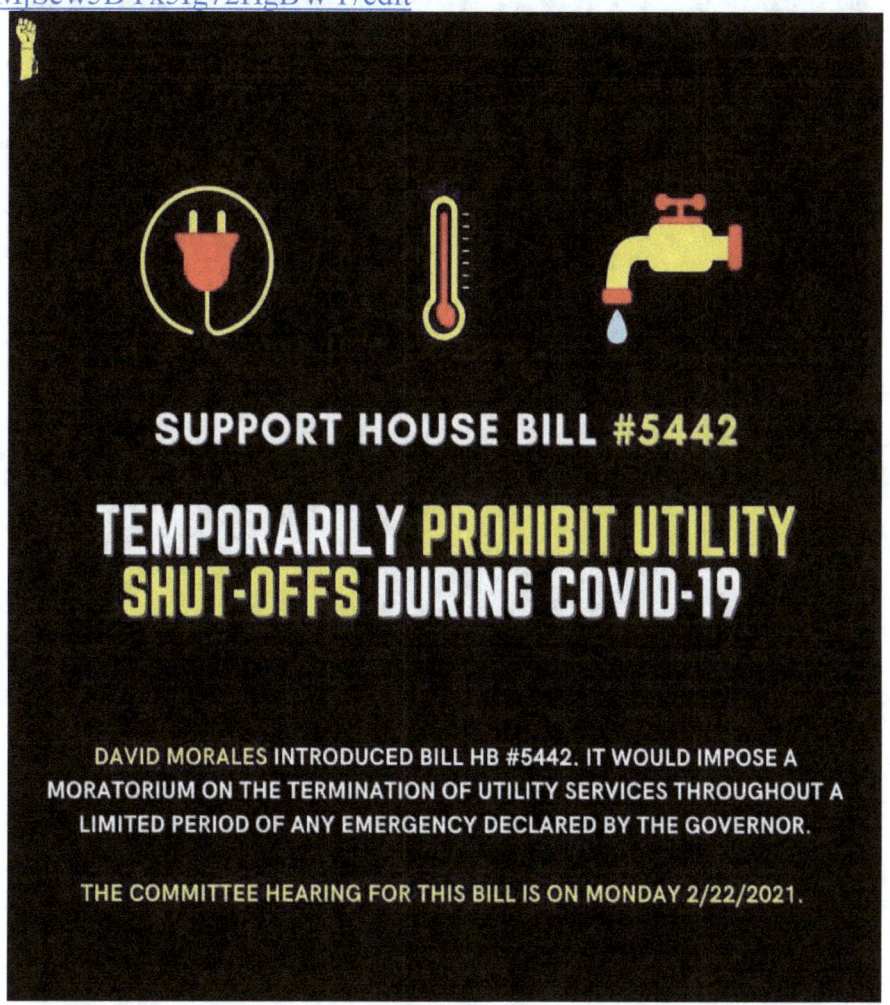

RHODE ISLAND

HAVE YOU BEEN AFFECTED BY THIS ISSUE?

PROVIDE A TESTIMONY!

VERBAL TESTIMONY:
GIVING VERBAL TESTIMONY IS THE BEST WAY TO HAVE YOUR VOICE HEARD. FOR VERBAL TESTIMONY, PREPARE TO TALK FOR 1-2 MINUTES ON WHY YOU SUPPORT HB #5442.
YOU CAN ALWAYS READ OFF A SCRIPT OR SPEAK FROM YOUR HEART.

IF YOU WOULD LIKE TO PROVIDE VERBAL TESTIMONY: INDIVIDUALS INTERESTED IN PROVIDING VERBAL TESTIMONY, SEND YOUR NAME, PHONE NUMBER, BILL NUMBER, AND POSITION ON LEGISLATION TO HOUSECORPORATIONS@RILEGISLATURE.GOV

WHAT TO EXPECT: ONCE YOU HAVE SIGNED UP, YOU WILL RECEIVE A CALL ON THE EVENING OF THE COMMITTEE HEARING TO PROVIDE YOUR TESTIMONY.

THE DEADLINE TO REQUEST VERBAL TESTIMONY IS MONDAY, FEBRUARY 22ND, 2021 AT 11 AM

WRITTEN TESTIMONY:
WRITTEN TESTIMONY SHOULD BE SUBMITTED TO HOUSECORPORATIONS@RILEGISLATURE.GOV
INDICATE YOUR NAME, BILL NUMBER, AND VIEWPOINT (FOR/AGAINST/NEITHER) AT TOP OF THE MESSAGE.

THE DEADLINE TO SUBMIT WRITTEN TESTIMONY IS 4 PM ON MONDAY THE 22ND

Outside the Lillian Feinstein Senior Center with David Morales

February 23, 2021
Sally Jane Wilson

Mexicanos en Rhode Island, unidos, jamás serán vencidos.

Ray Nuñez
March 7, 2021

After nearly a year of take-out only, it was reinvigorating to sit inside of Dolorespvd with this exceptional group of Mexican community leaders. Stay tuned y'all, we're cooking up some major systemic change over here.

The Rhode Island Legislative Black & Latino Caucus Book

Tomás Ávila
March 8, 2021

In celebration of my 25th Anniversary researching documenting and publishing RIMEO, I'm releasing my latest publication.

The Need Behind H-5781 Establishing An Elected And Appointed Minority Officials Commission

Tomás Ávila
March 8, 2021

{LC52/1} (Creates Elected/Appointed Minority Officials Commission to create record of minority officials from 1636 to present.)

Rhode Island Minority Elected, Officials (RIMEO)

Tomás Ávila
November 4, 2020

Back on February 2019, I decided to publish a collage once again about women in politics during Women History Month in Mach, and International Women Day, on March 8, and decided to make it about minority elected women. In preparation for such college, I decided to write an email to the librarian at the State Library, in the statehouse under the auspices of the of the Secretary of State, and also decided that instead of just asking about elected women in particular, I requested request information about all minorities who have been elected across the state throughout the years to state offices with the plan to start building a minority elected officials database from the data I was hoping to receive.

I received the response from the librarian, acknowledging receiving my request, and requesting some clarification "Do you want all minorities, or are there particular groups you're interested in (for example: people of color; women; LBGTQ community; a combination of these; etc.)? Based on the resources we have, I can only identify visually, and therefore I cannot identify religious or LBGTQ minority groups. We have the Rhode Island Owners Manuals which have Rhode Island's elected officials' photos from 1991 through present. We have a book of women elected officials from 1922--1992, but we do not have anything highlighting other elected officials who are part minority groups. Any additional information you can provide would be greatly appreciated. I will do as much as I can on your behalf and reach out to the State Archives once I hit a wall."

I responded that I was interested in minority people of color elected officials, black and Latinos. That was my interests, because that is where I focus my research and documentation over the past twenty-five years, and after a few email exchanges regarding the clarification about the context of what information I requested, I received the following response from the librarian, "Great, thank you for the clarification. We are working on this for you now."

A week after I received the following response "As *I began looking into your question regarding who have been all the people of color and minority elected in Rhode Island, I realized that I cannot accurately answer it. I can tell you that Rev. Mahlon van Horne was the first African American elected to the General Assembly in 1885.*

I recommend contacting the House and Senate to see if they are able to give you a list of the members of the Black and Latino Caucus. The Speaker of the House's office phone is 401-222-2466. I am more than happy to help you conduct research on this question with our resources. We do have the RI Owners' Manuals that do have black-and-white photos of elected officials dating back to 1991, which you are welcome to use in the library. We also have an index of all elected officials from 1879 through 1989 to get names of individuals, which can give you a list of names to research. The extent of our biographic information on elected officials is what is included in the Government Owner's Manual. The Rhode Island Historical Society and the Black Heritage Society both might have additional resources that would help figure out who identified/identifies as a minority, person of color, or Latino/a.

Thank You very much For sponsoring bill H-5781

Tomás Ávila
March 8, 2021

Rep. Anastasia P. Williams (D-Dist. 9, Providence)
Rep. Raymond A. Hull (D-Dist. 6, Providence, North Providence)
Rep. Karen Alzate (D-Dist. 60, Pawtucket)
Rep. Jean Philippe Barros (D-Dist. 59, Pawtucket)
Rep. David Morales (D-Dist. 7, Providence)
Rep. Jose F. Batista (D-Dist. 12, Providence)
Rep. Brianna E. Henries (D-Dist. 64, East Providence)
Rep. Joshua Giraldo (D-Dist. 56, Central Falls)
Rep. Leonela Felix (D-Dist. 61, Pawtucket)
Rep. Grace Diaz (D-Dist. 11, Providence)

For sponsoring bill H-5781 ESTABLISHING AN ELECTED AND APPOINTED MINORITY OFFICIALS COMMISSION {LC52/1} (Creates Elected/Appointed Minority Officials Commission to create record of minority officials from 1636 to present.)

http://webserver.rilin.state.ri.us/BillText/BillText21/HouseText21/H5781.pdf

2021 -- H 5781
LC000052

STATE OF RHODE ISLAND

IN GENERAL ASSEMBLY

JANUARY SESSION, A.D. 2021

AN ACT

RELATING TO STATE AFFAIRS AND GOVERNMENT -- ESTABLISHING AN ELECTED AND APPOINTED MINORITY OFFICIALS COMMISSION

Introduced By: Representatives Williams, Hull, Alzate, Barros, Morales, Batista, Henries, Giraldo, Felix, and Diaz
Date Introduced: February 24, 2021

Referred To: House Special Legislation

It is enacted by the General Assembly as follows:

1   SECTION 1. Title 42 of the General Laws entitled "STATE AFFAIRS AND
2   GOVERNMENT" is hereby amended by adding thereto the following chapter:
3   CHAPTER 160
4   THE ELECTED AND APPOINTED MINORITY OFFICIALS COMMISSION
5   **42-160-1. Short title.**
6   This chapter shall be known and may be cited as the "Elected and Appointed Minority
7   Officials Commission".
8   **42-160-2. Minority defined.**
9   (a) "Minority" means a person who is a citizen or lawful permanent resident of the United
10   States and who is:
11   (1) Black (a person having origins in any of the black racial groups of Africa);
12   (2) Hispanic (a person of Mexican, Puerto Rican, Cuban, Central or South American, or
13   other Spanish culture or origin, regardless of race);
14   (3) Portuguese (a person of Portuguese, Brazilian, or other Portuguese culture or origin,
15   regardless of race);
16   (4) Asian American (a person having origins in any of the original peoples of the Far East,
17   Southeast Asia, the Indian subcontinent, or the Pacific Islands);
18   (5) American Indian and Alaskan Native (a person having origins in any of the original

The Rhode Island Legislative Black & Latino Caucus: BIPOC Public Servants https://tinyurl.com/99tc5v34

The freshman House Reps dropping an album soon what should we name it?

José F. Batista
March 9, 2021

Tomás Ávila Legislative Testimony

March 10, 2021

COVID-19 Reflection: A positive pandemic outcome, is the efficiency and convenience of Legislative Testimony.

Instead of driving to the State House and wait in line for hours for your turn, you registered online and when your term comes up you receive a call and testify from the comfort of your home.

A Flippable Rhode Island 2022 Budget

Tomás Ávila
March 16, 2021

Tomás Ávila
Milenio Latino Institute

Executive Summary
https://book.designrr.co?id=68194&token=3625864976&type=FP

General Government & Quasi-Public Agencies
https://book.designrr.co?id=68177&token=2056951330&type=FP

General Government & Quasi-Public Agencies
https://book.designrr.co?id=68181&token=1975339924&type=FP

Education
https://book.designrr.co?id=68183&token=1074925915&type=FP

Public Safety, Natural Resources & Transportation
https://book.designrr.co?id=68186&token=1760263524&type=FP

Capital Budget
https://book.designrr.co?id=68189&token=442984905&type=FP

Morales and Cano bill would ensure all children have health care coverage regardless of status

March 16, 2021

STATE HOUSE – Legislation introduced by Rep. David Morales and Sen. Sandra Cano would ensure that all children, regardless of immigration status, qualify for health insurance under the state's RIte Track program.

"Health care is a human right, and all children, regardless of their immigration status deserve health care. Currently, there are about 3,000 uninsured children in our state who are not enrolled in the RIte Track program and are not able to access the health care services they need," said Representative Morales (D-Dist. 7, Providence). "Now more than ever, we need to ensure that all children in our state are healthy and have the ability to go to the doctor, especially as we continue to recover from the COVID-19 pandemic."

The legislation ([2021-H 5714](), [2021-S 0576]()) would establish Rhode Island's commitment to provide health insurance to all children who are residents of the state, regardless of immigration status. It would provide for the appropriation of state-only funds to pay for coverage if federal funds are not available.

RIte Track is the state's Medicaid program for children, providing health care coverage for those under age 19 whose family income does not exceed 250 percent of the federal poverty level. Rhode Island covered all children regardless of status for almost 10 years in the late 1990s and early 2000s, and it is time to restore this commitment to all children, the sponsors said.

Expanding coverage would allow parents to take their children to the doctor for preventive care, see specialists as necessary and buy critical medications that can help reduce higher health care costs for the state because if children are hospitalized, the hospital bills are covered by Medicaid, with the state paying its required share.

But more importantly, said Senator Cano (D-Dist. 8, Pawtucket), children should not suffer because of their legal status or socioeconomic background. In addition to lacking the health care that children need as they are growing up, children without health insurance may not receive emergency care as their families may fear that their status will be discovered. Having coverage for the children without regard to their immigration status would help alleviate some of those fears, keep kids healthier, and avoid preventable illnesses.

"All our kids need health care. They need immunizations. They need nutrition and medical treatment when they are sick. We are stronger and safer when everyone in Rhode Island has the health care they need," Senator Cano said.

The bill has strong support from over 20 organizations including Rhode Island KIDS COUNT, Economic Progress Institute, and The Latino Policy Institute.

"In 2019, 98.1% of Rhode Island children had health insurance coverage and Rhode Island ranked second for children's health insurance coverage," said Elizabeth Burke Bryant, Executive Director of Rhode Island KIDS COUNT. "To achieve our goal of covering all kids, we must restore access to RIte Care health insurance for income-eligible children who are undocumented immigrants. All children need access to health care that supports their healthy growth and development and promotes school success."

Linda Katz, policy director of Economic Progress Institute said, "COVID-19 has reinforced how interconnected and interdependent we are. Ensuring that *all* of Rhode Island's children have access to comprehensive health care through RIte Care enrollment not only helps those youngsters but protects all of us. EPI looks forward to working with Representative Morales and Senator Cano to enact this legislation."

"During the last year, we have experienced firsthand the impacts of health disparities on the educational and economic outcomes of our most vulnerable Black and Latino communities. Ensuring that our youngest Rhode Islanders have access to health coverage is a public health issue we cannot continue to ignore," said Marcela Betancur, Director of The Latino Policy Institute.

Dr. Gregory Fox, President of the Rhode Island Chapter of the American Academy of Pediatrics also expressed strong support. "The Rhode Island Chapter of the American Academy of Pediatrics enthusiastically supports this legislation, which opens Rite Care eligibility to all income eligible Rhode Island children. All children deserve access to the life-saving vaccines and quality preventative care which lay the groundwork for a healthy childhood and successful school career. Allowing for insurance coverage of all children of Rhode Island, regardless of immigration status, not only keeps kids in supportive medical homes and reduces costly emergency room care…it is the right thing to do."

The House bill was introduced Feb. 24 with over 20 cosponsors and has been assigned to the House Finance Committee. The Senate bill was introduced on March 11 and has been assigned to the Senate Finance Committee.

2021 -- H 5714

LC001720

STATE OF RHODE ISLAND

IN GENERAL ASSEMBLY

JANUARY SESSION, A.D. 2021

AN ACT

RELATING TO STATE AFFAIRS AND GOVERNMENT -- HEALTH CARE FOR CHILDREN AND PREGNANT WOMEN

Introduced By: Representatives Morales, Williams, Hull, Giraldo, Barros, Alzate, Tobon, Diaz, Kislak, and Kazarian
Date Introduced: February 24, 2021

Referred To: House Health & Human Services

It is enacted by the General Assembly as follows:

1 SECTION 1. Sections 42-12.3-4 and 42-12.3-15 of the General Laws in Chapter 42-12.3
2 entitled "Health Care for Children and Pregnant Women" are hereby amended to read as follows:
3 **42-12.3-4. "RIte track" program.**
4 (a) There is hereby established a payor of last resort program for comprehensive health
5 care for children until they reach nineteen (19) years of age, to be known as "RIte track." The
6 department of human services is hereby authorized to amend its title XIX state plan pursuant to
7 title XIX [42 U.S.C. § 1396 et seq.] and title XXI [42 U.S.C. § 1397 et seq.] of the Social Security
8 Act as necessary to provide for expanded Medicaid coverage through expanded family income
9 disregards for children, until they reach nineteen (19) years of age, whose family income levels are
10 up to two hundred fifty percent (250%) of the federal poverty level. Provided, however, that
11 healthcare coverage provided under this section shall also be provided without regard to availability
12 of federal financial participation in accordance to Title XIX of the Social Security Act, 42 U.S.C.
13 § 1396 et seq., to a noncitizen child who is a resident of Rhode Island lawfully residing in the
14 United States, and who is otherwise eligible for such assistance. The department is further
15 authorized to promulgate any regulations necessary, and in accord with title XIX [42 U.S.C. § 1396
16 et seq.] and title XXI [42 U.S.C. § 1397 et seq.] of the Social Security Act as necessary in order to
17 implement the state plan amendment. For those children who lack health insurance, and whose
18 family incomes are in excess of two hundred fifty percent (250%) of the federal poverty level, the

department of human services shall promulgate necessary regulations to implement the program. The department of human services is further directed to ascertain and promulgate the scope of services that will be available to those children whose family income exceeds the maximum family income specified in the approved title XIX [42 U.S.C. § 1396 et seq.] and title XXI [42 U.S.C. § 1397 et seq.] state plan amendment.

(b) The executive office of health and human services is directed to ensure that federal financial participation is assessed to the maximum extent allowable to provide coverage to children pursuant to this section, and that state-only funds will be used only if federal financial participation is not available.

42-12.3-15. Expansion of RIte track program.

(a) The Department of Human Services is hereby authorized and directed to submit to the United States Department of Health and Human Services an amendment to the "RIte Care" waiver project number 11-W-0004/1-01 to provide for expanded Medicaid coverage for children until they reach eight (8) years of age, whose family income levels are to two hundred fifty percent (250%) of the federal poverty level. Expansion of the RIte track program from the age of six (6) until they reach eighteen (18) years of age in accordance with this chapter shall be subject to the approval of the amended waiver by the United States Department of Health and Human Services. Healthcare coverage under this section shall also be provided to a noncitizen child who is a resident of Rhode Island ~~lawfully residing in the United States,~~ and who is otherwise eligible for such assistance under title XIX [42 U.S.C. § 1396 et seq.] or title XXI [42 U.S.C. § 1397 et seq.]

(b) The executive office of health and human services is directed to ensure that federal financial participation is assessed to the maximum extent allowable to provide coverage to children pursuant to this section, and that state-only funds will be used only if federal financial participation is not available.

SECTION 2. This act shall take effect upon passage.

LC001720

EXPLANATION

BY THE LEGISLATIVE COUNCIL

OF

AN ACT

RELATING TO STATE AFFAIRS AND GOVERNMENT -- HEALTH CARE FOR
CHILDREN AND PREGNANT WOMEN

***

1   This act would expand the Rite Track Program to provide health care coverage to children
2 up to age nineteen (19) funded by federal funds, if available, or if not available, by state funds.
3   This act would take effect upon passage.

LC001720

Capitol Spotlight: Representative David Morales with Margie O'Brien

March 17, 2021

SUMMARY KEYWORDS
Rhode island, people, constituents, work, address, phone calls, legislator, campaigning, representatives, priorities, opportunity, degree, representative, fulfilling career, frontline health care, untraditional, full time gig, committee hearings, passed, part

00:37
MO: Hi everyone and welcome to this Capitol spotlight, it's my pleasure to introduce you to one of our newest representatives, Representative David Morales Thanks for being here.

00:45
DM: Yeah, thank you so much for inviting me. I really do appreciate it.

MO: So first time running for office.?
DM: Yes.
MO: What was it like?

DM: it was definitely a unique experience in terms of campaigning during the times of COVID Sure, so definitely required a lot of adapting and being able to reach our constituents and working people in a non traditional way that we might have done before so that involved, of course, a lot of the door to door canvassing just that, a social distance that was appropriate that kept everyone safe, making sure that we use to social media to be able to reach different audiences, then ultimately just being able to make a lot of phone calls to our residents and our different constituents, but most importantly, going well beyond just campaigning for the purpose of winning an election, but also being able to provide people with resources that are adequately available such as services like Meals on Wheels such as nonprofits like Ahmad who are doing a lot of mutual aid work so I saw this campaign season as an opportunity to not only obviously win an election, but more so be able to provide services to people that they might have not been aware of otherwise.

01:46
MO: And not that you have anything to compare it with but do you feel like people were more needy this time. They wanted to talk to you they wanted answers, because many are isolated, many are stuck at home. I imagined they took the opportunity to come out with the safety precautions in place to speak with you.

02:06
DM: Yes, most definitely, as we've seen across different news coverages, we are often saying that COVID has exacerbated issues that already existed. So we have a health care program across our country that has been broken because it's a for profit health insurance industry. And so a lot of people are seeing how that has been exposed, because the moment they lost their job, they also lost their health insurance. So there are definitely a lot more grievances that people had expressions about, but most importantly, they wanted to know what our local government what our state government can do to address these needs because oftentimes people think it's a top bottom approach from the federal government, all the way down to the states and the states have no say on these decisions, however with COVID people are saying actually you know what our state government should be doing something to address the COVID outbreak to address health care to address the economy. So did these conversations help you form your priorities for this legislative session. Most definitely. I believe one of my main priorities has been an urgent response to COVID relief, that looks like having a moratorium on evictions that looks like making sure that we provide hazard pay to our frontline health care workers and Frontline essential workers, for months, it's really been sacrificing and risking their health and their lives of their families. in order to receive the compensation they deserve.

03:21
MO: So I know that a lot of people at home think this is your full time gig, but a legislator is actually a part time position here in Rhode

Island. **What is your other life look like and how did that shape your decision to run and maybe your perspective here.?**
03:35
DM: Yeah, of course, so it is technically a part time legislature, you're correct. I often say yes I often say that it is a full time responsibility though I'm answering phone calls from the moment I wake up to, before I go to sleep from constituents, or just being able to coordinate with other legislators but important priorities we need to work on. But beyond the legislature, I work full time as an employment and internship specialist with Year Up Rhode Island which is an employment training program so I have the opportunity and the privilege to work with young adults who want to enter a fulfilling career through the one year training program we put them through. Unfortunately, my employer has been very flexible with this new Adjustment going into the legislature so I have not seen much of a difference except the fact that maybe I have less time to walk my cat.

04:18
DM: I mentioned that one of the benefits of YearUp is the camaraderie between the people that are volunteering, the people that are getting sort of the benefit of their volunteerism, did you hope that that would be a similar camaraderie here in the house.

04:34
DM: Yeah I think it's always the idea that a group of people are working towards a common goal at Year Up, we're working towards the common goal of making sure young adults again enter fulfilling careers and have the skills to do so. Whereas here in the statehouse, our goal is to make sure that we are passing policies that prioritize the needs of working people here in Rhode Island.

04:52
MO: It's hard though, right, because you're not in the House chamber, you're not sitting right next to someone that you could really bond with they might become a mentor for you at the vets you're spaced out safely. At least you are still together. That is the positive.

05:07
DM: No, I definitely agree, it has been untraditional from what I've heard from different representatives in regards to their experience from previous years. Nevertheless, I am still making an effort to reach out to my colleagues so it looks a little different. It involves a lot of phone calls and a lot of video chat resume as opposed to an in person meeting where we could get to know each other a bit better and a bit more personally. And how have you found the session so far. So far I think we are going at a pace that is appropriate, and I would like to think that after we come back from break, we will accelerate that pace and really begin to get a couple bills on the floor. I understand that the Senate has passed very important legislation on their side, regarding the minimum wage, regarding safe staffing for nursing homes. So I would like for us to address those issues in our committee hearings and eventually get them onto the floor for a vote, and eventually be able to get the governor to sign them into law because again, a lot of these are urgent issues that we can't afford to wait on.

06:01
MO: So my last question we just met some folks out in the hallway. When someone says hello representative. What does it make you feel like?

06:10
DM: I haven't been who is into titles so it always does make to degree, a little bit of pride, just because my lived experiences I didn't grow up in poverty to a single mother. And for us, the expectation was, hopefully we'll be able to go to college and earn a bachelor's degree and make a self sustaining living. Never was the idea to get into politics or become a part of the legislative process. So like I said, to a degree, it doesn't make me feel proud. I always tell people they can simply call me, David. Nevertheless,

06:39
MO: well welcome Representative David mirallas to the house. We look forward to talking again during this session. Thank you so much, appreciate that. And thank you at home for joining us for this capital Spotlight.

Eight Months After Posting

Tomás Ávila
March 17, 2021

8 Months since I published this posting, this undocumented family still without permanent housing or Human Services despite COVID-19! Why? March 17, 2021

¡8 meses desde que publiqué esta publicación, esta familia indocumentada sigue sin vivienda permanente o servicios humanos a pesar de COVID-19! ¿Por qué?

July 7, 2020

Heartbreaking when you received this article from a Facebook Friend today. Started reaching out to my network trying to help Sucely J Murillo, and request everyone who can help to reachout to her. https://www.providencejournal.com/.../hundreds-in-ri-face...

Desgarrador cuando recibió este artículo de un amigo de Facebook hoy. Comencé a comunicarme con mi red tratando de ayudar a Sucely J Murillo, y solicitó a todos los que pueden ayudar a comunicarse con ella.

Ray-ality TV Episode 10: State Representative David Morales (D-Dist. 7)

March 21, 2021

00:00
Hello, welcome to Reality TV. I'm your host Ramond Bakary. And today I'm joined by the state representative for Rhode Island State House District seven. Representative David Morales Representative Morales. How are you today?

00:11
Raymond, it's a pleasure to see you. And I just want to thank you again for the invitation. I am feeling pretty well, we just finished a long legislative week. But I'm very excited with all the progress that we're making.

00:21
Yeah, of course, anytime you're always welcome on the show, and it's a pleasure to have you on just diving right into the first question here, what made you want to get into politics, I

00:28
think first and foremost lived experience, I grew up to a single mom. And watching her work, multiple jobs just to provide for me and my older sister really had an impact on me at a young age. Because Initially, I always thought it was normal to watch someone struggle because I was surrounded by working class neighbors. My friends, were not wealthy either. But as I got older, I began to realize that there is a high level of income inequality that forces people like my mom to be exploited in terms of working long hours for very minimal pay. And she worked multiple jobs, especially during the holiday, she would work up to three jobs, whether it was at a gas station, a grocery store, picking vegetables, or fruits from the fields. So I saw that hard labor directly. And it wasn't again, until I got older when I was roughly in high school that I began to realize and understand that the government could actually address a lot of those issues, most specifically low wages, most specifically, making sure that there's health care coverage for those who need it. Because I'm sure we'll get into it as the conversation goes along. Right. But oftentimes, we have

a lot of working people who don't necessarily qualify for Medicaid. But at the end of the day, they still can get health insurance from their employer, or if they do, it ends up being too expensive. But all that to say I'm indebted to my mom and all that she did for my sister. And I especially because something I don't know, we share often. But my dad was an alcoholic and was addicted to drugs, and unfortunately, did not necessarily have a safety net or a resource to access when he was struggling with those issues himself. But overall, I would like to say it's going to be lived experience that really pushes a lot of the policies that I'm advocating for, because I want to make sure that all working people are productive, protected, both socially and economically.

02:19
Yeah, and you had mentioned there are a lot of issues like health care and addressing the minimum wage, we're gonna get to that definitely in this in this conversation. Starting off, one of the big issues you have been fighting for as state reps so far is for a universal health care system here in Rhode Island. Why do you feel this would be beneficial for Rhode Islanders,

02:35
because right now, we have over 40,000 people who do not have any form of health care coverage. And for those individuals who do have health insurance, about 42% of them are underinsured, which essentially means that they technically have health insurance, but they do not receive medical treatment or go to the doctor, because the CO pays and out of pocket expenses are still too expensive. So in other words, I would say that, in a way, they still don't have the health care coverage that they need. Technically, that safety net is available for them to ever go to the emergency room, it's not going to be as expensive as if they were uninsured. But at the end of the day, if you can't go in for a basic checkup, because you are concerned about the costs. Or you are concerned that you're going to learn something about your health that will lead you into medical debt, that is not a sustainable model. And I do not believe that we should be enabling a for profit health care system, because that's going to lead to health disparities, which disproportionately affect poor people disproportionately affect communities of color. And furthermore, it

essentially in my mind, it goes back to the basic principles of I think it's immoral, I think it's immoral for there to be a system that benefits from disease from diseases, a system that benefits from people being ill and is dependent on that. So ultimately, I don't think it's a sustainable model, both for the actual people experiencing it. But also as a state, we're gonna recognize that's actually more and more expensive, because at the end of the day, the insurance companies are focused on profit. And they're going to continue trying to outsource Medicaid, they're going to continue trying to outsource health services, and tell the government that we're going to do it in a more efficient and cheaper way, despite the fact that it's less effective, and in some cases, actually more expensive. So ultimately, I think the best step to take as of right now is I do have a bill in place alongside representative john Lombardi and represent Brandon Potter to establish a study commission. And that was a bill I was very happy to co sponsor and this one would essentially, like I said, established a study commission to study the implementation and establishment of a single payer Medicare for all type system here in Rhode Island. I myself have the actual single payer Medicare for all system bill in the House as yet to receive a hearing in the finance committee. And while I understand that we are not going to transform our healthcare system overnight, I think it's important to have officials inside that state house who are advocates Eating for these changes.

05:03
In this, along with many issues that you're advocating for do have strong opinions on both sides. One of the big arguments from the critics of the universal health care system is mainly the cost and how it would be paid for what they like to argue is that something that could end up costing trillions on the national level in here on a local level, most likely billions, what they say would result in a tax crease in for those in the middle and working class. Just out of curiosity, how exactly would this get paid for if it were to pass and be signed into law? And would this result in any tax increases for middle and working class? Rhode Islanders?

05:29
Yes, thank you for asking that. So I think what you highlighted is the perfect example of fear mongering rhetoric that is spread throughout

the mainstream media. And that was my way of saying that that is essentially the taglines that wealthy people then tell the middle class and working people to convince them that an idea and a policy that will actually benefit them is going to be harmful to them. So they resort to misinformation and lies. Now, in terms of a Medicare for all health care system, it looks differently, whether you choose to do it at the federal level, or at the state level, I'm going to focus on the state level, because that is what would impact us here in Rhode Island. So if we are to do it at the state level, it would not result in a tax increase for working or middle class people. Because what would happen is we would request a waiver from the Biden administration or whoever the president, whoever the president is, at the time when we passed a system. And what that waiver would do is essentially any payments or cost that we received to cover Medicaid would not be going to the Medicaid fund. Instead, it would be going to what we call the Rhode Island comprehensive health care program fund. And that would be the fund that would essentially distribute that Medicare for all system to everyone who needs it, and again, would not necessarily be dependent on the Blue Cross Blue Shield, so the world to provide it to us. And what we would do is essentially a lot of the, what we call the middle person, that being the health insurance carrier between the hospital and the patient is we would break down that middle person and instead be able to connect that person directly with the healthcare provider that they need. And in terms of how this would be paid for as well. Specifically, it would be a 10% payroll tax on large corporations. Hence, in a life, the size large corporations, those who have 500 or more employers, not our small businesses, because again, that's another fear mongering rhetoric that people like to tag on to. And when you actually do the math, it would be a lot cheaper and more cost efficient for a large company to pay into this payroll tax, then to having to contract with the health insurance companies to provide their employees health care, which they are required to do already. So overall, when you actually again, it takes some explanation, and it took me about a minute and a half to really explain that to you in detail, it becomes very easy for the opponents of a Medicare for all system, those opponents being the ones whose profits would be impacted, to spread all of this misinformation and lies without actually explaining the real details in terms of how this program would work.

07:48
And the issue of health care is like a very big issue with with the umbrella of sub issues. And I just want to cover another one. Well, while we're still on the healthcare related issues, another one you've been advocating for is to fix, advocating to fix is lowering the prescription drug costs, what can be done to achieve that goal here in Rhode Island,

08:05
there are various ways we can do it. Um, I believe the most direct way to do it is just copying co pays. Because the way it works, and again, takes a little bit of explanation is the drug manufacturers develop a drug such as insulin only costs about $3 per vial to actually produce and manufacture and ship out. Unfortunately, however, this is marked up, and they will sell it to the insurance companies for about $300. And then the insurance companies will take it back to the patient and charge them about $600. So as you can see, everyone's kind of like, in a way, right, I'm gonna be a little informal, everyone's kind of like ripping each other off. And the person who's benefiting the most is the drug manufacturers and of course, the health insurance in entities also get a kick out of that profit as well. And the person who's hurt the most is the patient and the person who depends on. So I think the most direct way to do it, especially with drugs that do not cost that much to produce such as insulin is you just kept copays, you kept the out of pocket expenses, and you tell the health insurance companies, it is now your responsibility because you are the only entity in the country who has the privilege to directly negotiate with drug manufacturers Keep in mind, the government is not allowed to do it based on federal regulation. So the moment you start cutting into the health insurance profits, the health insurance company is then forced to go back to the drug manufacturer and tell them they are cutting into our profits, we are not going to pay these outrageous amounts that you've been charging us because now we can't benefit from it. Hence, the drug manufacturers are then forced to lower the prices as a result. And I say that because that has been a case study that has been seen in Colorado that has been seen in New Mexico, and has been seen in various other states where they have kept specifically I leaned back on to insulin but some states have also started doing the same caps on

what we call specialty medication, which is designed for chronic diseases and illnesses such as cancer and HIV. And again, the drug manufacturers become an Of these products of these drugs, and they are able to abuse the system. And since the federal government cannot intervene, or any form of government can intervene, they can do it. But that's why it's important to recognize what policies we could adopt. And alongside that one bill, I was very proud to co sponsor this year, representative. Ackerman introduced one that would allow us to have a regulation board. And what I mean by that is that there would be somewhere within the Office of the health insurance commissioner to work directly with the drug manufacturers and understand why they're pricing the drugs away they are so in other words, it's like calling for more transparency. And it holds the drug manufacturers feet to the fire, in terms of why they're increasing the outrageous amounts of drugs in terms of the price. Furthermore, we also have a bill in place or introduced by Representative Anastasio Williams, that would allow us to import prescription drugs from Canada. And I believe that's another again, another tool we have in terms of adopting policies to make medicine cheaper and affordable for those who need it and depend on it.

11:04
And this is one of those bipartisan issues I've had. I have heard of Republicans being supportive lowering prescription drug costs, I believe the former president, former President Trump was in favor of doing that, but I'm not sure what progress they had made on it. Has there been any republicans in the state legislature that you've been able to get on board with this?

11:20
So generally, when I introduce the two bills I've introduced in committee so far focused on prescription drug pricing, that being insulin at $25 a month, and that being specialty medication at $100 a month, I have not received any opposition from any Republicans, nor have I necessarily had any republicans come out loud and tell me Hey, this is a really good bill. I know I have had some more like conservative Democrats, come up to me and tell me, you know, I don't always agree with some of your ideas or the way you approach it. But I do think that these issues that you're fighting for, specifically,

the specialty medication are really important. And that's something that I'm in support of alongside you.

11:57

And you're also on board with raising the minimum wage to $15 an hour, one of the topics we had discussed a little bit at the top of this interview here in Rhode Island raising the minimum wage to $15. This is this has a really good chance of passing the General Assembly and then being signed into law by Governor McKee. Where is that because they're out there. As we mentioned before we went on camera there, like there was like 1000 bills submitted. And it's kind of a little tough for everybody to track the progress. Where's the $15 minimum wage bill currently in the process of being passed and signed into law?

12:24

Yeah, so there has already been a committee hearing for it in the House Committee of labor. And right now it is being held for further study. So when, in about a month or so I think we will see it being considered out of the Labor Committee and then ultimately going on to the House floor for a vote, which in and of itself is not a guaranteed actually pass. So we have to make sure we're ready to advocate. And I do want to mention something that's very important, especially in the context that we're talking right now. 2021, we're talking about raising the $15 minimum, the minimum wage to $15, by roughly 2024. The fight for 15 started back in 2009. The fight for 15 star back in 2010, I think we're really behind. And I'm optimistic that we are going to pass the $15 minimum wage, so I don't take anything for granted, we're gonna have to fight very hard for it. But I want to get us out of place where it doesn't stop at 2024. And following that, we're able to adjust for inflation, or the price index, whatever meter we want to use to measure. But essentially, we need to make sure that every year following 2024, there is an incremental increase to keep up with the cost of living, because rent continues to escalate. We all know that we're in an affordable housing crisis right now. Healthcare continues to get more expensive in terms of your annual premiums in terms of deductibles, groceries are getting more expensive, right? Milk costs more on an annual basis, even if it's nothing too significant, it adds up every year, gas is starting to increase as well. So my point is like things that we use in our daily lives increase naturally every single year, except for the wages. And that in and of itself just is not does not make any sense at all. So that's why for me, it's going to be really big that if we could add an amendment to make sure that after 2424, there's still an incremental increase, we need to take that, and we cannot just be settled and satisfied with $15 by 2024. Because at that point, I think it's already outdated, and it's definitely gonna help some people, but it's not helping them as much as it should be.

14:24
Then you had mentioned that there is going to be a big fight, you know, to get that bill signed into law. And also it's been on the goal since 2009. You said,

14:32
correct bite for 15 started by McDonald's workers back in Chicago.

14:36
And there's a lot of probably one of the big reasons is the common criticisms that you hear against raising the minimum wage, and this will probably be heard a lot during the testimony. A lot of those who are against it point out how they what they say how it could hurt small businesses, especially since the same businesses were being strangled to death during the pandemic as well as prices items going up to cancel out the growth in wages. And then they also bring up another argument of why not just lower taxes, what's your response to those comments? arguments heard in the discussion of raising the minimum wage? And are those common concerns being taken into consideration when the discussions are going on about raising the minimum wage?

15:09
So I just want to be clear that it is always very interesting to see how selective the Chamber of Commerce are. And these business Coalition's are when it comes to being concerned about the health of the small businesses, I think they'd like to use them as a scapegoat when it comes to raising the minimum wage for sure. Well, I do believe that the minimum wage should be considered in terms of the capacity of the small businesses, I think that also raises the issue of how we've been doing enough to support our small businesses during

the pandemic. And I would say no, I think the Restore Rhode Island grant was a good start did not go far enough was not accessible enough. Because we have a lot of Latino owned businesses here in district seven in the Mount Pleasant Valley in Elmhurst neighborhood. I could count on my fingers, the amount of them that actually got the restorer right grant, one of the main reasons they got it was because I went there directly with the application, and I had a consultant with me who was willing to help them on. In other words, they wouldn't have received the grant. Not every district has an official who is going to be knocking at their doors, telling them about this opportunity. There are a lot of small businesses of color that were left out of it. So my argument is, if someone wants to pose the issue of raising the minimum wage to $15, because of the impact it's going to have on our small businesses, I expect to see them on the front lines really trying to fight for more viable support for small businesses during the covid 19. pandemic. And following that, I think there will, there will be a more credible conversation in terms of that. And that's for cutting taxes. I have not heard that argument, I find that to be very humorous, because we often hear that like we're in a deficit or that we can't pay or that we can't pay for anything in our budget. So are we cutting more from our budget? Like who is intentionally again, I'm curious, who is telling us, hey, let's have less funding for our schools, especially during times like these, that to me makes no sense whatsoever? And it probably comes back down to who are the people saying, right, it's not working. People are not saying don't raise the minimum wage. working people aren't necessarily aside from property taxes, you're not really hearing working people complain too much about their income taxes. Yeah, it seems to be like the wealthy individuals are the ones who want that tax cut. And again, it always comes back to the basic principle of greed. And I think we highlighted it during our discussion about health care, whether it's drug manufacturers, health insurance companies, certain corporate lobbyists, it always comes back down to the profit margin. And again, I think they are concerned, they're scared that it passed the Senate. And now that's going over to the house. Yeah, we're gonna get ready for a lot of fear mongering rhetoric. I'm getting ready to hear a lot of officials spew the words that a corporate lobbyist would otherwise say, during a committee hearing.

18:01
And just shifting the focus a little bit while we're still on the topic of wages and all that a lot of people who are essential workers would also see their wages go up when the minimum wage goes up. And I kind of wanna shift the focus for a moment because one of the key issues that you have been advocating for to be addressed is hasn't paid for essential workers. Where's that bill currently when it comes to the legislative process? And what are some of the key details that Rhode Islanders should know about the bill? Like say, for example, how much is being proposed for hazard pay for essential workers?

18:26
Yes, thanks so much for asking Dounreay. So my bill to provide essential workers that being individuals at grocery stores that being individuals in health care facilities, janitorial staff, credit unions, banks, anyone who has been essential over this past year to provide us with services, and has been risking their health to do that deserves additional compensation. And what this looks like is 1.3 times one's base pay. So in other words, if you make $12 an hour under this hazard bait hazard pay bill, your wage would go up to $15.60 an hour. Now, I want to be specific in terms of who this would affect However, because again, as someone who does advocate for a lot of our small businesses, specifically, and especially those owned by people of color, I made sure to have the threshold at employers who have 50 or more employees. Most small businesses do not have 50 or more employees. Even restaurants usually cap it around 40 if they have multiple shifts, so this would not impact any of our small businesses. This will predominantly impact some of the larger entities in our state such as CVS such as Walmart, Target against Citizens Bank, all of these different institutions, price, right stop and shop, Trader Joe's all these the list can go on and on. But a lot of these large entities that rake in millions to billions in profit, are paying their workers less than $12 an hour despite the fact that they're forced to Wear a face mask for eight hours at a time and interact with dozens of people daily. I think at the very least deserve some additional compensation for it. And I know at the beginning of the pandemic, and again, it's really sad to say only at the beginning of the pandemic, from, from March to roughly mid June, it was for my understanding that stopping shop was providing some form of hazard pay. After

those three months, however, it went away. And, again, I personally believe that hazard pay hasn't been seen as a really credible policy. And it upsets me, it really upsets me that we have not actually considered it to be something where we can say, thank you for risking your health, risking the health of your loved ones, to provide us with these vital services, I believe you should receive a little bit more pay just for doing. Unfortunately, I don't think it's gained enough traction the way it should have. Especially because you drive around. And if you pass by any healthcare facility, specifically the nursing homes, you will always see banners that say we love our healthcare heroes, thank you healthcare heroes, when it comes down to actually providing them with the compensation they need to pay their daily expenses. There's no additional compensation to be found, there is no additional pay to be found. There is no additional benefits to be found. So I'm going to continue pushing for this bill, we did have a committee hearing for it back in February in the house Labor Committee, and actually think it was probably one of my better hearings of the year, we did have multiple questions asked by committee members, and I think they were all in good faith. But they realize that I had the answers to them. And that actually made a lot of sense. Because initially, some people asked me like, oh, what are you gonna do about small businesses? And of course, I told them, well, if you read the bill, it's 50. Plus, hence only impacting bigger businesses.

21:54
And just shifting the focus to others who because I have a couple more is still covered. Because there was a lot like, like I mentioned, there's a new like 1000 plus bills introduced. Other issues that you've also prioritize are affordable housing and ending source of income discrimination. There are other things that land or there are other things that landlords and homeowners have the right to use when it comes to renting to people aside from where income comes from. That's the point that doesn't get introduced a lot when it comes to the arguments that the critics bring up. What were the reactions from some of the homeowners, from some from some of the homeowners that you've heard when it comes to this issue in terms of source of income discrimination? Yeah, and affordable housing like that, that umbrella surprise,

22:31

I did not hear that much resistance towards it. And I think it's because this has been a fight that's been going on for so long that people are recognizing like, they're not really asking for much. They just want to make sure that working people poor people, and again, disproportionately people of color, have a safe space to live. The pushback you do receive is the fact that you know, some people don't want to have their units inspected, because they have to be in accordance with regulations from the United States Department of Housing and Urban Development. Right. So HUD does have to oversee the unit. And I know that for some people, certain property owners, they see it as a burden that they don't want to take on. However, if you want to call yourself a property owner or landlord, your unit should be up to code regardless of whether or not the person you're renting to has a housing voucher. So that's why I don't buy too much into that argument and of itself, because again, being a property owner is an investment. Therefore, you should be willing to take the investments if you're going to charge market rate for your unit. Especially because as we've discussed earlier, when affordable housing crisis, we have a lot of units aren't even market rate anymore. As for affordable housing, the way we are going to achieve affordable housing is going to be through the budget. That's as direct as it gets. I'm sorry, I don't think there needs to be that many complicated policies to really try to grasp and understand the issue of affordable housing. For me, it simply looks like devote at least $20 million a year into the Rhode Island State Budget, increase it incrementally every year and devote it towards the development of affordable housing. Use an encourager governments to use eminent domain as needed in order to develop some more dense housing. As opposed to trying to figure out some very wonky policies as to how we can incorporate affordable housing and meet the 10% threshold as long as you give the cities and the towns the money. And you direct them very specifically on how to best approach this issue. And you work with the city leaders, I think that we can get to 10% affordable housing across the state.

24:47

And you had mentioned the pushback. And it's interesting that you had mentioned that because I recall when this was being talked about on on Twitter, there was an interesting thread there was like a whole argument between one homeowner and the one person who was like very in favor The ending source of income discrimination. Their point was that there are the things that landlords and homeowners have the right to look at when it comes to renting to tenants, you know, like background checks and all that. And the homeowners who who weren't in favor of it, they're in the mind, they were in the mindset where they say, at the end of the day, if someone owns a house and doesn't want to rent us rent to someone income sources aside, and just the fact that they don't want to rent in theory shouldn't be forced to rent, they don't want to that was their argument on this thread. So the issue of where the income comes from aside if someone doesn't want to rent all at all, and they own the home. And you know, this was a concern that one of them had, can you assure those homeowners that they won't be forced to rent if they don't want to?

25:37
Well, they, it's because of the source of income, they know that that guarantee can be said, because that's what the law does. The law says that if you are intentionally telling an individual or you refuse to rent for them, to rent to them, because of the source of income that they receive, that being a legal source of income, then that is illegal. And they can be taken to court for

26:02
like, like in, like, in general, like the income sort of income aside, because like one of the common arguments I heard, and I don't know, if this was done sparking a chain reaction, they had mentioned that this is gonna open the door for them to be forced to run like, the income side or whenever they want to be forced out. And

26:16
it always comes back down to the details, the sometimes it's individuals who, again, didn't actually read the bill or understand. And again, I'm not poking fun at anyone, because I do think legal language is inaccessible to a large degree, but I don't think people

miss the point of the actual bill itself. So no, it's not causing this floodgate of like now, you are forced to rent to anyone and everyone.

26:41
Thank you. Yeah, no problem, because that was because like, one of my main goals, whenever it comes to these issues is you know, to give both sides the clear chance to give their argument and also, you know, any discrepancy discrepancies or logical fallacies gets left at the door. That's what that's kind of a little bit of a confusion on the way I worded that one but just want to know, no

26:59
worries. I mean, don't get me wrong. I do think there are a lot of slippery slope arguments when it comes to certain issues focused on socio economic mobility.

27:06
And another big issue. Quick segue to another big issue is shifting the focus to education. You're a big advocate for public schools, just out of curiosity, because this is going to be a big issue, especially since governor McKee said on newsmakers that he would veto the charter school moratorium, where do you stand on the expansion of charter schools,

27:21
I do not believe that. Charter School networks should be expanding in the state of Rhode Island. I want to emphasize charter school networks. I believe a single standing charter school like Paul cuffy provides very high quality education and program tailored to the students that they're serving on achievement first network however, and there may oral academies do not do that they teach to the test, it is a strict environment, they do not prioritize socio emotional value with their students. And all they want is to be able to enroll more and more students each and every single year in order to take it back to their charter management organizations. So they will teach to the test to ensure that the right cast scores are high, regardless of the social and emotional impact that has on their students. So I do not think organizations like them whose sole purpose is to expand as much as possible should be expanding our state. And again, those are charter

school networks, owned and controlled by charter management organizations. So that's my stance on I think it's just very straightforward. If we want to talk about single staying charter schools, I think there is room for that. Yes.

28:28
So just to kind of summarize that you're like when it comes to nonprofit charter schools, you'd be more in favor of those as opposed to for profit.

28:35
Yes, I mean, legally, I don't even know if we're using the right terms. Cuz I don't know if they're technically is like a for profit charter school. The right they're still registered as a nonprofit in a way. But again, if you're a charter school network, there is some profit coming in. So I would say, Yeah, they are technically for profit, legally speaking, though, technically not.

28:52
And this kind of also goes into the sub issues like school choice. And the common question that I that has been heard when it comes to expansion to charter schools, especially from those that are super in favor of it. They asked Why is it such a problem for there to be more charter schools, so parents can send their child to a school that isn't in a failing district, like Providence or Central Falls that required state takeovers after what they say were millions of dollars spent? What What would be your response to those common questions and concerns?

29:19
Yeah, so I think there is still flexibility of school choice within the public school system. Right. I mean, I think that's why you have a situation where, you know, unfortunately, there are some parents in our local school districts who are really trying their hardest to make sure their child is enrolled at classical High School, as opposed to Mount Pleasant High School. So there's still some flexibility there. I think the purpose that we're really trying to get at is we want to ensure that our children in our youth are being sent to academic institutions that again, prioritize their well being and are really making that push

to ensure that there's some form of academic achievement, as opposed to again, a larger charter management organization that doesn't necessarily prioritize the well being of their Youth in their children, but instead again are focused on what is the score on the next reicast exam going to be? What is the next student that we could highlight on our newsletter in order to convince the world that charter schools are better than public schools? So I don't think you're taking away choice necessarily when you put a moratorium on certain charter school institutions. And again, maybe that's something that we can look into when it comes to amending the law, because for my understanding, yes, McKee. Governor McKee has been very vocal that he would veto it, though the senate actually has enough votes to override that veto anyways, for what it's worth. But in terms of going to the House floor for that charter school moratorium, I will probably be voting in support of it.

30:40

And you had mentioned possible amendments that could be added to it. And the another big issue that I had kind of mentioned, the last question was school choice where the it would fund students and a lot of states have been on the bandwagon of passing. It's like Montana, I believe New Hampshire is another one Arizona, they're making the move on this, where they would fund the tax, I believe, is the tax dollars that would fund the students instead of the systems. And students want to be restricted what schools can go to by the zip code? Have you or your colleagues at the state legislature considered making an amendment or passing something like school choice where the textiles for the student instead of the school systems and children aren't restricted to their educational opportunities by zip code.

31:15

So that would require revising the education funding formula that for the past five years has not been touched, even though, you know, we have a study Commission on it. And officials are working very hard on analyzing and trying to see what works best for everyone. Again, I don't really think it's a very complicated issue. In my opinion, you ensure that school districts receive funding per English language learner pupil, and they're not combined alongside free and reduced lunch peoples, because they're not mutually exclusive. You make sure our transportation is covered as well, that every school district has the means to be able to transport. The students are going to be going in to the district from out of town. So in other words, like, yeah, I think we could adopt a model that is similar in terms of per pupil funding, and not necessarily district based. But again, I don't think it's a one size fits all model. I think some of the states that you cited, have actually seen decreases in education spending as a result of adopting a per pupil model. So I would never be in support of something that would reduce our education spending.

32:23
And moving on to another big issue that you've been advocating for when you were even when you were running for state rep. And now even more so since you've become state rep and that's passing a green new deal in Rhode Island. And here, this is like how we mentioned with probably a bunch of issues throughout this. There's a lot of like, tricky elements in certain language when it comes to the arguments on this on a national level. It was projected to cost at least $10 trillion a year when it was introduced by Congresswoman ocasio Cortez and Rhode Island. We are and here's when the when the arguments come in from those against it in Rhode Island, we already have an inflated budget of almost 13 billion for a state with little over a million residents. Well, the last one was 12 point 7 billion. So almost 13 billion the last budget for a state with a little over a million residents. And this is a bit of a multi part question. What would be in this green New Deal? refer Rhode Island proposal? How much would it cost? And kind of citing back to the earlier question, would middle class and working class Rhode Islanders see any tax increases? If it becomes law?

33:18
Yes, so I want to be clear, there's like no definite, green New Deal policy, like you're not gonna have a bill that is titled green New Deal. The green new deal is an intersectional approach to addressing the housing crisis, it is an intersectional approach to addressing the lack of high quality jobs. It is an intersectional approach towards environmental sustainability. Therefore, it is a combination of multiple programs, you will not get to the green New Deal unless you adequately fund affordable housing in the state budget annually,

which is why I mentioned that earlier, you will not get to the green New Deal unless you have carbon emission reduction goals, which thankfully, we're gonna see the act on climate pass very soon. And that's going to get us there, you see, so they all work together as my point, all of these policies are connected with each other. Because you are not going to get to 100% renewable energy unless you take away the interconnection authority of national grid, and you transfer it over to a public entity that will actually prioritize the general welfare of the state. As for some of these ambitious programs, in general, in the different policies, we've talked about how much it would cost. I always love having conversations about the budget, because if we want to really get serious about like any deficits or our concerns about how much we're spending in such a small state, then perhaps we should cut out some of the corporate welfare we have in place, perhaps we should start looking back at the fact that we cut the corporate tax rate and because of And furthermore, look at the fact that we have large institutions such as Brown University, which make up about 40% of the acreage in Providence and is essentially tax exempt, thus forcing taxes to increase on working and middle class people in terms of their property taxes. So we already have, we are I believe we have the tools in the budget to really invest in our people, but we self sabotage it. And by that I mean the influence of the lobbyists, den influencer and officials to make decisions that are not popular. For example, we're about a rip apart Kennedy Plaza. And we're gonna have one main bus hub split into three different bus hubs. And despite opposition and resistance from the people who actually ride the bus, were willing to spend over $30 million on this project that no one in terms of those who would be affected actually agree on. So I don't want to hear these conversations so much in terms of the budget and being irresponsible with spending, because I would argue that's irresponsible spending. But you don't see the watchdogs, pointing it out as much as when it comes to, you know, actually investing in health care and investing in education, all of a sudden, we become policy experts. And we become so so concerned about our budget, but that concern is nowhere to be seen when it comes to corporate welfare. Now in terms of taxes, again, no working person or middle class person is going to be hurt. As a result of these programs, the only individuals whose taxes should be impacted to fund these programs already stated, or large institutions like Brown University, who have millions and billions and assets, but do not pay their fair share. And alongside that, the wealthiest individuals in our state who make over $495,000 a year, and had been paying a 6% income tax rate, which is the same as a working person since 2006. This is a conversation we do not have enough, about 15 years ago, we cut taxes, income taxes for the wealthiest people in our state, they went from paying a 9.9% income tax rate 10%, essentially, to now a 6% income tax rate. And as a result of that, our state and projections have shown this to be true, we have lost over $1 billion in tax revenue, that's $1 billion, that we could have invested back into our into our communities, that is $1 billion dollars that we could have used to help jumpstart the green New Deal. So all that to say is I believe it is possible to create a better future and a better world for the people in our state. And it is not going to disrupt the economy in order for us to get there.

37:22
And just before I shift away from the political issues from my last two questions, this this follow up while we're still on the green New Deal topic, is there a ballpark figure that we could get for how much the green New Deal color Well, in with these proposals, how much would they cause like, just like a would be a ballpark figure. And you did mention all the only big corporations would receive the tax increase? Is there a certain income bracket where you would cap tax increases that and what would be the as I said earlier, you

37:46
if you are to repeal the 2006 tax cuts for the wealthy, what you would see is a situation where someone who makes over $495,000 a year, keep in mind, it's essentially half a million dollars, their taxes would go back to being 9.99%, the same way it was prior to 2006. If you do not make $495,000. And that is the vast majority of Rhode Island, I'd say probably you know, probably about 98 99% of the state, your taxes aren't being raised, we can see a tax increase. In terms of the corporate tax, I don't really see there being any political will to repeal the tax cuts that we made under speaker Matty yellow. So I believe down is going to stay put as is. Nevertheless, I do think we should get to a point where we really begin having more auditing and tax assessor's analyzing the use of nonprofits, and how they're using their

tax exemption status and their property that's tax exempt. In other words, I kind of want Brown University to start paying their fair share, again, not gonna impact the working person or middle class person, but I'm sure their lobbyists will tell you it will not weigh you can become concerned.

38:58
So for in terms of taxes, only the people make a 400k or more would receive the increases what I'm hearing for that 495k 495k or more. So if it's less like if someone's making like 60 70k no tax increase? No. Okay. And I'm just because I didn't I kind of want to get this one addressed as well. Before I moved on to the last two questions. ballpark figure, how much would this probably cost? Like, are we talking 1 billion, 5 billion 10 billion, like, what are we? Sorry? What would be the projected cost of things like the green new deal and all these proposals like just a ballpark figure if there's one because like I mentioned on the national level, it was projected 10 trillion a year? What would that look like for Rhode Island on a state level, like the bulk again,

39:37
only addressing certain pieces of it, if we're looking at affordable housing, if it's up to me, we're investing at least 20 million a year and affordable housing. As for other projects, again, that's going to be the I don't want to state what can and can't be because we haven't even gotten past interconnection. We are still under the control of national grid on whether or not a renewable energy projects going to receive a approval. So until we even get there, we can't have conversations about developing renewable energy. Therefore, I can't really put a price tag on it, because I don't know what that will is going to look like then.

40:09
And that is a fair point that is brought up because it's more of right now they're in the discussion phase of like getting this the getting these issues out to the public.

40:16

Yeah, like we're still building a framework. And because trust me, I would love to have a price tag to it. That way, we could compare how much it would cost versus like the corporate welfare we give out. And then like the combination of like, general obligation bonds as well, which interest rates are at an all time low? Oh, it'd be great. But no, we're still in the phase of getting that framework together.

40:35
And I know I had said the ballpark figure was the final one. But this is the one that brought up because, you know, the the argument of the budget being 12, like almost 13 billion the last year for state with a little over a million residents. Would this would to see the budget get inflated and go higher. Like if in a perfect world where you were able to get this all done like that, when we see the budget go up any higher?

40:58
Again, I think it depends on the leadership you have at the gubernatorial level. And how creative people want to be. I don't think all these projects are you know, the idea of a green new deal has to be dependent on the state budget. Yeah, bonds, general obligation bonds, you have revenue bonds, there are a lot of different resources you could try to extract, you could also start cutting the corporate welfare. So maybe that balances out the budget, right? Regardless, every year, the budget does increase. Like draw all of Gov among those 10 year each and every single year, the budget increased. Ironically, we're cutting Medicaid the entire time as well. But the budget naturally is going to increase. So a green New Deal or not, the budget will increase excellent, not exponentially, but it will increase each and every single year thereafter.

41:45
And then now shifting the focus, because we kind of did go extensively into that, which was the goal because I always like to go extensively into these because some of these issues could take hours to debate and all that shifting now shifting the focus away from politics, because I always like to get away from the political questions in the last couple of questions. This is something that we got, we've gone back and forth on Twitter about you're a big wrestling fan. I'm a

big wrestling fan. And I have to ask these five things in this next question that every wrestling fan nowadays has to answer and I'll kind of do it in like rapid fire lightning round format. So let's just let's just go for it. Favorite wrestler of all time. Right now Samoa Joe. All Time. All right, and favorite match of all time.

42:20
Bret Hart versus Stone Cold Steve Austin WrestleMania 13 submission match.

42:24
That was a good one. And that's kind of you know, we still don't know who walked up the hill people say Brett walked up the hill called Brett walk down the hill. No, no, that was Yeah, a lot of people like to argue that started the the rise of Austin's anti hero character persona persona, because like right after that's when it just went out of the app off the rails the mike tyson mike tyson referee match when he thought Michaels at 14, maybe 14. Are you an AWS or web guy or even impact because they're Alright,

42:51
so WWF WWE when it comes to nostalgia current product, I'm asked to give it out to a W. As you can see, I've been holding these belts. I'm prepared. I like that, though. And oh, yes, you're right. I was prepared for that one. So yeah, current product A w goes all out every single week. And like, I actually feel like the creative staff is thinking about scans when they develop the show. Yeah, whereas with WWE, I just feel like they kind of throw it out the wall and just wait till the next pay per view to produce quality, which again, is not consistent.

43:22
And sometimes not even every pay per view is good. Like, like, I think the last couple good pay views. If only they'd been the big four is like SummerSlam, the last one Survivor Series, we had Lesnar versus Daniel Bryan, then the I think that was the same one when NXT joined that little brand warfare thing where they had like the champs and they include NXT, which was really good idea. I don't know why they don't keep going with that even at WrestleMania. What's your one dream match? That hasn't happened yet?

43:46

Probably several, as I mentioned earlier, Samoa Joe is one of my favorite wrestlers. And they're giving his I hope it's not an early retirement. Given that he's been sidelined. For the past year and a half. There are a lot of matches he hasn't been able to have. I think a big one that we overlook is john cena versus Samoa Joe, because they both started together and up w back in 2001. A lot of people don't know that history. But they essentially got their start in professional wrestling together. And I think it'd be nice to have that full circle come together. Looking not so modern. However. Bret Hart versus Kurt Angle.

44:18

That would have been that would have been a towel making mission match. That would have been like, was it benwell Versa Jericho? I don't know if was the no it was um could have been a face that made you 17 was a Jericho no no Jericho face regalos benwell vs angle and then I don't know if the rematch of backlash was a submission match or two out of three falls. It's I can I can picture that being something like that. Mine personally, if we're going historical sting versus taker that should have happened. Oh, no, you got it. Yeah, Sting versus taker angle versus taker especially in oh six. I was. I don't know why that didn't happen. That would have been perfect. The money was right there. Even when sting came back from Kenya 31 to have sting versus Triple H that was garbage. No, I was I was let down especially with the outcome. Hunters don't have one. And it's like That was probably like in my opinion the last good years wV had like the last good year I feel like whatever you have is probably 2016 when the brand split first started and SmackDown had that goaded roster with Bray Wyatt AJ Styles going into Survivor Series. I'm working out a little I'm marking out a little hard right now for wb

45:18

is you set a perfectly the 2016 roster was so stacked that no one was ignored. Like everyone had a role in exactly. The ruthless aggression and the Attitude Era so special is that even someone like spike Dudley, who in today's world would just be like a jobber. And that's it. Yeah, otter roll back then

45:35
to play.

45:36
And Fun fact that you know, I respect spike Dudley even more after finding out this fact. He's from Rhode Island. He's one of the very few famous wrestlers from renowned Chuck Palumbo, and if we're going independency and Vega Scott, she does amazing work. And she I think she did commentary for a W this past summer, amazing talent, all of them. And a lot of people don't know that. When you look at famous wrestlers from Rhode Island, I find a question for this. Before I go to my final final question for the interview. What do you usually say and this gets me annoyed as a wrestling fan to when non wrestling fans when they find out where a wrestling fan they say you know, it's fake right? what's what's your go to response?

46:11
I say it is scripted. The same way that your favorite television show the same way that our favorite movies are scripted. The action and the punishment and the physical brutality they go through is all too real. And I kind of like to leave it at that. But if I have to I'll explain the fact that you know people have been severely injured in the rain

46:33
and that that's the harsh reality they they're on the road like three 300 days a year that one one wrong move one slip you can you can be paralyzed me

46:42
look at the Summer slam right? When you look at Stone Cold versus open heart.

46:46
I was just about to mention that or when Darren drove I don't know if this was on a dark matter if it was that one was was very sad and I and he did it for the business and he still has no hard feelings with everybody involved. And he's still you know, loves the business. And that's what people don't realize it's a business. We know it's scripted,

but the action is way more physically demanding than I would say even most of the sports like football to be honest with you 111 wrong move that can end a career like that. And harsh reality that also doesn't get addressed with things like the healthcare for the wrestlers at AWS is addresses the unionization that's why jesse ventura got fired in the 80s because Hulk Hogan ratted him out.

47:21
See this is this is that we're like wrestlers speaking each other's language now that's why I never included Hulk Hogan in the Mount Rushmore, Mount Rushmore anyways, because he stopped the unionizing efforts he had you know this case of racism etc etc

47:35
that's probably why he was the the golden boy in the 80s to when he ratted out jesse ventura. That's the the big rumor and innuendo going on about that. And to be fair, you know what now I'm going to ask this before I go to my final final question your Mount Rushmore wrestling the What's it for four on there the four Yeah, so

47:50
Undertaker's on it without a doubt. Stone Cold Steve Austin is on it. Without a doubt, john, john cena is on it. And now you have to go to someone the golden arrow by default. And again, it's very easy to pick Hogan, and I'm not gonna pick Hogan somat to go with the nature boy Ric Flair, just because of his longevity. I'd love to go macho man.

48:10
But at the end of the day, he didn't really get as much of the opportunities in his career was kind of short stopped a little bit before he went to WCW. And even his WCW run was it. It was underrated. Like every time you got the belt Hogan one at the next week and the next night. It's just crazy to think about and, and that was that was a that was a poor use of a great talent and even Bret Hart in WCW.

48:31
You know, we don't talk about Bret Hart. That was not a bad yeah, we know that was shameful. They had the hottest angle in professional wrestling and they just blew it.

48:41

Imagine it's just like you get the best of the best wrestler in the country in probably the whole world. Let's say contract is New Japan was really good in the 90s 2000s, etc. You get the best wrestler in the world who could put on the best match, he could carry anybody. He even carried that on that one guy forgot his name that Vince gave the trial and in Madison Square Garden, and the Vince was gonna push him to the moon. But we realize Bret Hart carried him in the tryout match. It's just like Bret Hart can make a nobody into a star. He can wrestle a broom and we'll be entertaining. You just make them he'll have joined the NW Oh, and then Goldberg ruined his career. That is a global he's a nice guy. I hadn't met him when we had the New England Fan Fest back in Providence, like seven years ago or something.

49:20

I remember that. Yeah.

49:21

We need to get more conventions and more like a wrestling scene in Rhode Island. Maybe we got a call spike dawn and Chuck Palumbo one of these days that professional wrestlers without a doubt my final question moving on from the wrestling top and my final question is one that I asked everyone here on the show to keep tradition that has some involvement with Rhode Island and that is in your opinion, what do you think Rhode Island is best known for?

49:42

In the spirit of spring? I'm going to say Dells lemonade right now,

49:45

when a close book there. That's one of the big answers. Now the real question is with or without a straw.

49:53

Without, okay, cuz if you say with a straw, that that no, that's actually gonna be a question but has to be without a straw. That's the ultimate road is to be without a straw. That's why when I hear with strong,

50:05
I remember I think, I think it was even on Twitter, Angie Yang, he got called for having a with a straw. He's he because he has a profound connection because he went to Brown University and he's been in Providence a couple times. It gives speeches back when he was an entrepreneur pre presidential run. And it's just you know, without a straw, that's the ultimate thing. Thank you once again, Rep. Morales for coming on the show. It's been a pleasure to have you on. Yeah, of course, Ray. Likewise. And thank you once again for watching this episode of reality TV. If you want to see future episodes, this is a post on this channel, please click the subscribe button down below along with the post notification bell icon to the right of it. I'm Raymond bakari. I'll see you on the next episode.

MEDIA ADVISORY: Legislators to participate in Third Annual RI Multilingual Education Advocacy Day tomorrow, March 23

March 22, 2021

STATE HOUSE – Several legislators will be joining the Coalition for a Multilingual RI **tomorrow, Tuesday, March 23 at 11 a.m.** for the third annual RI Multilingual Education Advocacy Day. Due to COVID-19 precautions, this year's event will be held virtually on Zoom. Those interested in participating can register at bit.ly/multilingualri2021 and the event will be live-streamed on Capitol TV and the Coalition for Multilingual RI Facebook page.

Multilingual Education Advocacy Day will bring legislators, students, parents, educators, community organizations and members of the public together to discuss challenges and advocate for resources to expand multilingual education opportunities to all Rhode Island students.

The Zoom press conference will begin with remarks from Sen. Frank A. Ciccone (D-Dist. 7, Providence, North Providence), Sen. Sandra Cano (D-Dist. 8, Pawtucket), Rep. Grace Diaz (D-Dist. 11, Providence), Rep. David Morales (D-Dist. 7, Providence), and Sen. Ana Quezada (D-Dist. 2, Providence).

The event will also feature remarks from Department of Elementary and Secondary Education Deputy Commissioner Dr. Kelvin Roldán; parents Fernanda and Andrew Poyant; multilingual students and educators; Aline Binyungu, Women's Refugee Care; Jonathan De Jesus and Jaqueline Agustín, Progreso Latino; Sandra Victorino, Care New England; Paige Clausius-Parks, Rhode Island KIDS COUNT; and Dr. Erin L. Papa on behalf of the Coalition for a Multilingual RI; along with closing remarks from Howie Berman, Executive Director of ACTFL.

The Coalition for a Multilingual RI is a coalition of organizations and community members dedicated to creating a culturally sustaining educational environment where all Rhode Island students learn in multiple languages from Pre-K to college.

Vaccines are now available for ALL 18+ Providence

March 22, 2021

Vaccinate Providence

ATTENTION NEIGHBORS / ATENCION VECINOS:

Vaccines are now available for ALL 18+ Providence residents in 02909, 02908, 02907, and 02905, and 02904. Appointments available now! New vaccine appointments are regularly updated below.

Si se tiene a lo menos 18 años de edad, y se vive en Providence en el 02909, el 02908, el 02907, el 02905, o el 02904, se puede obtener la vacuna. Hay citas disponibles ahora. Navígese a este sitio del internet:

Rhode Island's Act on Climate bill passes House, 53-22

Republicans and some Democrats objected to giving "faceless bureaucrats" rather than elected officials power over the climate change plan, which makes the state's greenhouse gas reduction goals mandatory.

By Edward Fitzpatrick Globe Staff,Updated
March 23, 2021, 8:52 p.m.

The Rhode Island State House Blake NISSEN FOR THE BOSTON GLOBE

PROVIDENCE — After more than four hours of debate, the state House of Representatives voted 53 to 22 on Tuesday to pass the "Act on Climate" bill, which makes the state's goals for reducing greenhouse gas emissions mandatory and enforceable.

The Senate has already approved a companion bill by a vote of 33 to 4, but each chamber must pass the other's version before attention turns to whether Governor Daniel J. McKee will sign the legislation, which updates state carbon-reduction goals set in 2014 and provides an enforcement mechanism.

"Fighting climate change is the challenge of our time," House Majority Leader Christopher R. Blazejewski said. "To ensure a safe and healthy future for all of us, and our children and grandchildren, we must embrace our shared responsibility to reduce emissions and bring greater accountability, urgency, and equity to governmental action on climate."

Blazejewski, a Providence Democrat, emphasized that the last seven years have been the warmest in recorded history, causing ice caps to melt and sea levels to rise.

"Rhode Island is the smallest state and the Ocean State, with 400 miles of coastline, and it is particularly prone to the dangerous impacts of climate change," he said. "Rhode Island is warming faster than any of the lower 48 states."

But a group of Republican lawmakers and some Democrats opposed the legislation, emphasizing that it would give power to unelected state officials.

"It's clear that this bill sets up a process whereby businesses, municipalities, and individuals will be regulated in a vast area of daily activities," said House Minority Leader Blake A. Filippi, a Block Island Republican. "I cannot accept what this bill does, and that is a massive delegation of our legislative authority to a body of unelected bureaucrats."

Deputy House Speaker Charlene M. Lima, a Cranston Democrat, raised similar objections, saying, "This is a total abrogation of legislative responsibilities we were elected to fulfill."

The bill sets mandatory goals for the state to reduce greenhouse gas emissions: 45 percent below 1990 levels by 2030, 80 percent below those levels by 2040, and at "net-zero emissions" by 2050. And it calls for the Executive Climate Change Coordinating Council, consisting of officials from a variety of state agencies, to come up with a plan to hit those targets.

"Think of this as the PUC on steroids," Lima said, referring to the Public Utilities Commission, suggesting citizen concerns would "fall on deaf ears."

The House rejected a proposed amendment that would have required legislators to vote on any plan adopted by the Executive Climate Change Coordinating Council before it is carried out by state agencies.

House Majority Katherine S. Kazarian, an East Providence Democrat, said the legislature regularly passes laws that require state agencies to create plans and enact regulations. "We are not abdicating any responsibility," she said. "If anything comes up, we jump in."

Representative Karen Alzate, a Pawtucket Democrat, said communities such as Pawtucket, Central Falls, Providence, and Woonsocket will benefit from the bill. "Climate change does not affect just coastal communities – it affects all of our Rhode Island communities," she said.

But Representative Patricia L. Morgan, a West Warwick Republican, contended that, "What we are doing will fall on the working poor hardest of all – the ones who pay the rents, the ones who pay the electric bill, the ones who will have to change their furnaces and their cars."

Morgan said she is concerned that "some faceless bureaucrats are going to make regulations and force people, with a carrot or a stick, to put electric heat in their homes and to buy electric vehicles because that is the only way we can meet the aggressive goals set out in this bill."

Advocates contended that nothing in the bill requires homeowners to install electric heat in their homes or to buy electric cars.

Representative Teresa Tanzi, a South Kingstown Democrat, said she was "disheartened to hear all the misinformation." She said Rhode Island would reach the greenhouse gas emission goals by "tried and true" methods such as using renewable energy sources like offshore wind projects and solar power, and it could purchase renewable energy credits.

The House debated the bill and batted down a series of proposed amendments over the course of four hours. At one point, House Speaker K. Joseph Shekarchi announced that the House might put off a final vote until Thursday because legislators' iPads were running low on power. But the House pushed ahead with Blazejewski moving to call a final vote.

In final arguments, Filippi said the debate was not about climate change or polls showing that people want action on climate change.

"It's about whose responsibility it is," he said. "The responsibility is ours. We are punting. It's a copout. People in this body are afraid because they know that the plan that is going to be presented by ECCC will be so expensive and draconian, they know this body would never vote for it."

But Representative Lauren Carson, the Newport Democrat who introduced the bill, said Rhode Island needs to adopt a plan to qualify for federal support and funding. She said states such as Massachusetts are far ahead in developing plans and meeting goals for addressing climate change.

"There is a new economy coming," Carson said. "There will be new jobs and business. This bill begins to position Rhode Island to be at the front of that kind of economy. I don't think we can afford to not do something on climate change."

So will the governor sign the bill if it comes to his desk? On Tuesday night, McKee's spokeswoman, Andrea Palagi, said, "The governor looks forward to reviewing the legislation."

Edward Fitzpatrick can be reached at edward.fitzpatrick@globe.com. Follow him on Twitter @FitzProv.

2021 -- H 5445 SUBSTITUTE A

http://webserver.rilin.state.ri.us/BillText/BillText21/HouseText21/H5445A.pdf

2021 -- H 5151

http://webserver.rilin.state.ri.us/BillText/BillText21/HouseText21/H5151.pdf

2021 -- H 5218

http://webserver.rilin.state.ri.us/BillText/BillText21/HouseText21/H5218.pdf

2021 -- H 5151

LC000246

STATE OF RHODE ISLAND

IN GENERAL ASSEMBLY

JANUARY SESSION, A.D. 2021

A N   A C T

RELATING TO FOOD AND DRUGS -- RHODE ISLAND FOOD, DRUGS, AND COSMETICS ACT

Introduced By: Representatives Morales, McGaw, Alzate, Ackerman, McNamara, Hull, Lombardi, Speakman, Felix, and Fogarty
Date Introduced: January 25, 2021

Referred To: House Health, Education & Welfare

It is enacted by the General Assembly as follows:

1   SECTION 1. Chapter 21-31 of the General Laws entitled "Rhode Island Food, Drugs, and
2 Cosmetics Act" is hereby amended by adding thereto the following section:
3   **21-31-16.2. Cost sharing in prescription insulin drugs - Limits - Definition - Rules.**
4   (a) As used in this section, unless the context otherwise requires, "prescription insulin drug"
5 means a prescription drug, as defined in §21-31-2, that contains insulin and is used to treat diabetes.
6   (b) A carrier that provides coverage for prescription insulin drugs pursuant to the terms of
7 a health coverage plan the carrier offers shall cap the total amount that a covered person is required
8 to pay for a covered prescription insulin drug at an amount not to exceed twenty-five dollars ($25)
9 per thirty (30) day supply of insulin, regardless of the amount or type of insulin needed to fill the
10 covered person's prescription.
11   (c) Nothing in this section prevents a carrier from reducing a covered person's cost sharing
12 by an amount greater than the amount specified in subsection (b) of this section.
13   (d) The insurance commissioner may use any of the commissioner's enforcement powers
14 to obtain a carrier's compliance with this section.
15   (e) The insurance commissioner may promulgate rules and regulations necessary to
16 implement and administer this section and to align with federal requirements.

1   SECTION 2. This act shall take effect on January 1, 2022.

LC000246

EXPLANATION

BY THE LEGISLATIVE COUNCIL

OF

AN ACT

RELATING TO FOOD AND DRUGS -- RHODE ISLAND FOOD, DRUGS, AND COSMETICS ACT

***

1   This act would limit the total amount that an insured person is required to pay for a covered
2   prescription insulin drug at an amount not to exceed twenty-five dollars ($25) per thirty (30) day
3   supply of insulin, regardless of the amount or type of insulin needed to fill the covered person's
4   prescription.
5   This act would take effect on January 1, 2022.

LC000246

2021 -- H 5218

LC000917

STATE OF RHODE ISLAND

IN GENERAL ASSEMBLY

JANUARY SESSION, A.D. 2021

AN ACT

RELATING TO LABOR AND LABOR RELATIONS -- MINIMUM WAGES

Introduced By: Representatives Morales, Alzate, Ranglin-Vassell, Vella-Wilkinson, Ajello, Lombardi, Henries, Potter, Batista, and Williams
Date Introduced: January 28, 2021

Referred To: House Labor

It is enacted by the General Assembly as follows:

1   SECTION 1. Chapter 28-12 of the General Laws entitled "Minimum Wages" is hereby
2   amended by adding thereto the following section:
3   **28-12-26. Public health disaster emergency hazard pay.**
4   (a) Except for the state and its political subdivisions, every employer employing eight (8)
5   or more employees shall pay any employee who performs essential services outside the employee's
6   home or residence, at a rate of one and one-third (1⅓) times the regular rate of pay during any
7   period of public health disaster emergency as declared by the governor pursuant to § 30-15-9.
8   (b) For purposes of this section, essential services include those provided by or related to
9   the operation of the following businesses:
10   (1) Agricultural equipment and supply;
11   (2) Auto repair and supply;
12   (3) Banks and credit unions;
13   (4) Electronics and telecommunications;
14   (5) Firearms;
15   (6) Food and beverage stores, supermarkets and distributors to include: liquor stores,
16   specialty food stores, bodegas and convenience stores, farmers' markets, food banks and pantries;
17   (7) Funeral homes;
18   (8) Gas stations;
19   (9) Harm reduction organizations, recovery and treatment organizations, and organizations

conducting in-person outreach with vulnerable populations such as those who use drugs, unhoused individuals and people recently released from incarceration;

(10) Health care;

(11) Industrial, construction equipment and supply, hardware stores, general power equipment;

(12) Laundromats;

(13) Pet supply;

(14) Pharmacies, medical supply stores and compassion centers;

(15) Printing shops, mail and delivery stores and operations and office supply businesses;

(16) Professional uniform suppliers and stores;

(17) Restaurants;

(18) Seafood equipment and supply;

(19) Security and public safety; and

(20) Any commercial business, operation or entity designated as providing essential services by the director of the department of labor.

SECTION 2. Section 28-5-7 of the General Laws in Chapter 28-5 entitled "Fair Employment Practices" is hereby amended to read as follows:

28-5-7. Unlawful employment practices.

It shall be an unlawful employment practice:

(1) For any employer:

(i) To refuse to hire any applicant for employment because of his or her race or color, religion, sex, sexual orientation, gender identity or expression, disability, age, or country of ancestral origin;

(ii) Because of those reasons, to discharge an employee or discriminate against him or her with respect to hire, tenure, compensation, terms, conditions or privileges of employment, or any other matter directly or indirectly related to employment. However, if an insurer or employer extends insurance related benefits to persons other than or in addition to the named employee, nothing in this subdivision shall require those benefits to be offered to unmarried partners of named employees;

(iii) In the recruiting of individuals for employment or in hiring them, to utilize any employment agency, placement service, training school or center, labor organization, or any other employee referring source which the employer knows, or has reasonable cause to know, discriminates against individuals because of their race or color, religion, sex, sexual orientation, gender identity or expression, disability, age, or country of ancestral origin.

(iv) To refuse to reasonably accommodate an employee's or prospective employee's disability unless the employer can demonstrate that the accommodation would pose a hardship on the employer's program, enterprise, or business; ~~or~~

(v) When an employee has presented to the employer an internal complaint alleging harassment in the workplace on the basis of race or color, religion, sex, disability, age, sexual orientation, gender identity or expression, or country of ancestral origin, to refuse to disclose in a timely manner in writing to that employee the disposition of the complaint, including a description of any action taken in resolution of the complaint; provided, however, no other personnel information shall be disclosed to the complainant; or

(vi) To take any adverse employment action against an employee for failure or refusal to work during any period of public health disaster emergency as declared by the governor pursuant to § 30-15-9.

(2)(i) For any employment agency to fail or refuse to properly classify or refer for employment or otherwise discriminate against any individual because of his or her race or color, religion, sex, sexual orientation, gender identity or expression, disability, age, or country of ancestral origin; or

(ii) For any employment agency, placement service, training school or center, labor organization, or any other employee referring source to comply with an employer's request for the referral of job applicants if the request indicates either directly or indirectly that the employer will not afford full and equal employment opportunities to individuals regardless of their race or color, religion, sex, sexual orientation, gender identity or expression, disability, age, or country of ancestral origin;

(3) For any labor organization:

(i) To deny full and equal membership rights to any applicant for membership because of his or her race or color, religion, sex, sexual orientation, gender identity or expression, disability, age, or country of ancestral origin;

(ii) Because of those reasons, to deny a member full and equal membership rights, expel him or her from membership, or otherwise discriminate in any manner against him or her with respect to his or her hire, tenure, compensation, terms, conditions or privileges of employment, or any other matter directly or indirectly related to membership or employment, whether or not authorized or required by the constitution or bylaws of the labor organization or by a collective labor agreement or other contract;

(iii) To fail or refuse to classify properly or refer for employment, or otherwise to discriminate against any member because of his or her race or color, religion, sex, sexual orientation, gender identity or expression, disability, age, or country of ancestral origin; or

(iv) To refuse to reasonably accommodate a member's or prospective member's disability unless the labor organization can demonstrate that the accommodation would pose a hardship on the labor organization's program, enterprise, or business;

(4) Except where based on a bona fide occupational qualification certified by the commission or where necessary to comply with any federal mandated affirmative action programs, for any employer or employment agency, labor organization, placement service, training school or center, or any other employee referring source, prior to employment or admission to membership of any individual, to:

(i) Elicit or attempt to elicit any information directly or indirectly pertaining to his or her race or color, religion, sex, sexual orientation, gender identity or expression, disability, age, or country of ancestral origin;

(ii) Make or keep a record of his or her race or color, religion, sex, sexual orientation, gender identity or expression, disability, age, or country of ancestral origin;

(iii) Use any form of application for employment, or personnel or membership blank containing questions or entries directly or indirectly pertaining to race or color, religion, sex, sexual orientation, gender identity or expression, disability, age, or country of ancestral origin;

(iv) Print or publish or cause to be printed or published any notice or advertisement relating to employment or membership indicating any preference, limitation, specification, or discrimination based upon race or color, religion, sex, sexual orientation, gender identity or expression, disability, age, or country of ancestral origin; or

(v) Establish, announce, or follow a policy of denying or limiting, through a quota system or otherwise, employment or membership opportunities of any group because of the race or color, religion, sex, sexual orientation, gender identity or expression, disability, age, or country of ancestral origin of that group;

(5) For any employer or employment agency, labor organization, placement service, training school or center, or any other employee referring source to discriminate in any manner against any individual because he or she has opposed any practice forbidden by this chapter, or because he or she has made a charge, testified, or assisted in any manner in any investigation, proceeding, or hearing under this chapter;

(6) For any person, whether or not an employer, employment agency, labor organization, or employee, to aid, abet, incite, compel, or coerce the doing of any act declared by this section to be an unlawful employment practice, or to obstruct or prevent any person from complying with the provisions of this chapter or any order issued pursuant to this chapter, or to attempt directly or

indirectly to commit any act declared by this section to be an unlawful employment practice;

(7) For any employer to include on any application for employment, except applications for law enforcement agency positions or positions related to law enforcement agencies, a question inquiring or to otherwise inquire either orally or in writing whether the applicant has ever been arrested, charged with or convicted of any crime; provided, that:

(i) If a federal or state law or regulation creates a mandatory or presumptive disqualification from employment based on a person's conviction of one or more specified criminal offenses, an employer may include a question or otherwise inquire whether the applicant has ever been convicted of any of those offenses; or

(ii) If a standard fidelity bond or an equivalent bond is required for the position for which the applicant is seeking employment and his or her conviction of one or more specified criminal offenses would disqualify the applicant from obtaining such a bond, an employer may include a question or otherwise inquire whether the applicant has ever been convicted of any of those offenses; and

(iii) Notwithstanding, any employer may ask an applicant for information about his or her criminal convictions at the first interview or thereafter, in accordance with all applicable state and federal laws;

(8)(i) For any person who, on June 7, 1988, is providing either by direct payment or by making contributions to a fringe benefit fund or insurance program, benefits in violation with §§ 28-5-6, 28-5-7 and 28-5-38, until the expiration of a period of one year from June 7, 1988 or if there is an applicable collective bargaining agreement in effect on June 7, 1988, until the termination of that agreement, in order to come into compliance with §§ 28-5-6, 28-5-7 and 28-5-38, to reduce the benefits or the compensation provided any employee on June 7, 1988, either directly or by failing to provide sufficient contributions to a fringe benefit fund or insurance program.

(ii) Where the costs of these benefits on June 7, 1988 are apportioned between employers and employees, the payments or contributions required to comply with §§ 28-5-6, 28-5-7 and 28-5-38 may be made by employers and employees in the same proportion.

(iii) Nothing in this section shall prevent the readjustment of benefits or compensation for reasons unrelated to compliance with §§ 28-5-6, 28-5-7 and 28-5-38.

SECTION 3. This act shall take effect upon passage.

EXPLANATION

BY THE LEGISLATIVE COUNCIL

OF

A N   A C T

RELATING TO LABOR AND LABOR RELATIONS -- MINIMUM WAGES

***

1   This act would require employers to pay "hazard pay" to employees involved in providing
2   essential services during a declared public health emergency. The hazard pay would be at a rate of
3   one and one-third (1⅓) times the regular rate of pay. Additionally employers would be prohibited
4   from taking adverse employment action against an employee who refuses to work during a public
5   health emergency.
6   This act would take effect upon passage.

LC000917

2021 -- H 5445 SUBSTITUTE A

LC001259/SUB A

STATE OF RHODE ISLAND

IN GENERAL ASSEMBLY

JANUARY SESSION, A.D. 2021

AN ACT

RELATING TO STATE AFFAIRS AND GOVERNMENT - 2021 ACT ON CLIMATE

Introduced By: Representatives Carson, Cortvriend, Blazejewski, Kazarian, Ruggiero, Donovan, Speakman, Knight, McEntee, and Alzate
Date Introduced: February 10, 2021

Referred To: House Environment and Natural Resources

It is enacted by the General Assembly as follows:

1 SECTION 1. The title of Chapter 42-6.2 of the General Laws entitled "Resilient Rhode
2 Island Act of 2014 - Climate Change Coordinating Council" is hereby amended to read as follows:
3 CHAPTER 42-6.2
4 Resilient Rhode Island Act of 2014 - Climate Change Coordinating Council
5 CHAPTER 42-6.2
6 2021 ACT ON CLIMATE
7 SECTION 2. Sections 42-6.2-1, 42-6.2-2, 42-6.2-3, 42-6.2-7 and 42-6.2-8 of the General
8 Laws in Chapter 42-6.2 entitled "Resilient Rhode Island Act of 2014 - Climate Change
9 Coordinating Council" are hereby amended to read as follows:
10 **42-6.2-1. Creation -- Members.**
11 There is hereby established within the executive branch of state government a Rhode Island
12 executive climate change coordinating council (the "council") comprised of officials from state
13 agencies with responsibility and oversight relating to assessing, integrating, and coordinating
14 climate change efforts. The council shall include, but not be limited to, the following members: the
15 director of the department of environmental management; the executive director of the coastal
16 resources management council; the director of the department of administration; the director of the
17 department of transportation; the director of the department of health; the director of the emergency
18 management agency; the commissioner of the office of energy resources; the director of the
19 division of planning; the executive director of the Rhode Island infrastructure bank; the

administrator of the division of public utilities and carriers; the chief executive officer of the Rhode Island public transit authority; the secretary of the executive office of health and human services; and the ~~chief executive officer~~ secretary of the Rhode Island commerce corporation.

42-6.2-2. Purpose of the council.

(a) The council shall have the following duties:

(1) Assess, integrate, and coordinate climate change efforts throughout state agencies to reduce emissions, strengthen the resilience of communities and infrastructure, and prepare for the effects on climate change, including, but not limited to, coordinating vulnerability assessments throughout state government;

(2)(i) No later than ~~December 31, 2017~~ December 31, 2025, and every five (5) years thereafter, submit to the governor and general assembly ~~a~~ an updated plan, following an opportunity for public comment, that includes strategies, programs, and actions to meet economy-wide enforceable targets for greenhouse gas emissions reductions as follows:

(A) Ten percent (10%) below 1990 levels by 2020;

(B) Forty-five percent (45%) below 1990 levels by ~~2035~~ 2030;

(C) Eighty percent (80%) below 1990 levels by ~~2050~~ 2040;

(D) Net-zero emissions by 2050.

No action shall be brought pursuant to: subsection (a)(2)(i)(B) of this section before 2031, pursuant to subsection (a)(2)(i)(C) of this section before 2041, and pursuant to subsection (a)(2)(i)(D) of this section before 2051.

(ii) The plan shall also include procedures and public metrics for periodic measurement, not less frequently than once every five (5) years, of progress necessary to meet these targets and for evaluating the possibility of meeting higher targets through cost-effective measures.

~~(ii) The plan shall specifically study the effectiveness of the state and/or multi-state carbon pricing program to incentivize institutions and industry to reduce carbon emissions. The study shall include the effectiveness of allocating revenues generated from such carbon pricing program to fund enhanced incentives to institutions and industry for targeted efficiency measures; projected emissions reductions; economic impact to businesses; any economic benefits to Rhode Island; and impacts to the state's economic competitiveness if the program were implemented.~~

(iii) The plan shall address in writing the annual input that is provided to the council by its advisory board, as set forth in § 42-6.2-4, and its science and technical advisory board, as set forth in § 42-6.2-5, in their reports to the council.

(iv) If a plan directs an agency to promulgate regulations, then the agency must do so by either issuing an advance notice of proposed rulemaking, as set forth in § 42-35-2.5, no later than six (6) months after the plan is released or by issuing a notice of proposed rulemaking, as set forth in § 42-35-2.7, no later than one year after the plan is released, unless the plan specifies another timeframe for an advance notice of rulemaking or a notice of rulemaking.

(v) The plan shall include an equitable transition to climate compliance for environmental justice populations, redress past environmental and public health inequities, and include a process where the interests of and people from populations most vulnerable to the effects of climate change and at risk of pollution, displacement, energy burden, and cost influence such plan.

(vi) The plan shall identify support for workers during this equitable transition to address inequity in the state by creating quality and family-sustaining clean energy jobs that pay wages and benefits consistent with or that exceed area wage and labor standards. The plan shall provide for the development of programs that directly recruit, train, and retain those underrepresented in the workforce, including women, people of color, indigenous people, veterans, formerly incarcerated people, and people living with disabilities.

(vii) The requirements under this subsection shall be subject to the enforcement provisions of § 42-6.2-10 effective in 2026.

(viii) No later than December 31, 2022, the council shall submit to the governor and the general assembly an update to the greenhouse gas emission's reduction plan dated "December 2016" which shall not be subject to the requirements of § 42-6.2-2(a)(2)(ii) through (a)(2)(vi). No action shall be brought pursuant to subsection (a)(2)(viii) of this section before 2023.

(3) Advance the state's understanding of the effects on climate change including, but not limited to, sea level rise, coastal and shoreline changes, severe weather events, critical infrastructure vulnerability, food security, and ecosystem, economic, and health impacts, including the effects of carbon pollution on children's health;

(4) Identify strategies to prepare for these effects and communicate them to Rhode Islanders, including strategies that incentivize businesses, institutions, and industry to adapt to climate change;

(5) Work with municipalities to support the development of sustainable and resilient communities;

(6) Identify and leverage federal, state, and private funding opportunities for emission reduction and climate change preparedness and adaption work in Rhode Island;

(7) Advise the governor, the general assembly, and the public on ways to ensure that Rhode Island continues to be a national leader in developing and implementing strategies that effectively address the challenges on climate change;

(8) Work with other New England states to explore areas of mutual interest to achieve

common goals; and

(9) Identify and facilitate opportunities to educate the public about climate change and efforts throughout state agencies and municipalities to address climate change.

(b) The council is encouraged to utilize the expertise of Rhode Island universities and colleges in carrying out the duties described in subsection (a) of this section, specifically to ensure that the state's efforts to mitigate and adapt to climate change are based on the best available scientific and technical information, and to optimize the contribution by the universities and colleges of their expertise and experience in research, analysis, modeling, mapping, applications to on-the-ground situations, technical assistance, community outreach, and public education.

42-6.2-3. Support for the council.

To support the council's work, state agencies shall:

(1) Assist the council in implementing the provisions of this chapter;

(2) Develop short-and long-term greenhouse gas emission reduction strategies and track the progress of these strategies;

(3) ~~To~~ Lead by example and, to the maximum extent feasible, purchase alternative fuel, hybrid, and electric vehicles that produce lower total emissions of greenhouse gases and develop programs to encourage state employees to reduce their vehicle miles and use sustainable transportation alternatives, including public transit systems;

(4) Implement programs to achieve energy savings in state and municipal buildings to reduce greenhouse gases, reduce expenditures on energy, and stimulate economic and job development;

(5) Increase the deployment of in-state generation of renewable energy and energy efficiency;

(6) Support efforts to expand Rhode Island's green economy and develop green infrastructure;

(7) Assess the vulnerability of infrastructure and natural systems, including, but not limited to, roads, bridges, dams, and wastewater and drinking water treatment facilities, and riverine and coastal habitats, to impacts on climate change and ~~recommend~~ implement strategies to relocate or protect and adapt these assets;

(8) Work with relevant academic institutions and federal agencies to assess the threats of sea level rise, erosion and storm surge, and communicate these assessments and threats, along with potential tools to address them, to state agencies and affected communities;

(9) Develop plans, policies, and solutions based on the latest science to ensure the state continues to have a vibrant coastal economy, including protection of critical infrastructure, and a

vibrant and resilient food system that can provide affordable access to healthy food for all Rhode Islanders;

(10) ~~Develop a climate and health profile report that documents the range of~~ Address recommendations to reduce health impacts associated with climate change and ~~identifies~~ protect the ~~most vulnerable~~ populations most vulnerable to the effects of climate change and at risk of pollution, displacement, energy burden, and cost;

(11) Encourages municipalities to incorporate climate change adaptation into local hazard mitigation plans and, when feasible, into hazard mitigation projects; ~~and~~

(12) Take affirmative steps to eliminate and avoid duplication of effort through consistent coordination between agencies and programs, and pooling of resources, so as to make the most cost-efficient use of the state resources and provide the most effective services~~.~~; and

(13) Foster public transparency by developing public metrics and an online public dashboard that shall track both emissions reductions and sources of energy consumed by the state. The metrics and the dashboard shall be updated at least annually.

42-6.2-7. Reporting.

No later than May 1, 2015, and annually thereafter, the council shall issue a report of its findings, recommendations, and progress on achieving the purposes and requirements of this chapter.

42-6.2-8. Powers and duties of state agencies – Exercise of existing authority.

~~Consideration of~~ Addressing the impacts on climate change shall be deemed to be within the powers, ~~and~~ duties, and obligations of all state departments, agencies, commissions, councils, and instrumentalities, including quasi-public agencies, and each shall ~~be deemed to have and to~~ exercise among its purposes in the exercise of its existing authority, the purposes set forth in this chapter pertaining to climate change mitigation, ~~adaption~~ adaptation, and resilience in so far as climate change affects ~~the~~ its mission, duties, responsibilities, projects, or programs ~~of the entity~~. Each agency shall have the authority to promulgate rules and regulations necessary to meet the greenhouse gas emission reduction mandate established by § 42-6.2-9.

SECTION 3. Chapter 42-6.2 of the General Laws entitled "Resilient Rhode Island Act of 2014 - Climate Change Coordinating Council" is hereby amended by adding thereto the following sections:

42-6.2-9. Statewide greenhouse gas emission reduction mandate.

Mandatory targets for emissions reduction:

It is hereby established that the state shall reduce its statewide greenhouse gas emissions to the targets set forth in § 42-6.2-2(a)(2)(i), as those targets may be from time to time be revised, and that achieving those targets shall be mandatory under the provisions of this chapter. The targets at the time of the enactment of this act are that greenhouse gas emissions shall be ten percent (10%) below 1990 levels by 2020, shall be forty-five percent (45%) below 1990 levels by 2030; eighty percent (80%) below 1990 levels by 2040, and shall be net-zero emissions by 2050.

42-6.2-10. Enforcement.

(a) The provisions of this chapter may be enforced by means of an action in the superior court seeking either injunctive relief, a declaratory judgment, a writ of mandamus or any combination thereof, for:

(1) Climate plans required by § 42-6.2-2(a)(2); or

(2) The greenhouse gas emissions reduction mandate required by § 42-6.2-9.

(b) No such action may be commenced without the plaintiff providing written notice of the violations of this chapter to defendants at least sixty (60) days prior to filing a legal action in superior court. Where the defendant is a government entity, no costs or fees shall be awarded if a court determines that substantive action was taken during the sixty (60) day period. No such action shall be brought before 2026.

(c) Unless otherwise authorized in this chapter, no such action shall be brought prior to 2026.

(d) Venue for such actions shall be proper in the superior court.

(e) The Rhode Island attorney general, any Rhode Island resident and any Rhode Island corporation, company, organization, nonprofit or other Rhode Island legal entity or organization registered with the Rhode Island secretary of state may bring a civil action to enforce this chapter.

(f) The court may award costs of litigation (including reasonable attorney and expert witness fees) to any substantially prevailing party. Provided, however, nothing in this section shall restrict any right which any person (or class of persons) may have under any statute or common law.

42-6.2-11. Liberal construction.

This chapter, being necessary for the welfare of the state and its inhabitants, shall be liberally construed so as to effectuate its purposes.

42-6.2-12. Severability.

If any clause, sentence, paragraph, section, or part of this chapter shall be adjudged by any court of competent jurisdiction to be invalid, that judgment shall not affect, impair, or invalidate the remainder of the chapter but shall be confined in its operation to the clause, sentence, paragraph, section, or part directly involved in the controversy in which that judgment shall have been rendered.

1   SECTION 4. This act shall take effect upon passage.

LC001259/SUB A

EXPLANATION

BY THE LEGISLATIVE COUNCIL

OF

A N   A C T

RELATING TO STATE AFFAIRS AND GOVERNMENT - 2021 ACT ON CLIMATE

***

1 This act would establish a statewide greenhouse gas emission reduction mandate.

2 This act would take effect upon passage.

LC001259/SUB A

The Progressives have won the Democratic Ideological Battle

Tomás Ávila
March 26, 2021

 Tomas Avila is with **David Morales** and 20 others in **Rhode Island**.
Mar 26

The Progresives have won the Democratic Ideological Battle

THEPUBLICSRADIO.ORG
In leftward move, RI Democrats hire progressive strategist to modernize the party

In leftward move, RI Democrats hire progressive strategist to modernize the party

March 26, 2021

Ian Donnis
by Ian Donnis

In a clear signal that the Rhode Island Democratic Party is moving to the left, the party has hired longtime progressive strategist Kate Coyne-McCoy to modernize the RIDP "and position Democrats to win from the top to the bottom of the ballot."

Coyne will lead the party through elections next year featuring contests for governor, four other general offices and the General Assembly, focusing on data, communications, grassroots organizing, and finance.

The move to hire a former lobbyist for Everytown for Gun Safety would have been inconceivable during the reign of former House Speaker Nicholas Mattiello, who had an A rating from the NRA.

But progressives have won steadily more legislative seats in recent election cycles, in a legislature long typified by socially conservative Democrats, and Mattiello lost his re-election race last year.

In a joint statement, House Speaker Joe Shekarchi and Senate President Dominick Ruggerio said Coyne-McCoy will give Democrats the "hands-on leadership and vision required to adapt our strategy to the new realities" of how the pandemic has changed voting and elections.

"She will make certain that Democrats up and down the ballot have the tools they need to build winning campaigns," the legislative leaders said.

Coyne-McCoy resides in Scituate and has operated her own firm, KCM Consulting, since 2012.

She has worked with candidates across the country. A former regional director for EMILY's List, the fundraising group for women candidates, Coyne-McCoy created a super PAC that supported Gina Raimondo's 2014 run for governor. She ran unsuccessfully in 2000 in a Democratic primary for an open seat in RI's second congressional district.

The RIDP hasn't had a full-time executive director since Cyd McKenna left in 2020 to join Michael Bloomberg's presidential campaign.

While Coyne-McCoy will not have the title of executive director, she will be the person responsible for leading the party's political efforts.

"I am eager to begin a building process that expands the reach of the party, that offers training and engagement for candidates, activists and voters," Coyne-McCoy said. "Moving into the post-COVID world, there is a great deal of work to do to prepare to win in 2022 and beyond. My goal is to build and modernize the Rhode Island Democratic Party and provide every tool needed to win campaigns to our candidates."

According to her bio, "Kate is widely recognized as an accomplished fundraiser, media trainer and campaign tactician. Coyne-McCoy's efforts contributed significantly to several historic victories in previous cycles including the election of Rhode Island's first female Governor, and first Latina Secretary of State, and the conversion of red to blue legislative seats in Florida."

Democrats have dominated Rhode Island politics since the "Bloodless Revolution" of 1935, with long-running super-majorities in both chambers of the legislature. At the same time, the mainstream of legislative Democrats has been dominated by social conservatives who largely opposed the legalization of same-sex marriage in 2013 and the establishment of state-based abortion rights in 2019, relenting only due to grassroots pressure from outside the Statehouse.

The RI Democratic Party has also come in for criticism for its endorsement process, including the backing of a former Donald

Trump supporter in 2018, and how it has allocated resources to candidates.

Top Democrats, including members of the state's congressional delegation, expressed support for Coyne-McCoy.

"I am looking forward to working closely with Kate as we build an even stronger party that is prepared for the challenges of the 2022 election cycle," said Democratic Party Chairman Joseph M. McNamara, a state representative from Warwick. "She will make sure Democrats in local, General Assembly and statewide races have a strong agenda and a grass-roots strategy to reflect the ever-changing needs of working Rhode Island families."

Ian Donnis can be reached at idonnis@ripr.org. Follow him on Twitter @IanDon. Sign up here for his weekly RI politics and media newsletter.

USHCC Virtual Legislative Summit on March 30-31, 2021

March 26, 2021
Tomás Ávila

USHCC 2021 Virtual Legislative Summit

Join us at the USHCC Virtual Legislative Summit on March 30-31, 2021!

On behalf of the United States Hispanic Chamber of Commerce, and our Board of Directors we invite you to join us as we connect America's Hispanic Business leaders with elected officials from both sides of the aisle in a bipartisan effort to influence legislative change.

This Summit creates a platform for ideas that help our economy grow, our businesses scale, and our country move forward to reestablish our economic vibrancy. Join us on Tuesday, March 30th and Wednesday, March 31st, 2021 for this important Hispanic business virtual event.

https://www.ushcclegislative.com

PCTA

April 11, 2021

What a busy and memorable weekend filled with friends, neighbors, and meaningful conversations.
On Saturday morning I received my vaccine at PCTA and I cannot thank our healthcare staff and volunteers enough for coordinating such a safe and efficient process. It was so nice to be alongside other community members as we waited to be vaccinated. Later that morning, we had a neighborhood clean-up at Pleasant Valley Parkway organized by some of our neighbors. The weather was ideal for picking up litter and collectively cleaning our park as a community.

In the afternoon, I had the honor of being the 'keynote' speaker for the MESA Program's Regional Finals Tournament! As an alumni of the program, it was a pleasure to connect with young first-generation middle school and high school students competing in mathematics, engineering, and speech contests. Fun fact: MESA was my introduction to public speaking as I debated the topic of 'Hydraulic Fracturing' (fracking) in 8th grade.

Later that afternoon, @DARE.PVD held an emotional protest against the inhumane treatment of incarcerated people in our State's ACI Facility. Let's be clear, there is a human rights crisis going on in there as there have been 4 unresolved deaths that have occurred alongside reports of abuse/mistreatment. It is absolutely wrong so alongside community advocates, I am calling on the Governor and his Administration to immediately address these issues.

It is a shame that we must remind our government that incarcerated people are humans.

This morning I joined Rep. Marcia Ranglin-Vassel (a champion for racial and socioeconomic justice) and my colleagues on a morning walk of reflection to honor and begin #BlackMaternalHealthWeek
Now is the time we finally pass policies rooted in lived experience!

Overall, it was a beautiful weekend of advocacy, solidarity, collective action, and community engagement. One cannot really ask for much more..

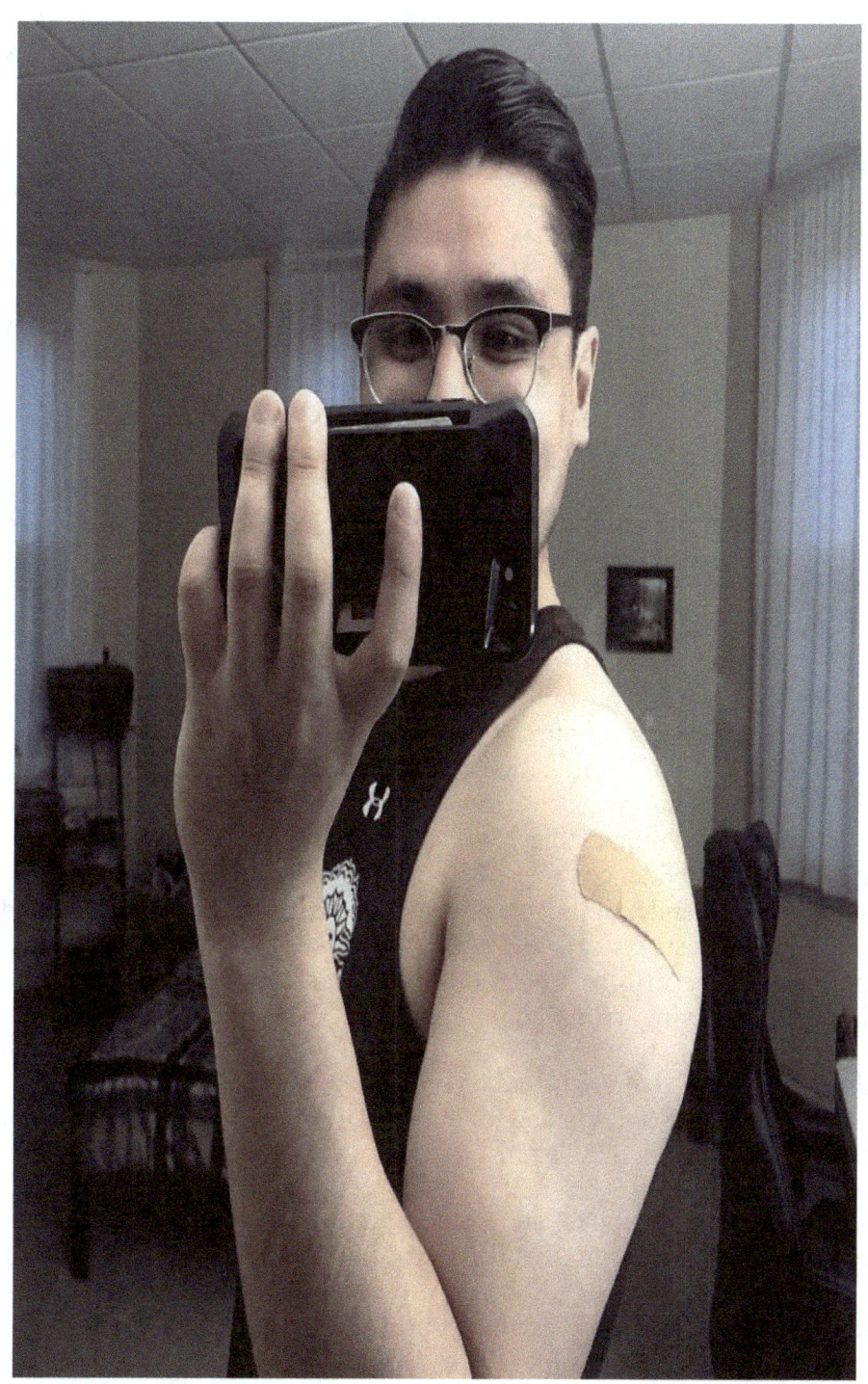

Morales and DiMario file bill to prohibit insurers from imposing cost-sharing for COVID services during emergency

April 12, 2021

STATE HOUSE – Rep. David Morales and Sen. Alana DiMario are sponsoring legislation to prevent health insurers from instituting cost-sharing for as long as the state of emergency remains in effect.

The House bill (2021-H 6208) was introduced April 7 with over 20 co-sponsors and has been assigned to the House Health and Human Services Committee with a hearing scheduled April 15. The Senate bill will be introduced soon.

"Ultimately, this is about protecting the health and safety of all Rhode Islanders. There should not be any financial barriers standing in the way of someone who thinks they might have COVID-19 and now requires testing or treatment. If cost-sharing is instituted, it will discourage people from getting tested or seeing a health professional. That is not what we need during a time when we are trying to collectively overcome this pandemic," said Representative Morales (D-Dist. 7, Providence. "Despite our progress with administering the vaccine, the pandemic is still here. We are still in an emergency and we need all insurers to stay on board and continue to be committed partners in the effort to overcome this pandemic and minimize the impact it is having on our communities."

The legislation stemmed from a recent announcement that Blue Cross Blue Shield of Rhode Island planned to allow its cost-sharing waiver to expire on March 31. The insurer later rescinded the plan.

Representative Morales and Senator DiMario say they filed the legislation to make sure that no such cost-sharing is instituted by any insurer, so Rhode Islanders are protected for the duration of the emergency. The bill prohibits insurers from requiring copayments, coinsurance or any out-of-pocket deductible for COVID-19 testing, vaccines, or COVID-19-related emergency services, inpatient services, office visits or hospital stays for the duration of the state of emergency. The prohibition on cost-sharing for COVID-19 testing and vaccines would remain in perpetuity.

"We are so close to the other side of this pandemic, and it's essential to keep up our efforts with testing, treatment, and vaccination without any cost barriers so we don't prolong it. Staying vigilant will save lives," said Senator DiMario (D-Dist. 36, North Kingstown, Narragansett).

2021 -- H 6208

LC002569

STATE OF RHODE ISLAND

IN GENERAL ASSEMBLY

JANUARY SESSION, A.D. 2021

AN ACT

RELATING TO INSURANCE

Introduced By: Representatives Morales, Williams, Kazarian, Potter, Nardone, McGaw, Solomon, Hull, Kislak, and Caldwell
Date Introduced: April 07, 2021

Referred To: House Health & Human Services

It is enacted by the General Assembly as follows:

1   SECTION 1. Chapter 27-18 of the General Laws entitled "Accident and Sickness Insurance
2   Policies" is hereby amended by adding thereto the following section:
3   **27-18-85. Health insurance contracts - copayments exemption for COVID-19**
4   **vaccinations.**
5   (a) Any individual or group health insurance plan or policy shall not impose any
6   copayment, coinsurance or charge any out-of-pocket deductible to the insured for COVID-19
7   related services, including, but not limited to, emergency services, inpatient services, provider
8   office visits, and inpatient hospital stays, as long as the COVID-19 state of emergency remains in
9   effect.
10 (b) Any individual or group health insurance plan or policy shall not impose any
11 copayment, coinsurance or charge any out-of-pocket deductible to the insured for the
12 administration of the COVID-19 vaccine or a COVID-19 test.
13 (c) The health insurance commissioner shall promulgate rules and regulations to enforce a
14 carrier's compliance with this section.
15 SECTION 2. Chapter 27-19 of the General Laws entitled "Nonprofit Hospital Service
16 Corporations" is hereby amended by adding thereto the following section:
17 **27-19-77. Health insurance contracts - copayments exemption for COVID-19**
18 **vaccinations.**
19 (a) Any individual or group health insurance plan or policy shall not impose any

copayment, coinsurance or charge any out-of-pocket deductible to the insured for COVID-19 related services, including, but not limited to, emergency services, inpatient services, provider office visits, and inpatient hospital stays, as long as the COVID-19 state of emergency remains in effect.

(b) Any individual or group health insurance plan or policy shall not impose any copayment, coinsurance or charge any out-of-pocket deductible to the insured for the administration of the COVID-19 vaccine or a COVID-19 test.

(c) The health insurance commissioner shall promulgate rules and regulations to enforce a carrier's compliance with this section.

SECTION 3. Chapter 27-20 of the General Laws entitled "Nonprofit Medical Service Corporations" is hereby amended by adding thereto the following section:

27-20-73. Health insurance contracts - copayments exemption for COVID-19 vaccinations.

(a) Any individual or group health insurance plan or policy shall not impose any copayment, coinsurance or charge any out-of-pocket deductible to the insured for COVID-19 related services, including, but not limited to, emergency services, inpatient services, provider office visits, and inpatient hospital stays, as long as the COVID-19 state of emergency remains in effect.

(b) Any individual or group health insurance plan or policy shall not impose any copayment, coinsurance or charge any out-of-pocket deductible to the insured for the administration of the COVID-19 vaccine or a COVID-19 test.

(c) The health insurance commissioner shall promulgate rules and regulations to enforce a carrier's compliance with this section.

SECTION 4. Chapter 27-41 of the General Laws entitled "Health Maintenance Organizations" is hereby amended by adding thereto the following section:

27-41-90. Health insurance contracts - copayments exemption for COVID-19 vaccinations.

(a) Any individual or group health insurance plan or policy shall not impose any copayment, coinsurance or charge any out-of-pocket deductible to the insured for COVID-19 related services, including, but not limited to, emergency services, inpatient services, provider office visits, and inpatient hospital stays, as long as the COVID-19 state of emergency remains in effect.

(b) Any individual or group health insurance plan or policy shall not impose any copayment, coinsurance or charge any out-of-pocket deductible to the insured for the

1 administration of the COVID-19 vaccine or a COVID-19 test.

2 (c) The health insurance commissioner shall promulgate rules and regulations to enforce a
3 carrier's compliance with this section.

4 SECTION 5. This act shall take effect upon passage.

LC002569

EXPLANATION

BY THE LEGISLATIVE COUNCIL

OF

AN ACT

RELATING TO INSURANCE

***

1   This act would prohibit insurance carriers from charging any out-of-pocket expenses to the
2   insured for treatment related to the COVID-19 pandemic while the state of emergency order is in
3   effect. This act would further mandate that all COVID-19 testing or vaccination is free during and
4   upon the expiration of the state of emergency order.
5   This act would take effect upon passage.

LC002569

Rhode Island's youngest state legislator: An advocate for the working class

Representative David Morales, 22, brings a "Power to the Workers" message to the State House – and a Spider-Man costume to community events

By Edward Fitzpatrick Globe Staff, Updated April 14, 2021, 6:00 a.m.

State Representative David Morales, a Providence Democrat who, at age 22, is Rhode Island's youngest legislator and one of the youngest Latino legislators in the country. SUZANNE KRIETER/GLOBE STAFF

PROVIDENCE — He's not much older than Peter Parker, and he's been known to wear a Spider-Man costume at community events in the Mount Pleasant neighborhood.

While state Representative David Morales has yet to wear the Spider-Man mask at the State House, the 22-year-old Providence Democrat does regularly don a "Power to the Workers" face mask. And he has emerged as an advocate for the working class since swinging onto the

Rhode Island political scene last year and trouncing the incumbent in a primary.

A Democratic Socialist who counts Bernie Sanders, Malcolm X and Shirley Chisholm among his heroes, Morales is part of a newly elected group of young, progressive legislators of color who have helped to make this year's General Assembly the most diverse in state history.

"To me, Peter Parker represents the working class," Morales said in explaining his choice of the Spider-Man costume. "If you follow the comic, he's usually poor and struggling. The average person can relate to him, and that's what makes his story so beautiful."

State Representative David Morales, right, wears a Spider-Man costume as he greets children at the Mount Pleasant Easter egg hunt in Providence.COURTESY OF REPRESENTATIVE DAVID MORA

So who is the man behind the mask?

The son of Mexican immigrants, Morales was born in 1998 in the rural, working-class, majority-Latino town of Soledad, Calif. – the setting for the John Steinbeck novel "Of Mice and Men."
He said his father struggled with "alcohol issues and an addiction to drugs, notably crack cocaine" and left the family to return to Mexico when Morales was 8. His mother raised him and his sister on her own, he said, working up to three jobs at a time, including running a cash register at a gas station and picking fruits and vegetables in the fields.

"Our goal was always to make our mom proud," Morales said.

He took college courses while in high school, so he was able to graduate from the University of California-Irvine in two years, with a bachelor's degree in urban studies. At age 20, he became the youngest graduate in the history of the Brown University public affairs master's program, he said.

In September's Democratic primary in House District 7, Morales received 49 percent of the vote, topping six-year incumbent Daniel P. McKiernan, a deputy majority leader, who received 28 percent, and the endorsed Democrat, Angel Subervi, who had 23 percent.

The victory was not without plenty of effort. Morales said he knocked multiple times on every door in the district, which includes Providence's Mount Pleasant, Valley and Elmhurst neighborhoods. He said he talked about issues such as affordable housing and the quality of public schools, while giving out his phone number and a list of local resources to help people amid the pandemic.

"Most importantly, our grassroots campaign did not just focus on 'super voters' who traditionally voted in primaries as we were determined to engage hundreds of new people into the political process who did not always feel like local politics was accessible," Morales said. "This included working people, poor people, young people, and people of color who ended up voting for the first time this past September and November."

At 22, Morales is now the youngest legislator in the General Assembly, and he is among the youngest Latino legislators in the country.

(The youngest legislator in Rhode Island history is believed to be former Representative Jeffrey J. Teitz, who was 19 when first elected in 1972, according to State Librarian Megan Hamlin Black, who consulted records dating back to the 1890s. Former Congressman Patrick J. Kennedy was 21 when he was first elected to the General Assembly in 1988.)

Morales said the election results reflect a growing acceptance for progressive ideas regarding health care, housing, and climate change. And he said the influx of new voices is changing a Rhode Island political landscape long dominated by more conservative or moderate Democrats.

"We are seeing a paradigm shift where you have an opportunity to adapt to these ideas that are considered more progressive or you risk a challenge from the 'left,' " Morales said.

In Rhode Island, some politicians hold conservative views but run as Democrats because it boosts their chances of getting elected, he said. "There are not too many other states where you will find a Democrat who is anti-choice or receives contributions from the NRA," he said. "They are called Republicans in other states."

Former House Speaker Nicholas A. Mattiello, a Cranston Democrat who had an "A" rating from the NRA and who voted against an abortion rights bill, lost November's election. So one of the first decisions Morales faced was whether to support K. Joseph Shekarchi, a Warwick Democrat, in his successful bid to become the next House Speaker.

Morales said he abstained from the leadership vote based on conversations with constituents, who noted that House leaders had not outlined the kind of progressive agenda touted by Senate leaders, who called for legalizing marijuana, taxing the rich, and boosting the minimum wage.

But Morales said he has been pleased that House leaders have supported the Act on Climate, which makes greenhouse gas reduction goals mandatory and enforceable, and a bill that prohibits landlords from discriminating against people who receive housing subsidies.

"It shows leadership is listening a lot more than in previous years in terms of what communities want and the needs of working people," he said.

Morales has introduced 23 bills during his first three months in office, and he said his priorities include legislation to ensure that all children, regardless of immigration status, qualify for health insurance under the state's "RIte Track" healthcare program program.

"Right now, we have 3,000 children in the state uninsured and the vast majority are low income or undocumented," he said. "A lot of people don't know this, but from 1996 to 2008 Rhode Island was one of the few states to provide universal health care to children. But because of the recession, it was slashed from the budget and not restored."

Restoring the program would cost about $7 million, which he said is relatively small chunk of the state's $11.7-billion budget.

Morales also has introduced a bill to cap the amount that insured people pay for insulin at $25 per month, and a bill that would provide "hazard pay" to those who provide "essential services" during the pandemic, including workers in supermarkets and restaurants.

State Representative David Morales, a Providence Democrat, on the steps of the State House.SUZANNE KRIETER/GLOBE STAFF

House Minority Leader Blake A. Filippi, a Block Island Republican, said he has very different political views than Morales. "Obviously, I disagree with a Democratic Socialist philosophy," he said.

Community Service

April 25. 2021
Dhana Whiteing

Dhana Whiteing

Apr 21 ·

So nice! I have received one of these at 30 yrs, this is a little different but equally special. Thank you David Morales~

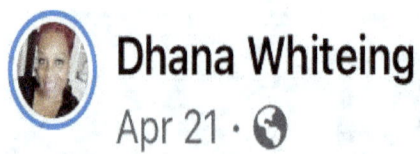

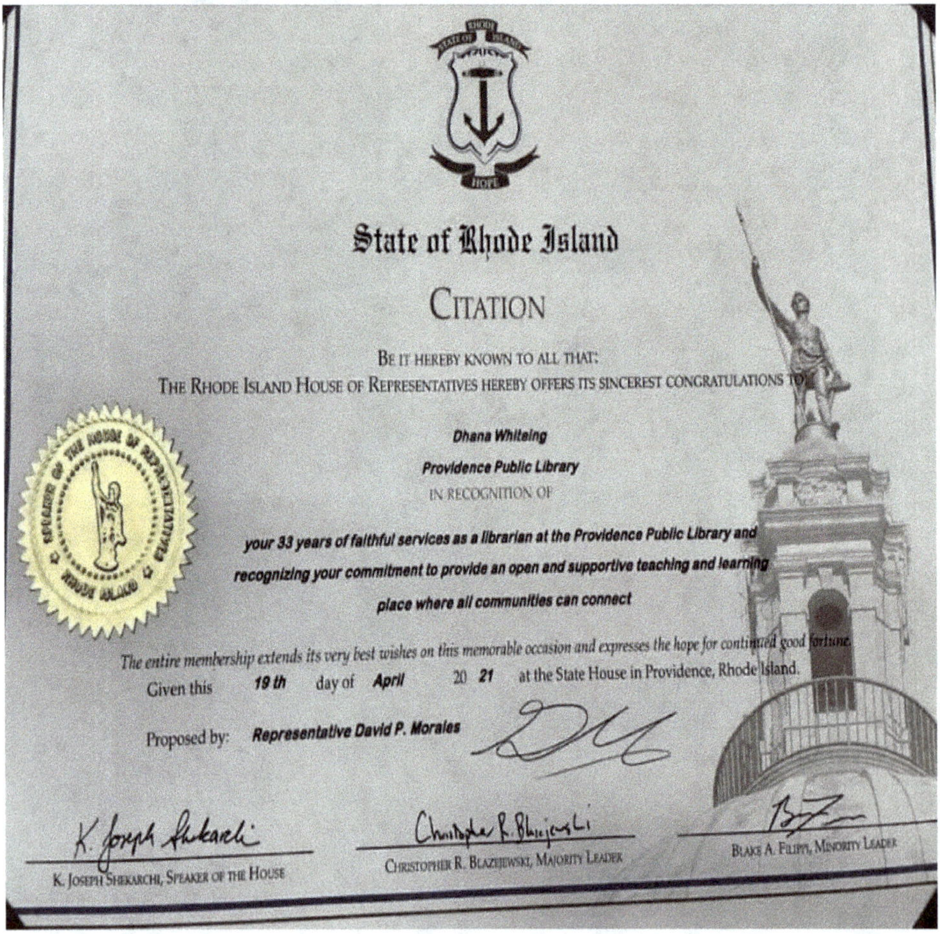

State of Rhode Island

CITATION

BE IT HEREBY KNOWN TO ALL THAT:

THE RHODE ISLAND HOUSE OF REPRESENTATIVES HEREBY OFFERS ITS SINCEREST CONGRATULATIONS TO

Dhana Whiteing

Providence Public Library

IN RECOGNITION OF

your 33 years of faithful services as a librarian at the Providence Public Library and recognizing your commitment to provide an open and supportive teaching and learning place where all communities can connect

The entire membership extends its very best wishes on this memorable occasion and expresses the hope for continued good fortune.

Given this ***19 th*** day of ***April*** 20 ***21*** at the State House in Providence, Rhode Island.

Proposed by: ***Representative David P. Morales***

K. Joseph Shekarchi — K. JOSEPH SHEKARCHI, SPEAKER OF THE HOUSE

Christopher R. Blazejewski — CHRISTOPHER R. BLAZEJEWSKI, MAJORITY LEADER

BLAKE A. FILIPPI, MINORITY LEADER

3 years ago, I was running for City Council and David was one of my amazing volunteers. Today, I'm Mayor and he is the elected State Rep in Rhode Island!

Farah N. Khan
May 3, 2021
So proud of David and all he's doing!!

3 Years Ago
See Your Memories >

 **David Morales** is with **Farrah N Khan** in Irvine, California.
May 3, 2018

My last two years in Orange County will always have a special place in my heart. I appreciate all the experiences and people I met along the way. In particular, I would like to thank this special woman - Farrah Khan.

Shortly after I arrived to the OC, I began working on Farrah's campaign for Irvine City Council. During the campaign trail, I learned countless lessons which helped me grow professionally and as an individual. Farrah has always served as a mentor and I am grateful for that.

Her advocation and grassroots approach towards providing a public service to the community is admirable. She understands that it is the responsibility of government and elected officials to represent and provide a public service. As such, I am confident she will be successful this election cycle for Irvine City Council. Thank you again for everything Farrah! #OurRevolution

Call Speaker Joseph Shekarchi (401) 222-2447 and tell him we are sick of paying taxes for colleges and now high schools????

Lisa Scorpio
May 4, 2021

PROVIDENCEJOURNAL.COM
La Salle tax bill revives debate over exemption for nonprofits

Call Speaker Joseph Shekarchi (401) 222-2447 and tell him we are sick of paying taxes for colleges and now highschools????

David Morales keep up the good work!
LaSalle is worth 59million and crying about paying 98k

We have to vote out these old, corrupt poltiicans.

Senate President Dominick Ruggerio introduced a bill that would provide a full tax exemption in state law. Senators are slated to vote on it Tuesday.

Rhode Island Interfaith Coalition to Reduce Poverty

May 6, 2021

Thank you to all the community residents, small business owners, advocates, faith leaders and elected officials, who came out today to support having a more just tax system in RI which means having the 1% pay their fair share of taxes. Thank you to Rhode Island Working Families Party The Economic Progress Institute. Direct Action for Rights and Equality and all the organizers that are part of the Revenue for Rhode Island coalition. And Representative Karen Alzate Senator Melissa Murray for sponsoring the legislation and all the other elected officials that came out to support it including RI State Representative David Morales Rep. Rebecca Kislak - Dist. 4 RI. Thank you to Pastor Santiago Rodriguez and Rabbi Jefferey Goldwasser for taking action today on this issue.

Rhode Island 2030

May 6, 2021
https://youtu.be/I-_i20kS_X8

"vale la pena

May 9, 2031

"vale la pena" — a strong independent mom who sacrificed everything for her children

Neighbors, this has been a heavy week of emotions in our City of Providence as we experienced multiple shootings and a scandal in our Providence Public Schools

May 16, 2021

Neighbors, this has been a heavy week of emotions in our City of Providence as we experienced multiple shootings and a scandal in our Providence Public Schools.

People are in critical conditions and families are hurting as a result of the shootings. Our communities are worried about this ongoing gun violence and their own safety.

As for our schools, despite being under a 'State Takeover' a man with a track-record of inappropriately touching children was hired as an Administrator in our School District and is once again in trouble for acting inappropriately towards a minor.

These are difficult times. I promise to do all that we can within government alongside support from community groups/leaders to address these issues and develop actual solutions. Solutions that involve *real economic investments* and *true accountability* in our school system. There must be accountability and there must be investments.

2021-H 5130A, 2021-S 0001aa Raising the Minimum Wage to $15.00

Tomás Ávila
May 20, 2021

Legislation sponsored by Rep. David A. Bennett and Sen. Ana B. Quezada to raise the minimum wage in Rhode Island from $11.50 to $15 over the next four years was signed into law by Gov. Dan McKee today, two days after passage by the General Assembly.

Flanked by the sponsors, House Speaker K. Joseph Shekarchi, Senate President Dominick J. Ruggerio, Lt. Gov. Sabina Matos and many legislators, Governor McKee signed the bill (2021-H 5130A, 2021-S 0001aa) in a ceremony outside the State House this morning

http://www.rilin.state.ri.us/pressrelease/_layouts/RIL.PressRelease.ListStructure/Forms/DisplayForm.aspx?List=c8baae31-3c10-431c-8dcd-9dbbe21ce3e9&ID=371658

For years, minimum wage earners and community advocates have been fighting for higher wages — today, we finally signed a pathway to a $15 minimum wage into State Law.

This is a victory for our working people and families! All our people deserve a higher standard of living and the only way that is possible is through decent wages. We are now heading in the right direction and we are just getting started!

Fun Fact: The minimum wage was the first issue I ever debated in my high school speech and debate program. Given my lived experience, I have fought hard for this issue for years alongside grassroots advocates. The work never ends, however, and I look forward to continue this organizing work. #FightFor15 @ Rhode Island State House

Overdose" Prevention Site" display model yesterday.

May 29, 2021

Thank you again to the kind and hard-working advocates of RI CARES for providing me and my colleagues a tour of their Overdose" Prevention Site" display model yesterday.

For context, Overdose Prevention Sites (OPS) are facilities where people can use previously purchased drugs under trained medical supervision. Through the provision of sterile needles, healthcare services, and referrals to drug treatment — these sites are effective with reducing the harms associated with drug use. Given the stigma associated with substance use disorder and a lack of resources to help our most vulnerable who are suffering — this is a severe public health issue that requires us to invest in solutions like OPS Facilities!

While these facilities have proven to be effective across the world along with proposed facilities across the country, no State has adopted this solution yet. This is why it is so important we pass HB #5245 which would allow us to authorize the use of OPS Facilities in our State.

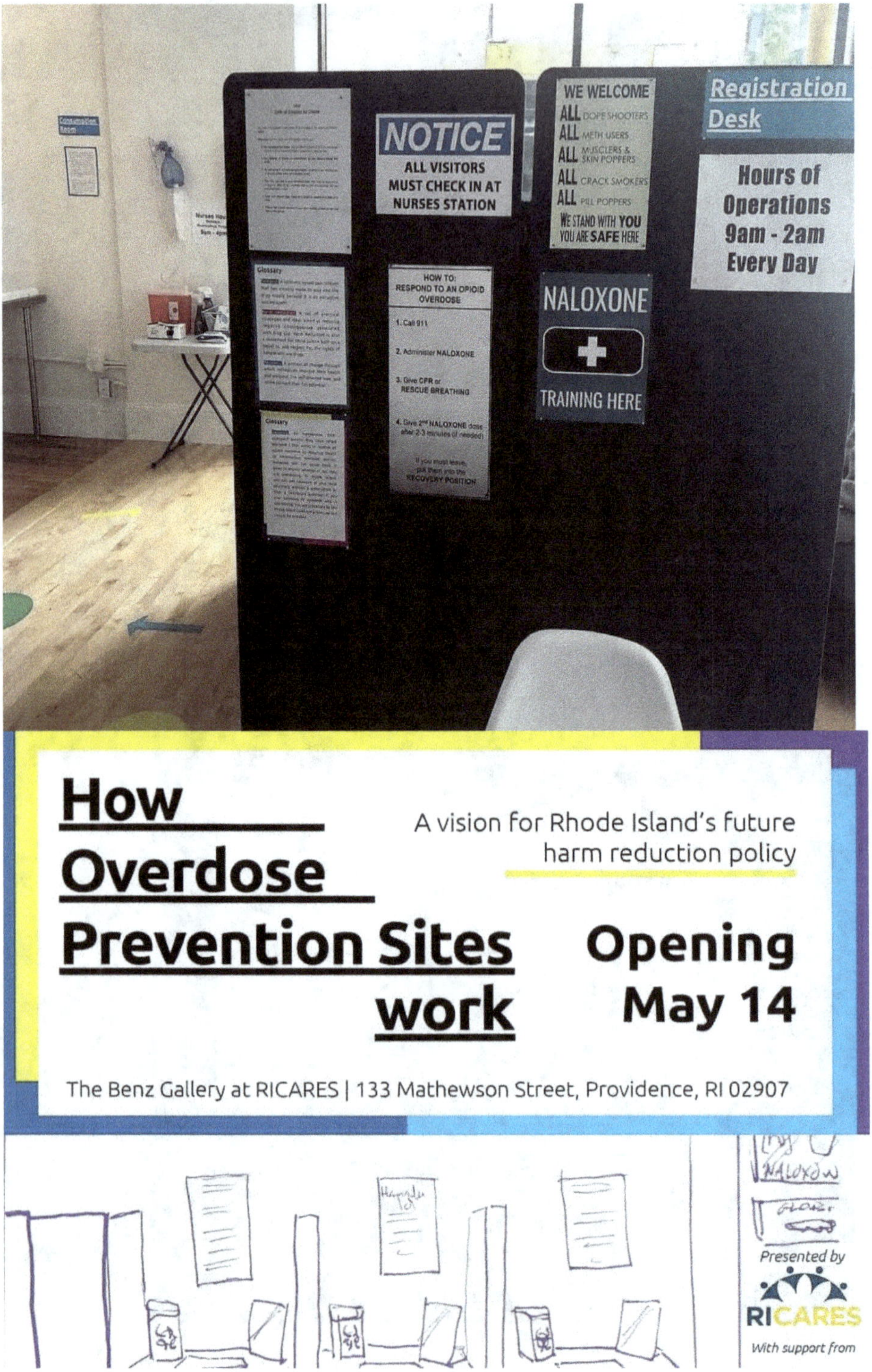

How Overdose Prevention Sites work

A vision for Rhode Island's future harm reduction policy

Opening May 14

The Benz Gallery at RICARES | 133 Mathewson Street, Providence, RI 02907

Presented by
RICARES
With support from

It is so important that our community take pride in the neighborhood we live in!

May 30, 2021

It is so important that our community take pride in the neighborhood we live in! That begins with streets free of litter and debris (alongside decent road conditions but that's another issue itself).

I've always believed that when you take care of your neighborhood, the neighborhood will help take care of itself. Thank you again to the dozen of neighbors came together to clean up the heart of Academy Avenue and Atwells Avenue.

I love Mt. Pleasant and it always makes me upset to see how divested our area has been along with other neighborhoods. This is why myself, our local Senator, and neighbors will continue to host these clean-ups throughout the year because our neighborhood deserves these investments!

Neighbors — if there is a street you would like to see cleaned up, please contact me and we will schedule one in your area!

I also want to be clear however — an invested neighborhood involves: quality public schools, decent road conditions, parks, and supported small businesses.

Helping our neighborhoods thrive is not just about clean-ups, it is about public policy and budget priorities.

¡COMMUNITY CLEAN UP IN MT. PLEASANT!

SUNDAY, MAY 23rd
10:00 AM – 11:30 AM

MT. PLEASANT MEMORIAL PARK
(28 ACADEMY AVENUE)

RI State Representative David Morales and Sen. Sandra Cano will be joined by community advocates at a State House even

June 1, 2021

RI State Representative David Morales and Sen. Sandra Cano will be joined by community advocates at a State House event Thursday to call for passage of their "Cover All Kids" legislation to ensure that all low-income children, regardless of immigration status, qualify for health insurance under the state's RIte Care program.

The event is scheduled Thursday, June 3, at 2:30 p.m. outside on the Smith Street side of the State House.

The legislation would establish Rhode Island's commitment to provide health insurance to all low-income children who are residents of the state, regardless of immigration status.

Central Falls Mayor Maria Rivera is scheduled to participate, and organizations attending the event include Rhode Island KIDS COUNT, Economic Progress Institute, the Latino Policy Institute, the Rhode Island Interfaith Coalition to Reduce Poverty, the Rhode Island Health Center Association and Dorcas International Institute of Rhode Island.

More info: http://www.rilin.state.ri.us/pressrelease/_layouts/RIL.PressRelease.ListStructure/Forms/DisplayForm.aspx?List=c8baae31-3c10-431c-8dcd-9dbbe21ce3e9&ID=371703

RI State Representative David Morales is sponsoring legislation to protect Rhode Islanders from workplace bullying and harassment.

May 27, 2021

STATE HOUSE – Rep. David Morales is sponsoring legislation to protect Rhode Islanders from workplace bullying and harassment.

The Dignity at Work Act ([2021-H 6352](#)) would require employers to take appropriate steps to prevent bullying or harassment, and would create a cause of action for those who face such abuse at work.

"All our people deserve the right to feel respected and safe at work. Sadly, there are many abusive tactics, from verbal abuse to sabotage, that are commonly deployed and tolerated in workplaces, sometimes between employees and sometimes by supervisors. Unfortunately, it is often women, people of color, and low-wage workers who are victims to this workplace abuse, which in turn, hurts their mental and emotional health. This is why it is so important that as a government, we stand up for our most vulnerable workers and pass legislation to address this unacceptable behavior. Through the Dignity at Work Act, we will urgently provide workers and employers with the resources they need to prevent and confront workplace bullying and harassment," said Representative Morales (D-Dist. 7, Providence).

The purpose of the legislation is to recognize and protect a person's right to dignity in the workplace, and to prevent, detect, remedy and eliminate all forms of workplace bullying and harassment that infringe upon that right. The bill provides legal remedies for workers who are targets of workplace bullying, moral, psychological or general harassment or other forms of workplace abuse. The bill also provides an incentive for employers to prevent, detect, remedy and eliminate workplace bullying in order that such behaviors shall be addressed and eliminated before they cause harm to the targets of such behaviors.

According to the Workplace Bullying Institute, 30 percent of American adults report having been bullied at work, and another 19 percent report having witnessed workplace bullying. Often it is the victim, not the bully, who either leaves or is fired or pressured to leave their job. The institute estimates that being a target of workplace bullying makes a worker 67 percent more likely to lose their job.

"With suicide and violent retaliation being the worst-case scenarios as a result of abuse at work, I'm afraid to be in a workplace where employees are mistreated, many of which are abruptly terminated when they try to speak up," said Emilia DaSilva-Tavarez, State Director for the Dignity at Work Act campaign. "Over the last several years, there have been too many cases where a disgruntled and mistreated employee enters the workplace with the intent to hurt their colleagues and employer in act of retaliation. Let's help employers understand the urgent need to address this epidemic, further exposed by the pandemic, so they can ensure safety for themselves and their employees. We need and deserve toxic-free and safe workplaces."

Besides the profound negative effects on targets, which can include anxiety, depression, substance abuse, post-traumatic stress disorder, stress-induced illnesses, suicide and more, bullying also harms employers. Each year, American employers lose billions of dollars in lost productivity, turnover, absenteeism, decreased morale, increased insurance premiums, workers' compensation, medical and legal costs.

The bill is cosponsored by Rep. Marcia Ranglin-Vassell (D-Dist. 5, Providence), Rep. Brianna E. Henries (D-Dist. 64, East Providence), Rep. Brandon Potter (D-Dist. 16, Cranston), Rep. Rebecca Kislak (D-Dist. 4, Providence), Rep. Anastasia P. Williams (D-Dist. 9, Providence), Rep. Michelle E. McGaw (D-Dist. 71, Portsmouth, Tiverton, Little Compton), Rep. June S. Speakman (D-Dist. 68, Warren, Bristol) and Rep. José F. Batista (D-Dist. 12, Providence).

Representative Morales introduced the bill in the House on May 20. Companion legislation (2021-S 0196) sponsored by Sen. Frank Ciccone (D-Dist. 7, Providence) passed the Senate on March 9. Both bills are currently before the House Labor Committee.

2021 -- H 6352

LC002813

STATE OF RHODE ISLAND

IN GENERAL ASSEMBLY

JANUARY SESSION, A.D. 2021

A N   A C T

RELATING TO LABOR AND LABOR RELATIONS -- DIGNITY AT WORK ACT

Introduced By: Representatives Morales, Slater, Ranglin-Vassell, Henries, Potter, Kislak, Williams, McGaw, Speakman, and Batista
Date Introduced: May 20, 2021
Referred To: House Labor

It is enacted by the General Assembly as follows:

1   SECTION 1. Title 28 of the General Laws entitled "LABOR AND LABOR RELATIONS"
2   is hereby amended by adding thereto the following chapter:
3   CHAPTER 52.1
4   DIGNITY AT WORK ACT
5   **28-52.1-1. Short title.**
6   This act shall be known and may be cited as "The Dignity at Work Act of 2021".
7   **28-52.1-2. Legislative findings.**
8   The general assembly hereby finds as follows:
9   (1) Generalized workplace harassment and bullying is a severe and pervasive problem. At
10 least one third of workers in the United States will face workplace bullying during their careers.
11 Workplace bullying leads to a loss of esteem, dignity and self-worth for targets and witnesses.
12 Workplace bullying also leads to severe emotional, psychological, economic and physical harm to
13 targets. Such harms include feelings of shame and humiliation, anxiety, depression, insomnia,
14 hypertension, substance abuse, post-traumatic stress disorder, suicidal ideation, heart disease,
15 stress-induced illnesses, suicide, workplace violence and job loss.
16 (2) Generalized workplace harassment and bullying costs American employers billions of
17 dollars in lost productivity, turnover, absenteeism, presentism, decreased morale, increased
18 insurance premiums, workers' compensation, medical and legal costs.
19 (3) Workplace bullying and general harassment has been studied in the United States since

at least the 1970s, when psychiatrist Carroll Brodsky published the earliest examination of workplace bullying in America in 1976. Since then, a multitude of employer systems have been made available to address the problem. Despite these decades of work and awareness, employer policies alone have been ineffective in preventing, remedying and eliminating workplace bullying.

(4) Since the 1980s, the United States Supreme Court has determined that discriminatory harassment in the workplace that creates a hostile work environment is prohibited under federal law. Hostile work environments are prohibited under various federal anti-discrimination statutes, such as Title VII of the Civil Rights Act of 1964, the Americans with Disabilities Act of 1990 (ADA), and the Age Discrimination in Employment Act of 1967 (ADEA). However, a hostile work environment that is unconnected to an employee's membership in a protected group is not actionable under these laws. The Legislature hereby finds that if mistreated employees who have been subjected to harassment cannot establish that the behavior was motivated by race, color, sex, sexual orientation, national origin or age, such employees are unlikely to be protected by the law against such mistreatment.

(5) Existing workers' compensation provisions and common law tort law are inadequate to discourage workplace bullying or to provide adequate redress to employees who have been harmed by workplace bullying.

(6) Since the 1940s, the right to dignity has been recognized as an inalienable human right and the foundation of freedom, justice and peace in the world. A typical adult will spend at least a third of their waking hours at work. Therefore, the right to dignity must be assured in the workplace. In order to protect workers' right to dignity, legislation must be passed protecting this right and providing legal recourse for targets of workplace bullying and/or general harassment and other abusive behaviors.

28-52.1-3. Purpose.

(a) The purpose of this chapter is to recognize and protect the right to dignity in the workplace, and to prevent, detect, remedy and eliminate all forms of workplace bullying and harassment that infringe upon that right. Accordingly, the provisions of this chapter shall be construed liberally and given broad interpretation consistent with this purpose.

(b) It is also the purpose of this chapter to:

(1) Prevent, detect, remedy and eliminate workplace bullying, moral, psychological and general harassment and other abusive behavior from the American workplace.

(2) Provide a remedy for workers who are targets of workplace bullying, moral, psychological or general harassment and/or other forms of workplace abuse in order to make whole such targets of workplace abuse.

(3) Provide an incentive for employers to prevent, detect, remedy and eliminate workplace bullying, moral, psychological and general harassment and other forms of abuse in the workplace, in order that such behaviors shall be addressed and eliminated before they cause harm to the targets of such behaviors.

28-52.1-4. Definitions.

(a) For the purposes of this chapter, the following words and phrases shall have the following meanings:

(1) "Employer" means any organization or individual employing an individual to engage in any work on their behalf or on behalf of their subsidiaries, customers or clients, whether such work is paid or unpaid. This shall include non-profit agencies employing volunteers. This shall also include organizations hiring workers through a temporary agency or other such organization to perform work on their behalf. Employers who exert control over the means, methods, payroll or personnel practices of their suppliers shall be considered joint employers with said supplier for the purpose of this act. Where more than one organization or individual meets the definition of employer under this act, for the purpose of a claim by a targeted employee, such organizations shall have joint and several liability as co-employers.

(2) "Employee" means a person who engages in work for another, whether such work is paid or unpaid, or whether such other directly employs said employee. "Employees" includes individuals who perform work in any capacity, including apprentices, trainees, unpaid interns, volunteers, or independent contractors.

(3) "Right to dignity" means the fundamental right to receive respect for one's dignity as a human being and the right to enjoy the conditions necessary for human dignity to flourish. Respect for dignity implies the right not to be treated in a degrading or humiliating manner.

(4) "Workplace bullying" means an abuse or misuse of power through means that undermine, humiliate, denigrate, or sabotage a person in the workplace, and which has the purpose or effect of threatening, intimidating, dominating, or otherwise infringing upon a person's right to dignity. The source of power shall not be considered as limited to formal organizational power or authority.

(i) Workplace bullying may take the form of interpersonal interactions, organizational practices, or management actions. Workplace bullying may take the form of harassment, incivility, abusive supervision, physical violence, aggressions and other types of objectionable behaviors. The behaviors may come from any level of the organization, including supervision, co-workers, subordinates, customers and even direct reports.

(ii) Workplace bullying can encompass a broad spectrum of conduct. Examples of workplace bullying include, but are not limited to:

(A) Persistent or egregious use of abusive, insulting, or offensive language;

(B) Unwarranted physical contact or threatening gestures;

(C) Interfering with a person's personal property or work equipment;

(D) The use of humiliation, personal criticism, ridicule, and demeaning comments

(E) Overbearing or intimidating levels of supervision;

(F) Withholding information, supervision, training or resources to prevent someone from doing their job;

(G) Changing work arrangements, such as rosters, offices, assignments, leave, and schedules to deliberately inconvenience someone;

(H) Isolating, or marginalizing a person from normal work activities;

(I) Inconsistently following or enforcing rules, to the detriment of an employee;

(J) Unjustifiably excluding colleagues from meetings or communications;

(K) Intruding on a person's privacy by pestering, spying or stalking; and

(L) Spreading misinformation or malicious rumors.

(iii) While the offender's intent is relevant to the remedy phase of a claim, it shall not be a required element to support a claim of workplace bullying. The decision on whether bullying has occurred is not to be determined by the intent of the offender, but rather by the nature of the behavior itself, and whether it has the effect of infringing upon a worker's right to dignity. An infringement upon the right to dignity shall be assessed by the impact the behavior has on the recipient. This includes, but is not limited to:

(A) Effects on the target's self-esteem (e.g., caused when an employee is subjected to excessively harsh criticism and repeated reminders of past mistakes);

(B) Effects on the target's social relations (e.g., caused when an employee is isolated by others or ignored);

(C) Effects on the target's reputation (e.g., caused when an employee is ridiculed, demeaned, or the subject of gossip or lies);

(D) Effects on the target's professional life (e.g., caused when an employee is given meaningless work assignments, no work assignments at all, or unreasonably difficult assignments or schedules); and

(E) Effects on the target's psychological and physical health (e.g., caused when the employee is threatened, attacked, or receives unsafe work assignments, including during pregnancy or a temporary health issue.).

(5) "Moral, Psychological, or General Harassment" means unwelcome, objectionable

conduct that is severe or pervasive enough to create an intimidating, hostile or abusive environment. Such analysis will be conducted from the view of a reasonable person under the totality of the circumstances

(i) For harassment to be legally actionable, a victim must demonstrate one or more of the following:

(A) The harassment disturbed their emotional tranquility in the workplace.

(B) The harassment affected their ability to perform their job as usual, or up to standard.

(C) The harassment interfered with and undermined their personal sense of well-being.

(ii) A single incident of harassment is sufficient to create a triable issue regarding the existence of a hostile work environment, if the harassing conduct creates an intimidating, hostile, or offensive working environment. The question of whether an environment is objectively hostile or abusive must be answered by reference to all the circumstances. These kinds of questions are especially well-suited for jury determination and are rarely appropriate for disposition on summary judgment, unless a complaint is clearly frivolous, unreasonable or totally without foundation.

(6) "Supervisor" means any individual who is empowered by the employer with the ability to change the employment status of an employee or who directs an employee's daily work activities.

(i) The term "supervisor" shall not be limited to only those with the power to hire, fire, demote, promote, transfer or discipline. It includes those with the power to set schedules, make task assignments, mediate complaints, distribute rewards and punishments, or assert other intangible forms of authority.

(7) "Management Action" means a course of action that is taken by an employer or its supervisors or its agents, to direct and control the way work is done. A management action shall not be considered bullying if it is carried out with just cause and is conducted in a reasonable manner. Examples of management action include, but are not limited to:

(i) Conducting performance appraisals;

(ii) Holding meetings to address underperformance;

(iii) Disciplining a worker for misconduct;

(iv) Investigating alleged misconduct;

(v) Transferring a worker for operational reasons; or

(vi) Implementing organizational change or restructuring out of economic necessity.

(8) "Just Cause" means a standard of reasonableness used to evaluate a person's actions in a given set of circumstances. If a person acts with just cause, his or her actions are based on reasonable grounds and committed in good faith.

(9) "Retaliation" means a materially adverse action that might deter a reasonable person

from engaging in protected activity such as submitting a complaint or reporting abuse.

(i) "Materially adverse" includes any form of unfavorable treatment that rises above trivial harms, petty slights, or minor annoyances. Materially Adverse action need not be job-related or occur in the workplace to constitute unlawful retaliation.

(10) "Constructive discharge" - an adverse employment action where:

(i) The employee reasonably believed he or she was subjected to an abusive work environment;

(ii) The employee resigned because of that conduct; and

(iii) The employer knew or should have known of the abusive conduct prior to the resignation and failed to stop it.

28-52.1-5. Worker right to dignity in the workplace.

Every worker shall have the right to a workplace environment that affords them the dignity to which all human beings are entitled.

28-52.1-6. Prohibition against bullying, moral, psychological, and general harassment and other abusive behaviors.

(a) It shall be unlawful for any person to engage in workplace bullying, moral, psychological or general harassment of a co-worker or other employee in the working environment.

(1) Bullying, moral, psychological or general harassment shall be prohibited without regard to its subject matter or motivating animus. There is no requirement that the bullying behavior be extreme, outrageous, or repetitive to be unlawful under this chapter.

(2) It shall be unlawful for an employee to be bullied to the point of resignation. If an employer's action or inaction makes the situation at work so intolerable for the employee that the employee resigns, it may be considered a constructive dismissal.

(3) It shall be unlawful for any person to aid, abet, incite, compel or coerce the doing of an act forbidden under this chapter, or to attempt to do so.

(4) It shall be an unlawful employment practice to coerce, intimidate, threaten, or interfere with any person in the exercise of, or on account of having exercised, or on account of having aided or encouraged any other person in the exercise of, any right granted or protected under this chapter.

28-52.1-7. Employer responsibility to assure worker dignity and protect against workplace bullying, moral, psychological and general harassment and other abusive behaviors.

(a) Employers shall have a general duty to provide a workplace free from bullying and moral, psychological or general harassment and to provide a workplace that protects each employee's personal integrity, dignity and human rights.

1   (1) If bullying or harassment occurs at work, the employer shall make available the means
2   and measures for remedying the situation. Any employer who does not take all reasonable steps
3   necessary to prevent, detect and eliminate such behavior in their workplace shall be in violation of
4   this law and shall be liable for damages to make the targets of such bullying whole, including but
5   not limited to economic damages, damages for pain and suffering and equitable relief.

6   (2) Employers shall be required to post notice of employee's rights under this law, to
7   distribute the employer's anti-bullying policy including an explanation of reporting measures,
8   investigation process and remedial processes.

9   (3) Employers shall have a general duty to ensure, so far as is reasonably practical, that
10 they provide a work environment free from the risks associated with workplace bullying, that they
11 put in place a system to monitor, prevent and manage workplace bullying, and that workers are
12 adequately informed and trained on the topic of workplace bullying prevention and management.

13   (4) Employers shall take all necessary steps to assure that there be no retaliation against
14 any complainant who has filed a complaint under this chapter in good faith.

15   (5) Employers shall take all necessary steps to assure that there be no retaliation against
16 any individual for participating in a complaint as a witness, or for taking action as a bystander to
17 prevent or eliminate bullying of a target, or for opposing any behavior made unlawful by this Act.

18 **28-52.1-8. Vicarious liability for wrongful exercise of power.**

19   (a) Supervisory or managerial authority, in any form, shall not be used to abuse, bully,
20 manipulate or denigrate a worker. Employers shall be strictly liable for any wrongful exercise of
21 power by individuals who have the ability to make decisions regarding employee's employment
22 status or by those who direct, supervise, or evaluate employees.

23   (1) This chapter does not prohibit management action taken out of economic necessity or
24 as a reasonable response to incidents of misconduct or poor performance. Employers retain a
25 prerogative to direct and control the way work is carried out, respond to poor performance and, if
26 necessary, take disciplinary action.

27   (b) A complainant who is aggrieved by a management action must carry the initial burden
28 of showing that the management action was objectionable in order to support the presumption of
29 bullying.

30   (1) Objectionable behavior means behavior that a reasonable person, having regard for all
31 the circumstances, would view as unreasonable, unwanted, and potentially harmful. An
32 objectionable management action consists of two elements:

33   (i) The behavior must be a management action and
34   (ii) Either it must be objectionable for the action to be taken or the action itself must be

conducted in an objectionable manner, with an adverse effect on the target or his or her employment terms and conditions.

(2) Examples of objectionable management action, whether intentional or unintentional, include but are not limited to:

(i) Subjecting individuals to excessive supervision and unwarranted monitoring;

(ii) The inappropriate use of disciplinary procedures, including using performance reviews to misrepresent an employee's work history;

(iii) Arbitrarily withholding information that is vital for effective work performance;

(iv) Unjustifiably removing whole areas of work responsibility from a person;

(v) Setting impossible targets and objectives, or changing targets without telling the person;

(vi) Deliberate isolation by ignoring or excluding a person;

(vii) Setting tasks that are unreasonably below or beyond a person's skill level;

(viii) Denying access to information, supervision, consultation or resources to the detriment of the worker; and

(ix) Conducting an unfair workplace investigation;

(c) The complainant is only obliged to present evidence of objectionable behavior to support the presumption of bullying. When there are facts from which it may be presumed that there has been bullying, it shall be for the respondent to prove that the actions that led to the complaint did not constitute bullying.

(d) Once the employee has provided facts to support the presumption of bullying, the burden of proof shall be on the employer to show that the management action was not guided by unlawful motives. For a management action to be considered reasonable and therefore not classified as bullying, it must be a legitimate business action based on just cause. There must also be some line of cause and effect tied to the conduct, behavior or performance of an employee. Furthermore, the relevant management action must at all times be a reasonable and proportionate response to the attributes of the employee to which it is directed.

(1) Examples of management actions that are reasonable include, but are not limited to:

(i) Setting realistic and achievable performance goals;

(ii) Expecting employees to maintain reasonable workplace standards;

(iii) Fair and appropriate rostering and allocation of working hours;

(iv) Transferring a worker to another area or role for operational reasons;

(v) Deciding not to select a worker for promotion where a fair and transparent process is followed;

(vi) Informing a worker about unsatisfactory work performance in an honest, fair and constructive way;

(vii) Informing a worker about unreasonable behavior in an objective and confidential way, and

(viii) Taking disciplinary action where it is appropriate or justified in the circumstances.

(e) If the employer can show that its actions were reasonable and unrelated to bullying, the complainant shall have the opportunity to refute that assertion as pretext for unlawful behavior. To establish pretext in the absence of direct evidence, a complainant can offer many different forms of circumstantial evidence. An inquiry into pretext requires that the fact-finder evaluate the credibility of the employer's explanation.

(f) The facts required to establish objectionable behavior must be made on a case-by-case basis, taking into account the following:

(i) What the action is;

(ii) How the action came about;

(iii) How the action was carried out; and

(iv) The way in which the action affects a worker;

(v) A court will look at the overall conduct surrounding the management action;

(vi) Consideration may also be given as to whether the management action involved a significant departure from established policies or procedures and, if so, whether the departure was objectionable in the circumstances. In certain cases, reasonable management action may constitute bullying if the manner, form or frequency it is engaged in is objectionable.

28-52.1-9. Vicarious liability for moral, psychological, and general harassment.

(a) An employer shall be vicariously liable for acts committed by employees with respect to the harassment of employees, if the employer, or its agents, or its supervisors, knew or should have known about the misconduct and failed to take immediate and appropriate corrective action.

(b) An employer may also be responsible for the acts committed by customers, clients, and other non-employees, with respect to harassment of employees, if the employer, or its agents or supervisors, knew or should have known about the conduct and failed to take immediate and appropriate corrective action. In reviewing cases involving the acts of nonemployees, the extent of the employer's control and any other legal responsibility that the employer may have with respect to the conduct of those nonemployees shall be considered.

(c) An employer shall be strictly liable for the acts committed by its supervisors, with respect to harassment of employees. This liability includes harassment that results in a tangible employment action such as termination, failure to promote or hire, and loss of wages.

(d) When a supervisor's harassment does not include a tangible employment action, an employer can reduce damages if it can demonstrate that it exercised reasonable care to prevent and promptly correct any harassing behavior. An employer who exercises reasonable care shall not be compelled to pay damages if the aggrieved employee could have avoided all of the actionable harm, for example by taking advantage of employer provided complaint procedures. If some but not all of the harm could have been avoided, then an award of damages shall be mitigated accordingly.

(e) To succeed in reducing the employee's damages, the employer must prove three elements:

(1) The employer took reasonable steps to prevent and correct workplace harassment;

(2) The employee unreasonably failed to use the preventive and corrective measures that the employer provided or otherwise avoid or mitigate harm; and

(3) Reasonable use of the employer's procedures would have prevented at least some of the harm that the employee suffered.

If the employer establishes that the employee, by taking reasonable steps to utilize internal complaint procedures, could have caused the harassing conduct to cease, the employer will only remain liable for any compensable harm that was unavoidable.

(f) A victim of harassment has a general duty to use such means as are reasonable under the circumstances to avoid or minimize the damages that result from violations of this Act. However, an employee's failure to report harassment may be reasonable given the employee's genuinely held, subjective belief of potential retaliation. The reasonableness of the employee's actions shall be considered in light of the circumstances facing him or her at the time, including the ability to report the conduct without facing undue risk, expense, or humiliation. Fears that are substantiated by evidence will excuse a victim's failure to take advantage of the employer's anti-harassment policy.

(g) A target of psychological, moral, and general harassment does not have to suffer psychological injuries to recover under this chapter. As long as a work environment is reasonably perceived to be hostile or abusive, there is no need for it also to be psychologically injurious.

28-52.1-10. Retaliation.

(a) No employer or employee shall retaliate in any manner against an employee who has opposed any unlawful employment practice under this chapter, or who has made a charge, testified, assisted or participated in any manner in an investigation or proceeding under this chapter, including, but not limited to, internal complaints and proceedings, arbitration and mediation proceedings, and legal actions. Furthermore, an employee who promptly reports in good faith an act of bullying before it becomes actionable shall also be protected from retaliation.

(b) No employer shall silence an employee through the use of a non-disclosure agreement, including in a settlement agreement. All employees shall have the freedom to share their stories free from consequences from the employer.

28-52.1-11. Individual liability.

Any individual who engages in workplace bullying or moral, psychological or general harassment shall be jointly and severally liable along with their employer.

28-52.1-12. Remedies.

(a) Targets of workplace bullying shall be entitled to all remedies necessary to make such targets whole. Such remedies shall include:

(1) Economic damages for lost wages, both back pay and front pay, and any expenses related to treatment related to the bullying;

(2) Compensable damages to compensate for the pain and suffering, emotional and psychological damages resulting from such workplace bullying;

(3) Punitive damages as deemed necessary to deter future acts of workplace bullying;

(4) Injunctive relief, whereby the court may enjoin the defendant from engaging in the unlawful employment practice; and

(5) And any other relief that is deemed appropriate, including, but not limited to: medical expenses, psychological treatment, restorative measures, organizational training and attorney's fees.

(b) Courts may also require employers to implement effective anti-bullying policies, including investigation and training policies, and require bullies to engage in training and other remedial measures.

(c) A complaining party may recover punitive damages under this Chapter only if the complaining party can demonstrate that the employer engaged in prohibited conduct with intent to injure or with knowing disregard of the protected rights of an aggrieved individual.

(d) The remedies provided in this chapter shall be in addition to any remedies provided under any other law, and nothing in this chapter shall relieve any person from any liability, duty, penalty or punishment provided by any other law.

28-52.1-13. Causes of action.

(a) There is hereby established a Fair Work Commission (the "commission"), consisting of seven (7) members to be appointed by the governor, to address workplace bullying and to enforce this act. In the enforcement of this chapter, the Commission shall have the following powers and duties:

(1) To issue enforcement guidance and formulate policies to effectuate the purposes of this Chapter and make recommendations to agencies and officers of the state or its political subdivisions

in aid of such policies and purposes.

(2) To receive, initiate, investigate, seek to conciliate, hold hearings, and issue orders on complaints alleging violations of this chapter.

(3) To require answers to interrogatories, compel the attendance of witnesses, examine witnesses under oath or affirmation in person by deposition, and require the production of documents relevant to the complaint, in accordance with this chapter.

(4) To make available to the public information on this Act, grievance procedures, and public records of the Commission and any other information that would further the purposes and intentions of this chapter.

(b) The commission shall also have the right to represent claimants in judicial proceedings and during the ALJ process. At the conclusion of the investigation, the Commission may bring the complaint in front of an ALJ to litigate the Commission's determination, recommend appropriate penalties against an employer and/or engage in mediation between the claimant and employer or issue the claimant a right to sue letter to bring a private claim of action.

28-52.1-14. Applicable statute of limitations.

(a) Claimants shall have three years from the last act of bullying or moral, psychological or general harassment to either file a complaint with the Fair Work Commission or to file litigation

(b) If a claimant files a complaint with the Fair Work Commission the statute of limitations for filing a private cause of action is tolled.

(c) Claimants who file with the Fair Work Commission shall have ninety (90) days to file a private cause of action after the Commission issues a right to sue determination.

(d) Under this subsection, apprentices, trainees, unpaid interns, volunteers, and independent contractors may file a complaint alleging unlawful bullying and harassment.

Nothing in this subsection shall create an employment relationship under wage and hour provision, workers' compensation, or unemployment insurance.

28-52.1-15. Conflicts with other laws.

(a) Nothing in this law should be construed as limiting employee rights under any other law including rights under Title VII of the Civil Rights Act, The Americans with Disabilities Act, the Age Discrimination in Employment Act and state EEO laws.

(b) Nothing in this law should be construed as limiting employee rights under the National Labor Relations Act (NLRA) and/or State Labor Rights laws. Concerted Activity/Section 7 activity under the NLRA as interpreted by the NLRB shall not be construed as workplace bullying or moral, psychological or general harassment.

(c) Nothing under this law shall restrict workers from negotiating broader protections of their dignity or protections against workplace bullying or harassment under via collective bargaining or other concerted activity.

SECTION 2. This act shall take effect upon passage.

LC002813

EXPLANATION

BY THE LEGISLATIVE COUNCIL

OF

AN ACT

RELATING TO LABOR AND LABOR RELATIONS -- DIGNITY AT WORK ACT

***

1   This act would establish the Dignity at Work Act, to provide workers with more protection
2   from bullying and harassment in the workplace.
3   This act would take effect upon passage.

LC002813

Media Advisory: Event slated Thursday to push for 'Cover All Kids' bill to expand Medicaid to all children, regardless of immigration status

June 1, 2021

STATE HOUSE – Rep. David Morales and Sen. Sandra Cano will be joined by community advocates at a State House event Thursday to call for passage of their "Cover All Kids" legislation to ensure that all low-income children, regardless of immigration status, qualify for health insurance under the state's RIte Care program.

The event is scheduled **Thursday, June 3, at 2:30 p.m. outside on the Smith Street side of the State House.**

The legislation ([2021-H 5714](), [2021-S 0576]()) would establish Rhode Island's commitment to provide health insurance to all low-income children who are residents of the state, regardless of immigration status.

Central Falls Mayor Maria Rivera is scheduled to participate, and organizations attending the event include Rhode Island KIDS COUNT, Economic Progress Institute, the Latino Policy Institute, the Rhode Island Interfaith Coalition to Reduce Poverty, the Rhode Island Health Center Association and Dorcas International Institute of Rhode Island.

2021-H 5714

2021 -- H 5714

LC001720

STATE OF RHODE ISLAND

IN GENERAL ASSEMBLY

JANUARY SESSION, A.D. 2021

AN ACT

RELATING TO STATE AFFAIRS AND GOVERNMENT -- HEALTH CARE FOR CHILDREN AND PREGNANT WOMEN

Introduced By: Representatives Morales, Williams, Hull, Giraldo, Barros, Alzate, Tobon, Diaz, Kislak, and Kazarian
Date Introduced: February 24, 2021

Referred To: House Health & Human Services

It is enacted by the General Assembly as follows:

1   SECTION 1. Sections 42-12.3-4 and 42-12.3-15 of the General Laws in Chapter 42-12.3
2 entitled "Health Care for Children and Pregnant Women" are hereby amended to read as follows:
3   **42-12.3-4. "RIte track" program.**
4   (a) There is hereby established a payor of last resort program for comprehensive health
5 care for children until they reach nineteen (19) years of age, to be known as "RIte track." The
6 department of human services is hereby authorized to amend its title XIX state plan pursuant to
7 title XIX [42 U.S.C. § 1396 et seq.] and title XXI [42 U.S.C. § 1397 et seq.] of the Social Security
8 Act as necessary to provide for expanded Medicaid coverage through expanded family income
9 disregards for children, until they reach nineteen (19) years of age, whose family income levels are
10 up to two hundred fifty percent (250%) of the federal poverty level. Provided, however, that
11 healthcare coverage provided under this section shall also be provided without regard to availability
12 of federal financial participation in accordance to Title XIX of the Social Security Act, 42 U.S.C.
13 § 1396 et seq., to a noncitizen child who is a resident of Rhode Island lawfully residing in the
14 United States, and who is otherwise eligible for such assistance. The department is further
15 authorized to promulgate any regulations necessary, and in accord with title XIX [42 U.S.C. § 1396
16 et seq.] and title XXI [42 U.S.C. § 1397 et seq.] of the Social Security Act as necessary in order to
17 implement the state plan amendment. For those children who lack health insurance, and whose
18 family incomes are in excess of two hundred fifty percent (250%) of the federal poverty level, the

department of human services shall promulgate necessary regulations to implement the program. The department of human services is further directed to ascertain and promulgate the scope of services that will be available to those children whose family income exceeds the maximum family income specified in the approved title XIX [42 U.S.C. § 1396 et seq.] and title XXI [42 U.S.C. § 1397 et seq.] state plan amendment.

(b) The executive office of health and human services is directed to ensure that federal financial participation is assessed to the maximum extent allowable to provide coverage to children pursuant to this section, and that state-only funds will be used only if federal financial participation is not available.

42-12.3-15. Expansion of RIte track program.

(a) The Department of Human Services is hereby authorized and directed to submit to the United States Department of Health and Human Services an amendment to the "RIte Care" waiver project number 11-W-0004/1-01 to provide for expanded Medicaid coverage for children until they reach eight (8) years of age, whose family income levels are to two hundred fifty percent (250%) of the federal poverty level. Expansion of the RIte track program from the age of six (6) until they reach eighteen (18) years of age in accordance with this chapter shall be subject to the approval of the amended waiver by the United States Department of Health and Human Services. Healthcare coverage under this section shall also be provided to a noncitizen child who is a resident of Rhode Island ~~lawfully residing in the United States,~~ and who is otherwise eligible for such assistance under title XIX [42 U.S.C. § 1396 et seq.] or title XXI [42 U.S.C. § 1397 et seq.]

(b) The executive office of health and human services is directed to ensure that federal financial participation is assessed to the maximum extent allowable to provide coverage to children pursuant to this section, and that state-only funds will be used only if federal financial participation is not available.

SECTION 2. This act shall take effect upon passage.

LC001720

EXPLANATION

BY THE LEGISLATIVE COUNCIL

OF

AN ACT

RELATING TO STATE AFFAIRS AND GOVERNMENT -- HEALTH CARE FOR CHILDREN AND PREGNANT WOMEN

***

1 This act would expand the Rite Track Program to provide health care coverage to children
2 up to age nineteen (19) funded by federal funds, if available, or if not available, by state funds.
3 This act would take effect upon passage.

LC001720

It was great to be back on the House Floor yesterday! Looking forward to the rest of the session!

June 2, 2021

Flanked by advocates, Morales and Cano call for passage of bill to expand Medicaid to 'Cover All Kids'

June 3, 2021

STATE HOUSE – Backed by a broad group of community and health advocates at a State House event today, Rep. David Morales and Sen. Sandra Cano today called for passage of their legislation to ensure that all low-income children, regardless of immigration status, qualify for health insurance under the state's RIte Track program.

"As we work to recover from the COVID-19 pandemic, we can't afford to leave any children without health care. All public health is at risk when there are some people who can't seek health care when they need it. But above all, health care is a human right, and all children deserve safety. Healthy kids should be a high priority of Rhode Island," said Representative Morales (D-Dist. 7, Providence).

The legislation ([2021-H 5714](#), [2021-S 0576](#)) would establish Rhode Island's commitment to provide health insurance to all children who are residents of the state, regardless of immigration status. It would provide for the appropriation of state-only funds to pay for coverage if federal funds are not available.

RIte Track is the state's Medicaid program for children, providing health care coverage for those under age 19 whose family income does not exceed 250 percent of the federal poverty level. Rhode Island covered all children regardless of status for almost 10 years in the late 1990s and early 2000s, and it is time to restore this commitment to all children, the sponsors said. Currently, there are about 3,000 uninsured children in our state who are not enrolled in the RIte Track program and are not able to access the health care services they need.

Expanding coverage would allow parents to take their children to the doctor for preventive care, see specialists as necessary and buy critical medications that can help reduce higher health care costs for the state because if children are hospitalized, the hospital bills are covered by Medicaid, with the state paying its required share.

But more importantly, said Senator Cano (D-Dist. 8, Pawtucket), children should not suffer because of their legal status or socioeconomic background. In addition to lacking the health care that children need as they are growing up, children without health insurance may not receive emergency care as their families may fear that their status will be discovered. Having coverage for the children without regard to their immigration status would help alleviate some of those fears, keep kids healthier, and avoid preventable illnesses.

"Every child needs regular health care. Of course they should have immunizations, attention to their development and medical treatment when they are sick. We are stronger and safer when everyone in Rhode Island has the health care they need," said Senator Cano.

The bill has strong support from over 20 organizations including Rhode Island KIDS COUNT, Economic Progress Institute, and The Latino Policy Institute.

"In 2019, 98.1% of Rhode Island children had health insurance coverage and Rhode Island ranked second for children's health insurance coverage," said Elizabeth Burke Bryant, Executive Director of Rhode Island KIDS COUNT. "To achieve our goal of covering all kids, we must restore access to RIte Care health insurance for income-eligible children who are undocumented immigrants. All children need access to health care that supports their healthy growth and development and promotes school success."

Linda Katz, policy director of Economic Progress Institute said, "COVID-19 has reinforced how interconnected and interdependent we are. Ensuring that *all* of Rhode Island's children have access to comprehensive health care through RIte Care enrollment not only helps those youngsters but protects all of us. EPI looks forward to working with Representative Morales and Senator Cano to enact this legislation."

"During the last year, we have experienced firsthand the impacts of health disparities on the educational and economic outcomes of our most vulnerable Black and Latino communities. Ensuring that our youngest Rhode Islanders have access to health coverage is a public health issue we cannot continue to ignore," said Marcela Betancur, Director of The Latino Policy Institute.

Dr. Gregory Fox, President of the Rhode Island Chapter of the American Academy of Pediatrics also expressed strong support. "The Rhode Island Chapter of the American Academy of Pediatrics enthusiastically supports this legislation, which opens Rite Care eligibility to all income eligible Rhode Island children. All children deserve access to the life-saving vaccines and quality preventative care which lay the groundwork for a healthy childhood and successful school career. Allowing for insurance coverage of all children of Rhode Island, regardless of immigration status, not only keeps kids in supportive medical homes and reduces costly emergency room care…it is the right thing to do."

The House bill was introduced Feb. 24 with over 20 cosponsors and has been assigned to the House Finance Committee. The Senate bill was introduced on March 11 and has been assigned to the Senate Finance Committee.

A few months ago when session first started, Senator Sandra Cano and I introduced legislation (Cover all Kids) to expand healthcare coverage to ALL low-income children in our State, regardless of immigration status.

June 3, 2021

Today, alongside community advocates, healthcare providers, public policy experts, families, and legislators we held a press conference in support of this bill because it is absolutely we pass it this year. Thank you again

RI KIDS COUNT, Economic Progress Institute, the Latino Policy Institute, the RI Interfaith Coalition to Reduce Poverty, the RI Health Center Association and Dorcas International Institute of RI for all of advocacy on this issue.

On a more personal note, it was an absolute honor to lead a press conference surrounded by such dedicated advocates who believe that healthcare is a basic human right. ¡Thank you again community — Muchas gracias a nuestra communidad!

What an honor to be surrounded by amazing leaders!

June 3, 2021
Glendaliz Colon

What an honor to be surrounded by amazing leaders! I had the pleasure of speaking at the Cover All Kids Press Conference in support of Rep. David Morales and Senator Sandra Cano who are fiercely fighting for health coverage for all of our children regardless of their immigration status!! To leave these children without proper health coverage is NEGLECT!

Gracias Sucely J Murillo for speaking today! You are NOT alone!

I would like to thank Councilwoman Adamaris Villar for sponsoring the resolution in support of House Bill 5714 and Senate Bill 576, and to my fellow colleagues on the Central Falls City Council for voting unanimously in full support! Mayor Maria Rivera, Senator Jonathon Acosta, Rep. Joshua Giraldo, Rep. Karen Alzate thank you for always fighting for our community!

#JuntosSomosMas

Last week, we unanimously passed HB #5196 to limit monthly out-of-pocket expenses for Insulin at $40 — one of the lowest rates in the entire country!

Given that over 80,000 RI adults have diabetes, 10% of our adult population, this is a major victory for our working families!

This was a very special moment for me because shortly after taking office, I immediately introduced a bill to limit monthly out-of-pocket expenses for Insulin, as it is a common and expensive medication for people with diabetes. Following my first committee hearing, I collaborated with my colleagues, Rep. Brian Kennedy and Rep. Grace Diaz, to help advocate for this comprehensive bill.

I'm proud to have helped lead this effort and ensure that all our people can afford the life-saving medication they need!

Legislation to ensure that all low-income children,

RI Black & Latino Legislative Caucus
June 3, 2021

Backed by a broad group of community and health advocates at a State House event today,
RI State Representative David Morales and Sen. Sandra Cano today called for passage of their legislation to ensure that all low-income children, regardless of immigration status, qualify for health insurance under the state's RIte Track program.

"As we work to recover from the COVID-19 pandemic, we can't afford to leave any children without health care. All public health is at risk when there are some people who can't seek health care when they need it. But above all, health care is a human right, and all children deserve safety. Healthy kids should be a high priority of Rhode Island," said Rep. Morales.

The legislation would establish Rhode Island's commitment to provide health insurance to all children who are residents of the state, regardless of immigration status. It would provide for the appropriation of state-only funds to pay for coverage if federal funds are not available.

RIte Track is the state's Medicaid program for children, providing health care coverage for those under age 19 whose family income does not exceed 250 percent of the federal poverty level. Rhode Island covered all children regardless of status for almost 10 years in the late 1990s and early 2000s, and it is time to restore this commitment to all children, the sponsors said. Currently, there are about 3,000 uninsured children in our state who are not enrolled in the RIte Track program and are not able to access the health care services they need.

Expanding coverage would allow parents to take their children to the doctor for preventive care, see specialists as necessary and buy critical medications that can help reduce higher health care costs for the state because if children are hospitalized, the hospital bills are covered by Medicaid, with the state paying its required share.

But more importantly, said Senator Cano, children should not suffer because of their legal status or socioeconomic background. In addition to lacking the health care that children need as they are growing up, children without health insurance may not receive emergency care as their families may fear that their status will be discovered. Having coverage for the children without regard to their immigration status would help alleviate some of those fears, keep kids healthier, and avoid preventable illnesses.

"Every child needs regular health care. Of course they should have immunizations, attention to their development and medical treatment when they are sick. We are stronger and safer when everyone in Rhode Island has the health care they need," said Senator Cano.

The bill has strong support from over 20 organizations including Rhode Island KIDS COUNT, Economic Progress Institute, and The Latino Policy Institute.

More information: http://www.rilin.state.ri.us/pressrelease/_layouts/RIL.PressRelease.ListStructure/Forms/DisplayForm.aspx?List=c8baae31-3c10-431c-8dcd-9dbbe21ce3e9&ID=371730

Introduced and passed a resolution thanking our Senior Centers

June 5, 2020

Earlier this week, alongside House colleagues, I introduced and passed a resolution thanking our Senior Centers for all the important services they've provided to our communities throughout the pandemic. From community gatherings, counseling services to referrals for government programs — our Senior Centers are clearly invested in the well-being of our seniors and their families.

Yesterday was another example as our own Lillian Feinstein Senior Center hosted an open house celebration with music and food! It was a pleasure to see so many friends again. @ Lillian Feinstein Senior Center

2021 — H 6380

LC002939

STATE OF RHODE ISLAND

IN GENERAL ASSEMBLY

JANUARY SESSION, A.D. 2021

HOUSE RESOLUTION

RECOGNIZING AND THANKING RHODE ISLAND'S SENIOR CENTERS FOR THEIR DEDICATION TO PROVIDING VITAL SERVICES DURING THE COVID PANDEMIC

Introduced By: Representatives Morales, Shekarchi, Blazejewski, Filippi, McEntee, Caldwell, Craven, Kennedy, Cortvriend, and Ranglin-Vassell
Date Introduced: June 01, 2021

Referred To: House read and passed

1   WHEREAS, Senior Centers are community gathering places that provide some of the
2   most widely used programs and essential services to enrich and assist the lives of Rhode Islanders
3   over the age of fifty; and

4   WHEREAS, Some of the invaluable services provided by Rhode Island Senior Centers
5   include: meal and nutrition programs, health & wellness programs, information on community
6   resources, eligibility screening for local, State & Federal assistance programs, assistance
7   identifying employment or volunteer opportunities, and limited transportation; and

8   WHEREAS, For more than a year, the world has been grappling with the devastating
9   physical, financial, and emotional toll of the COVID-19 pandemic, and one of the hardest
10 affected age groups has been our seniors; and

11 WHEREAS, Many of Rhode Island's Senior Centers have provided crucial information,
12 testing, and clinics for COVID vaccinations as well as continuing services to individuals in our
13 State's most hard-hit areas, such as the Lillian Feinstein Senior Center in Providence that provides

Thank you again to all our community members who came together to clean our Valley neighborhood!

June 12, 2021

Thank you again to all our community members who came together to clean our Valley neighborhood!

Together, we took the time to re-invest in Valley by cleaning our streets and engaging with fellow neighbors. Unfortunately, Valley has been neglected for decades as there has been a lack of attention towards the conditions of our streets and community engagement efforts. This is why these community events are so important, however, because through collective action we will make sure our community is well taken care of! Thank you again to everyone who showed up and made this possible.

Fue un fin de semana de mucha ayuda voluntaria y inversión comunitaria en nuestras comunidades de Providence.

June 13, 2021

Primero estuvimos limpiando las calles y vecindarios del distrito 7 con el Senador Sam Bell, Representante Estatal David Morales y mi hermano Miguel Sanchez quien se postula para consejo municipal de Ward 6 en Providence.

También tuvimos la oportunidad de participar y estar con el consulado Mexicano en Providence durante el proceso en donde estaban ayudando a nuestro pueblo Mexicano renovar pasaportes y documentos etc. Gracias a Emma Villa por organizar este evento para nuestra comunidad. Se respeta mucho su trabajo en nuestra ciudad.

Y para cerrar este fin de semana de mucho éxito, tuvimos un partido de futbol en Central Falls con nuestras comunidades de esa area. Tuvimos una carne azada y evento familiar con nuestra comunidad del sur de Providence. Nuestras comunidades más vulnerables merecen la ayuda y el apoyó directamente para ellos. Fue un placer conectar mas con nuestros residents de esa area.

House passes bill prohibiting insurers from charging copays for COVID services and vaccines

June 16, 2021

STATE HOUSE – The House today approved legislation sponsored by Rep. David Morales to prevent health insurers from instituting cost-sharing for COVID services for as long as the state of emergency remains in effect. The bill also prohibits insurers from requiring copayments, coinsurance or any out-of-pocket deductible for COVID-19 testing or the vaccine even after the state of emergency.

"As a state, protecting the health and safety of all Rhode Islanders, especially working people, should be our top priority. There should not be any financial barriers standing in the way of someone who thinks that they have COVID-19 from accessing testing or treatment," said Representative Morales (D-Dist. 7, Providence). "While we are fortunate to be one of the leading states in terms of vaccination rates, this pandemic is not over by any means, and we put our progress at risk if we relax the measures that have encouraged people to get tested, treated and vaccinated. We are still in an emergency and we need all insurers to stay on board and continue to be committed partners in our effort to overcome this pandemic and minimize the impact it is having on our communities."

The bill (2021-H 6208A), which has over 20 co-sponsors in the House, stemmed from an announcement this spring that Blue Cross Blue Shield of Rhode Island planned to allow its cost-sharing waiver to expire on March 31. The insurer later rescinded the plan.

Representative Morales filed the legislation to make sure that no such cost-sharing is instituted by any insurer, so Rhode Islanders are protected for the duration of the emergency.

The bill prohibits insurers from requiring copayments, coinsurance or any out-of-pocket deductible for COVID-19 testing, vaccines, or COVID-19-related emergency services, inpatient services, office visits or hospital stays for the duration of the state of emergency. The prohibition on cost-sharing for COVID-19 testing and vaccines would remain in perpetuity.

The legislation now goes to the Senate, which on June 1 passed companion legislation (2021-S 0877A) sponsored by Sen. Alana M. DiMario (D-Dist. 36, Narragansett, North Kingstown).

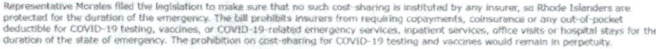

House passes bill prohibiting insurers from charging copays for COVID services, vaccines

SUZANNE KRIETER/GLOBE STAFF R.I.
ALEXA GAGOSZ
June 16 at 6:10 PM ET

House passes bill prohibiting insurers from charging copays for COVID services, vaccines

Representative David Morales, a Providence Democrat who, at age 22, is Rhode Island's youngest legislator and one of the youngest Latino legislators in the country.

Providence — The House Wednesday approved legislation that would prevent health insurers from instituting cost-sharing for services related to COVID-19 for as long as the state of emergency remains in effect. Some of these services also includes COVID-19-related emergency services, inpatient services, office visits and hospital stays. The bill, sponsored by Rep. David Morales, a Providence Democrat, also prohibits health insurance companies from requiring copayments, coinsurance, or any out-of-pocket deductible for COVID-19 testing or the vaccine— even after the state of emergency.

"Protecting the health and safety of all Rhode Islanders, especially working people, should be our top priority.

There should not be any financial barriers standing in the way of someone who thinks that they have COVID-19 from accessing testing or treatment," said Morales after the bill passed. The bill, which had more than 20 co-sponsors in the House, was filed after the state's largest health insurer announced that it would stop its full coverage of COVID-19 treatment.

Blue Cross & Blue Shield of Rhode Island sent an email in mid-March to its 415,000 members that it would end its no-cost coverage of treatment for COVID-19 on March 31, which was still weeks before most Rhode Islanders were even eligible for their first shot of the COVID-19 vaccine under the state's vaccine timeline. After discussions with Governor Dan McKee and state Health Insurance Commissioner Patrick Tigue, the insurance company reversed course.

"More recently, a year into the pandemic, with vaccines becoming more widely available, we felt it was appropriate to let the cost sharing waiver expire as had been planned," a statement from the insurance company read at the time. During that same week, Neighborhood Health Plan of Rhode Island put out a statement that said it would continue to fully cover expenses related to COVID-19 treatment. But at the time, the catch for both insurers is that they would continue full coverage "for the duration of the state of emergency.

"Elizabeth McClaine, Neighborhood's vice president of commercial products, said in a prepared statement sent to the Globe that the insurer has "no plans" to begin charging co-payments on testing or vaccines. "We have no plans to begin charging copayments on testing or vaccines and regard the COVID-19 vaccine in the same manner we do other state supplied vaccines, which do not require coinsurance," said McClaine Wednesday night.

"Our expectation is that the COVID-19 vaccine will become a state supplied vaccine in the near future." She did not say if

Neighborhood planned on charging co-payments for any other COVID-19 related services that this bill would prohibit the insurer from charging for. A spokesperson for Blue Cross & Blue Shield of Rhode Island could not be immediately reached for comment.

While Governor Charlie Baker recently ended Massachusetts' state of emergency order this past week, McKee extended Rhode Island's until July 9. It first went into effect in March 2020 at the start of the coronavirus pandemic and was signed by former Gov. Gina Raimondo. Globe reporters have asked McKee previously if he was extending state of emergency orders because thousands of Rhode Islanders would lose their full insurance coverage for COVID-19 treatment otherwise, but he said it was because the pandemic was still "ongoing."

As of Wednesday night, more than 56 percent of eligible Rhode Islanders (including children as young as 12) have been fully vaccinated against COVID-19. More than 67 percent of Rhode Island adults over the age of 18, who largely became eligible to receive the shot on April 19, are fully vaccinated. While more state residents continue to get vaccinated, the number of new confirmed COVID-19 cases, hospitalizations, and deaths have continued to decrease. However, certain towns and populations have been labeled as vaccine "cold spots" by the state's health department.

New data by the state health department recently revealed that two communities have the state's lowest vaccination rates, which are Woonsocket and Tiverton. "While we are fortunate to be one of the leading states in terms of vaccination rates, this pandemic is not over by any means, and we put our progress at risk if we relax the measures that have encouraged people to get tested, treated and vaccinated," said Morales. "We are still in an emergency and we need all insurers to stay on board and continue to be committed partners in our effort to overcome this pandemic and minimize the impact it is having on our communities." The legislation will now go to the Senate, which passed companion legislation sponsored by Sen. Alana DiMario, a Narragansett Democrat, on June 1.

As we continue to recover from COVID-19

June 17, 2021

As we continue to recover from this pandemic, it is absolutely necessary our State Government do everything we can to help our communities get vaccinated and receive the medical treatment they need!

Yesterday, we passed my bill (HB 6208) to ensure that COVID-19 related healthcare services be free of charge throughout our declared state of emergency. In addition, this bill will ensure that COVID Testing and Vaccinations *always* be free! This is important because contrary to popular belief, there are thousands of people being charged for the vaccine due to the limitations of their health insurance plans.

Having been a firm advocate for COVID relief since the start of this pandemic last year — it was an honor to have lead this effort to provide all our communities, especially our working people, the reassurance that they will not have to experience any financial barriers if they ever contract the virus or choose to receive the vaccine. Thank you again to all my colleagues for the overwhelming support on this issue! #COVIDRelief

```
                    CALENDAR
         ITEM 5           2021-H 6208 SUB A
         Morales                        HHS
              RELATING TO INSURANCE
                     PASSAGE
```

Y ABNEY	Y CASEY	Y FOGARTY	Y MCGAW	Y QUATTROCCHI
Y ACKERMAN	CASIMIRO	Y GIRALDO	Y MCLAUGHLIN	RANGLIN-VASSELL
Y AJELLO	Y CASSAR	Y HANDY	Y MCNAMARA	Y ROBERTS
ALZATE	Y CHIPPENDALE	Y HAWKINS	Y MESSIER	Y RUGGIERO
Y AMORE	Y CORTVRIEND	Y HENRIES	Y MORALES	Y SERPA
Y AZZINARO	Y CORVESE	HULL	Y MORGAN	Y SHALLCROSSSMITH
Y DAGINSKI	Y COSTANTINO	Y KAZARIAN	Y NARDONE	Y SHANLEY
Y BARROS	Y CRAVEN	Y KENNEDY	Y NEWBERRY	Y SLATER
Y BATISTA	Y DIAZ	Y KISLAK	Y NORET	Y SOLOMON
Y BENNETT	Y DONOVAN	Y KNIGHT	Y O'BRIEN	Y SPEAKMAN
Y BIAH	Y EDWARDS	Y LIMA C	Y PEREZ	Y TANZI
Y BLAZEJEWSKI	FELIX	Y LIMA S	Y PHILLIPS	Y TOBON
Y CALDWELL	Y FELLELA	Y LOMBARDI	Y PLACE	Y VELLA-WILKINSON
Y CARDILLO	Y FENTON-FUNG	Y MARSZALKOWSKI	Y POTTER	Y WILLIAMS
Y CARSON	Y FILIPPI	Y MCENTEE		Y MR. SPEAKER

The Boston Globe

RI HEALTH

R.I. House passes bill prohibiting insurers from charging copays for COVID services, vaccines

"There should not be any financial barriers standing in the way of someone who thinks that they have COVID-19 from accessing testing or treatment," said the bill's sponsor.

By Alexa Gagosz Globe Staff,
Updated June 16, 2021, 6:10 p.m.

Representative David Morales, a Providence Democrat who, at age 22, is Rhode Island's youngest legislator and one of the youngest Latino legislators in the country. SUZANNE KRIETER/GLOBE

2021 -- H 6208 SUBSTITUTE A

LC002569/SUB A/2

STATE OF RHODE ISLAND

IN GENERAL ASSEMBLY

JANUARY SESSION, A.D. 2021

AN ACT

RELATING TO INSURANCE

Introduced By: Representatives Morales, Williams, Kazarian, Potter, Nardone, McGaw, Solomon, Hull, Kislak, and Caldwell
Date Introduced: April 07, 2021

Referred To: House Health & Human Services

It is enacted by the General Assembly as follows:

1   SECTION 1. Chapter 27-18 of the General Laws entitled "Accident and Sickness Insurance
2 Policies" is hereby amended by adding thereto the following section:
3   **27-18-85. Health insurance contracts - copayments exemption for COVID-19**
4 **vaccinations.**
5   (a) Any individual or group health insurance plan or policy shall not impose any
6 copayment, coinsurance or charge any out-of-pocket deductible to the insured for COVID-19
7 related services, including, but not limited to, emergency services, inpatient services, provider
8 office visits, and inpatient hospital stays, as long as the COVID-19 state of emergency remains in

RI State Rep Wants Less Money in Budget for New State Police Barracks, More for Children's Health

Wednesday, June 23, 2021
GoLocalProv News Team

A State Representative is calling for less money for a new state police barracks in the approved Rhode Island House Finance budget making its way through the General Assembly — and more money for children's healthcare.

Last week, the House Finance Committee approved a Fiscal Year 2022 budget that included Governor Dan McKee's recently revised proposal to replace the North Kingstown and Richmond State Police barracks with a single new $28.1 million barracks to be built in East Greenwich. The revised proposal would no longer require voter approval due to a different funding mechanism.

Now, Representative David Morales (D-Dist. 7, Providence) told GoLocal he is looking to put forth an amendment that would divert some of that funding to go toward healthcare for undocumented children.

"The Governor had originally wanted the barracks funding to be a bond. It wasn't until three or four weeks ago his office came back and said they wanted the line item [in the budget]," said Morales. "Their rationale was the current barracks are in very rough condition and they needed to 'expedite the process.'"

"Given the fact that almost every year we see an increase in police budgeting at the state and local level, I think when it comes to a significant investment to determine whether this is something we want for our communities — and whether here's a good return on investment — it should have been a bond," said Morales.

"I had a bill this year to expand Medicaid to cover all kids," said Morales. "Currently any child in a household under 250% of the federal poverty level is eligible. But we currently we children who are not eligible due to their immigration status."

According to the statement from bill sponsors when the legislation was introduced, there are about 3,000 uninsured children in our state who are not enrolled in the RIte Track program and are not able to access the health care services they need.

"The fiscal estimate to expand eligibility I was told would be $1.6 to $5.5 million," Morales. "The way the amendment has been proposed, we would strip some money from the barracks, around $6 million [to fund the program]."

"From my understanding, leadership is aware of this — we're still having conversations," said Morales.

Hi neighbors, tomorrow (6/24) our State Legislature will be voting on the State Budget for this year.

June 23, 2021

As our State Representative, I want to provide you with my findings and thoughts! I hope you find this helpful.

Overall, this year's budget is worth $13.2 billion and addresses several important issues from improving social services to protecting Medicaid to funding affordable housing development.

I. Medicaid:

In the Governor's original budget proposal in March there were proposals to cut Medicaid by $5 million through eliminating the Upper Payment Limit (UPL) for outpatient hospital services and eliminating the Graduate Medical Education (GME). For context, the Upper Payment Limit is the reimbursement the State pays our hospitals for treating Medicaid patients (the federal government pays the other half). The Graduate Medical Education is funding we provide to hospitals so they can receive support from Medical students with treating Medicaid patients. Both these programs are important as they help ensure our Medicaid recipients are receiving the highest quality of care possible.

Given that we will not be cutting UPL or the GME -- this will be first time in years we will be voting on a budget that does not contain cuts Medicaid!

II. Affordable Housing:

For the first time ever, we will be allocating funding towards the construction of affordable housing! This year, we will be investing $25 million.

In addition, we have established an annual funding stream for affordable housing by increasing the 'conveyance tax' on all home sales over $800,000. This generated revenue will be allocated for affordable housing in future years.

III. Public Education:

This year's budget continues to fully fund our K-12 funding formula (until we revise this formula, however, I will continue to argue that our Providence Public Schools deserve more funding).

In addition, the budget will now require that school districts that see a student leave their traditional public school system for a charter school receive a reimbursement of $500 per student in the first year after the student switches.

As for higher education, Rhode Island College (RIC) will be receiving an additional $5.9 million in order to meet contract obligations and pay faculty. Given the important work RIC does for our communities, especially for our students of color, I'm glad we are properly investing in higher education.

IV. Social Services and Programs:

I'm so excited to see the investments we are making towards our State Agencies that provide social services along with increased funding for important social programs that help working people and our most vulnerable.

RI Works: RI Works is a cash-benefit program that helps over 2,400 low-income families and provides them with wraparound services. The budget proposes a 30% increase in benefits and expanded eligibility. This is the first time in about a decade, RI Works has seen an increase in benefits.

Supporting People with Developmental Disabilities: After years of stagnant pay, we will be providing an increase in wages to workers who support people with developmental disabilities at $15.75!

Child Care: The payment rates for child-care providers are being increased and the co-payments for parents will be capped at 7% of their household income! As a result, this will help expand accessibility to childcare for our working families.

Funding for Doulas: For the first time ever, we are including doula funding for people covered by Medicaid.

For context, Doulas are non-medical birth attendants who support pregnant individuals to ensure that their maternal health is protected (this is an issue that disproportionately affects women of color).

Pay for Success: Starting this year and for the next 5 years, alongside federal funds, we will begin the 'Pay for Success' program. At $1 million per year, this program is focused on providing wraparound services to unhoused people.

V. An Overview of Taxes:

Overall, the budget does not make any significant adjustments to our State's Tax Code, though there are some noteworthy tax initiatives.

Car Tax: This budget fully funds the fifth year of our six-year phaseout of our State's 'Car Tax'. Therefore, this will further reduce the number of cars that are taxed and the amount owed.

Taxes on Profitable PPP Loans: We will be mandating taxes on PPP loans over $250,000 if the business recipient was profitable. Overall, this will impact a very small number of businesses since it will only be for those who received loans over $250,000 and had profit during COVID.

Income Taxes: Despite recommendations from the Economic Progress Institute, several other advocacy organizations, and Legislators (including myself) to repeal our State's 2006 tax-cuts for the wealthy and establish a 8.99% income tax-rate for people earning over $475,000, this proposed budget does not adjust our income tax structure.

VI. Funding for Providence via PILOT Program:

One of the only areas of concern I have with this budget is the money Providence will receive from the PILOT (Payment In Lieu Of Taxes) Program.

For context, PILOT is the State's program to compensate cities and towns for property taxes not mandated on non-profit and government properties (an example is Brown University). According to State Law, the State is required to reimburse cities and towns 27% of 'foregone' tax-revenue.

Unfortunately, this year's budget only funds PILOT by 26.1.% as opposed to the mandated 27%. As a result, Providence will receive less money from the State, which we desperately need to improve city services and recover from this pandemic. If it were fully funded at 27%, it would be $1.8 million more in the budget to be shared by communities that also have PILOT agreements, which the state has the resources to do.

Therefore, I will be advocating to restore this funding and stop cuts to our City!

House approves 2022 state budget bill

June 24, 2021

STATE HOUSE – The House of Representatives voted 64-10 today to approve a $13.1 billion state budget for the 2022 fiscal year that boosts key supports for vulnerable Rhode Islanders — particularly affordable housing — makes body cameras available for every uniformed police officer statewide and does not rely on the $1.1 billion in one-time federal American Rescue Plan funding for ongoing expenses.

The bill ([2021-H 6122Aaa](#)), which now goes to the Senate, fully funds state aid to education, does not include any broad-based tax increases and continues the scheduled phase-out of the automobile excise tax, which is set to be fully eliminated after the 2023 fiscal year.

"I am immensely proud of this budget, which addresses the important needs in our state, including housing and education, while raising no broad-based taxes. This has been a collaborative effort with the Senate and Governor McKee, and I particularly want to acknowledge the dedication and hard work of the members of the House Finance Committee, who listened to hundreds of hours of public testimony that was incorporated into a budget that is compassionate, responsible and fulfills the obligations we've made to the people of Rhode Island," said House Speaker K. Joseph Shekarchi (D-Dist. 23, Warwick).

Said House Finance Committee Chairman Marvin L. Abney (D-Dist. 73, Newport, Middletown), "After experiencing the devastation of the COVID-19 pandemic, this budget not only protects and helps Rhode Island's struggling residents, but it will also drive Rhode Island's pandemic recovery into a successful future. Without broad-based tax increases and through the preservation and strengthening of services and programs that help the vulnerable, this budget is a bill that will support most Rhode Islanders attempting to get back to their normal way of life. I thank Speaker Shekarchi, Senate President Ruggerio and Governor McKee for their collaboration and leadership, as well as the dedicated members of the House Finance Committee who have spent countless hours vetting the budget and listening to the needs of the public during the committee process."

To help address the state's housing crisis, the bill creates a permanent funding stream for affordable housing creation through an increase in the conveyance tax on high-end real estate. The bill doubles the existing $2.30 rate on each $500 of the purchase price over $800,000. Gov. Dan McKee had included the provision in his budget proposal, but set the threshold at $700,000. The new funding is expected to generate about $4 million annually for affordable housing creation. Currently, Rhode Island is the only New England state that doesn't have a permanent funding mechanism for affordable housing.

The House added another affordable housing provision, a proposal introduced by Speaker Shekarchi in February as a separate bill (2021-H 5951) to create within the Executive Office of Commerce a deputy secretary of commerce and housing who will oversee housing initiatives and develop a housing plan that will include affordable housing, strong community building and neighborhood revitalization efforts.

The House added a third new housing initiative, a $6 million pilot program that would use a "Pay for Success" model to create supportive housing with wraparound services for the chronically homeless population. The program is intended to improve the wellbeing of the individuals while also reducing their reliance on expensive emergency medical services and interactions with law enforcement.

The House added a 30-percent benefit increase for Rhode Island Works, the state's cash assistance and work-readiness program for low-income families. The rate has not been increased in 30 years. The current benefit, averaging $6 per person per day, is the lowest in New England. In February, 2,400 families were receiving Rhode Island Works benefits, including 5,578 people. Additionally, the House included plans to ensure that the $100 yearly clothing allowance is paid to infants and toddlers, who are excluded from eligibility under current law. To improve parents' readiness for employment and retention, the bill would exempt income from employment for six months when a parent starts a job, or until a household income exceeds 185 percent of the federal poverty line.

The House also included funding to raise rates to subsidized child care providers above the governor's proposed amount, and caps parents' copays at 7 percent of income. Additionally, the House included language keeping the emergency rate being paid to providers during the pandemic for the next six months, even if the emergency order is allowed to expire.

The proposal includes full payment of the scheduled cost of living increase for nursing home caregiver rates and $600,000 for training CNAs.

The House committed an additional $10 million above the governor's recommendation to help the Department of Children Youth and Families address ongoing issues, including heavy caseloads and greater population needs resulting from the impacts of COVID. Included in the additional funds are authorization for 91 additional employees, 75 more than the 16 in the governor's proposal. To attract a qualified candidate for the vacant DCYF director's position, the budget includes authority to raise the salary, plus a commitment to a three-year contract. Health and Human Services Secretary Womazetta Jones told the House Oversight Committee last year that she'd been unable to find a qualified candidate who was willing to take the position for the salary offered.

The bill includes $15 million that would also leverage federal grants to provide enough body cameras for all patrol officers for every municipal police department statewide that does not already have them, and the State Police. That funding would deploy the cameras for a 5-year, state-supported implementation period, giving cities and towns the runway they need to budget for future maintenance. Legislative leaders announced the initiative in partnership with Governor McKee and Attorney General Peter F. Nerhona last week, and both chambers this week voted in favor of legislation ([2021-H 6463](), [2021-S 0954]()) sponsored by Rep. José F. Batista (D-Dist. 12, Providence) and Sen. Jonathon Acosta (D-Dist. 16, Central Falls, Pawtucket) to establish policies on use of the cameras and distribution of the funds.

Besides fully funding state aid to education, the House also included funding to help school districts that already have particularly high numbers of students going to charter schools and will lose more in the coming year, giving them a one-time boost of $500 per charter student. The House restored funding to the Paul V. Sherlock Center on Disabilities, which provides services to the state's blind and visually-impaired students, as announced last month. The sole source contract with the Sherlock Center was slated to expire on June 30, and it was announced earlier this spring that, under a master pricing agreement, the Rhode Island Department of Education would solicit bids from qualified vendors, which sparked an outcry from students and families.

In higher education, the House added an additional $5.9 million beyond the governor's proposal to help Rhode Island College address its financial difficulties.

The budget includes the $7.7 million needed to fund the Rhode Island Promise program, which provides two years of free tuition at CCRI to Rhode Islanders graduating high school. That program was made permanent by lawmakers earlier this year under legislation ([2021-H 5224A](), [2021-H 0097A]()) sponsored by Speaker Shekarchi and Senate President Dominick J. Ruggerio (D-Dist. 4, North Providence, Providence).

For business, the House softened the impact of the governor's proposal to tax businesses on their forgivable Payroll Protection Program loans provided by the federal government to keep them afloat during the pandemic. The House moved the exemption $100,000 higher than the governor proposed, so PPP loans would be taxable income only for businesses receiving a forgivable PPP loan of $250,000 or higher. Under the new limit, 93 percent of the approximately 30,000 Rhode Island businesses that received a total of $2.6 billion in PPP loans will not be taxed on them. An amendment approved in the House gave businesses more time – until March 31, 2022 — to pay any such taxes they owe on loans received in 2020.

The House renewed the expiring historic properties tax credit for one additional year with $20 million in new funding.

The House included a one-time $10 million increase for the film and tax credit in 2022, making $30 million available for new productions next year.

The House added $40 million to fund Eleanor Slater Hospital in its current form, without closing any of its buildings. The House declined to include any of the proposal to reorganize ESH, which includes the Zambarano campus in Burrillville as well as the campus in Cranston. House Speaker Shekarchi said lawmakers need to vet that proposal more fully.

The House included the governor's recently revised proposal to replace the North Kingstown and Richmond State Police barracks with a single new $28.1 million barracks to be built in East Greenwich. The revised proposal would no longer require voter approval due to a different funding mechanism. The House also concurred with the governor's revised request to for $2 million over two years to renovate the Portsmouth State Police barracks.

The bill pays back all of the $120 million borrowed from the state's "rainy day" fund at the early part of the pandemic in 2020. The House included the entire amount in 2021, instead of spreading it over three years, as the governor proposed.

Although the House declined to include funding for a proposal recently offered by the administration to use $82 million in federal coronavirus aid to build a new state laboratory on a parcel of the state-owned former Route 195 land, House leaders have indicated their willingness to move forward with the proposal when the state receives more guidance on how its federal American Rescue Plan funding can be used.

The budget did not include any proposal to legalize, regulate and tax marijuana. House leaders intend to continue working on the bills concerning cannabis legalization.

Also not included is a proposed tax on sweetened beverages, nor the creation of a new tax bracket on the highest earners, neither of which were contained in the governor's budget proposal either.

Federal funds allotted to Rhode Island account for the overwhelming majority of the $1.9 billion increase over the governor's original proposal.

General Assembly OKs bill prohibiting insurers from charging copays for COVID treatments

June 25, 2021

STATE HOUSE — The General Assembly today passed legislation introduced by Sen. Alana M. DiMario (D-Dist. 36, Narragansett, North Kingstown) and Rep. David Morales (D-Dist. 7, Providence) that would prohibit health insurance companies from charging copays for COVID-related treatments.

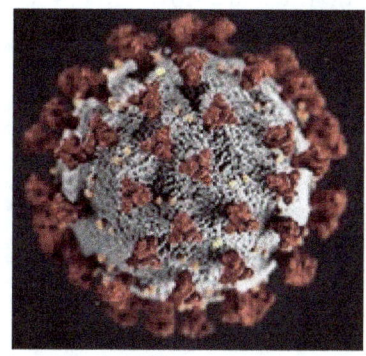

The bill ([2021-S 0877A](#), [2021-H 6208A](#)) would prohibit insurance carriers from charging any out-of-pocket expenses to the insured for treatment related to the COVID-19 pandemic while the state of emergency order is in effect.

"Out-of-pocket expenses can be a huge financial barrier for many when it comes to seeking medical treatment," said Senator DiMario. "We want to remove as many barriers as possible for people who are trying to access testing, vaccination and treatment. From a public health perspective, we need to continue to have a collective response to this pandemic in terms of the health of our communities."

The legislation would also mandate that all COVID-19 testing or vaccination is free during and upon the expiration of the state of emergency order.

"As a state, protecting the health and safety of all Rhode Islanders, especially working people, should be our top priority. There should not be any financial barriers standing in the way of someone who thinks that they have COVID-19 from accessing testing or treatment," said Representative Morales. "While we are fortunate to be one of the leading states in terms of vaccination rates, this pandemic is not over by any means, and we put our progress at risk if we relax the measures that have encouraged people to get tested, treated and vaccinated. We are still in an emergency and we need all insurers to stay on board and continue to be committed partners in our effort to overcome this pandemic and minimize the impact it is having on our communities."

The measure now moves to the governor's office.

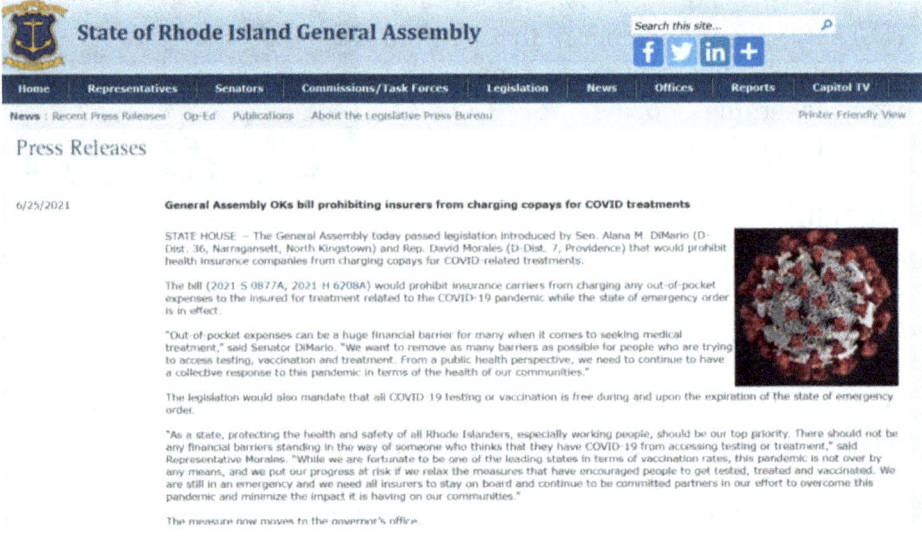

2021 -- H 6081

LC002192

STATE OF RHODE ISLAND

IN GENERAL ASSEMBLY

JANUARY SESSION, A.D. 2021

AN ACT

RELATING TO COURTS AND CIVIL PROCEDURE -- COURTS

Introduced By: Representatives Casimiro, Shanley, Hawkins, and Noret

Date Introduced: March 03, 2021

Referred To: House Judiciary

(Judiciary)

It is enacted by the General Assembly as follows:

1 SECTION 1. Sections 8-8.1-1 and 8-8.1-3 of the General Laws in Chapter 8-8.1 entitled
2 "Domestic Assault" are hereby amended to read as follows:
3 **8-8.1-1. Definitions.**
4 The following words as used in this chapter shall have the following meanings:
5 (1) "Cohabitants" means emancipated minors or persons eighteen (18) years of age or older,
6 not related by blood or marriage, who together are not the legal parents of one or more children,
7 and who have resided together within the preceding three (3) years or who are residing in the same
8 living quarters.
9 (2) "Course of conduct" means a pattern of conduct composed of a series of acts over a
10 period of time, evidencing a continuity of purpose. Constitutionally protected activity is not
11 included within the meaning of "course of conduct."
12 (3) "Courts" means the district court.
13 (4) "Cyberstalking" means transmitting any communication by computer to any person or
14 causing any person to be contacted for the sole purpose of harassing that person or his or her family.
15 (5) "Domestic abuse" means the occurrence of one or more of the following acts between
16 cohabitants ~~or against the minor child of a cohabitant,~~ or the occurrence of one or more of the
17 following acts between persons who are or have been in a substantive dating or engagement
18 relationship within the past one year ~~or against a minor child in the custody of the plaintiff~~;
19 "domestic abuse" shall be determined by the court's consideration of the following factors:

(i) The length of time of the relationship;

(ii) The type of the relationship;

(iii) The frequency of the interaction between the parties;

(iv) Attempting to cause or causing physical harm;

(v) Placing another in fear of imminent serious physical harm;

(vi) Causing another to engage involuntarily in sexual relations by force, threat of force, or duress; or

(vii) Stalking or cyberstalking.

(6) "Harassing" means following a knowing and willful course of conduct directed at a specific person with the intent to seriously alarm, annoy, or bother the person, and which serves no legitimate purpose. The course of conduct must be such as would cause a reasonable person to suffer substantial emotional distress, or be in fear of bodily injury.

(7) "Sole legal interest" means defendant has an ownership interest in the residence and plaintiff does not; or defendant's name is on the lease and plaintiff's is not.

(8) "Stalking" means harassing another person or willfully, maliciously and repeatedly following another person with the intent to place that person in reasonable fear of bodily injury.

8-8.1-3. Protective orders -- Penalty -- Jurisdiction.

(a) A person suffering from domestic abuse may file a complaint in the district court requesting any order which will protect her or him from the abuse, including but not limited to the following:

(1) Ordering that the defendant be restrained and enjoined from contacting, assaulting, molesting, or otherwise interfering with the plaintiff at home, on the street, or elsewhere, ~~whether the defendant is an adult or minor~~;

(2) Ordering the defendant to vacate the household forthwith, unless the defendant holds sole legal interest in the household;

(3) Upon motion by the plaintiff, his or her address shall be released only at the discretion of the district court judge;

(4) Ordering the defendant to surrender physical possession of all firearms in his or her possession, care, custody, or control and shall further order a person restrained not to purchase or receive, or attempt to purchase or receive, any firearms while the protective order is in effect. The defendant shall surrender said firearms within twenty-four (24) hours of notice of the protective order to the Rhode Island state police or local police department or to a federally licensed firearms dealer.

(i) A person ordered to surrender possession of any firearm(s) pursuant to this section shall, within seventy-two (72) hours after being served with the order, either:

(A) File with the court a receipt showing the firearm(s) was physically surrendered to the Rhode Island state police or local police department, or to a federally licensed firearm dealer; or

(B) Attest to the court that, at the time of the order, the person had no firearms in his or her immediate physical possession or control, or subject to his or her immediate physical possession or control, and that the person, at the time of the attestation, has no firearms in his or her immediate physical possession or control or subject to his or her immediate physical possession or control.

(ii) If a person restrained under this section transfers a firearm(s) to a federally licensed firearms dealer pursuant to this section, the person restrained under this section may instruct the federally licensed firearms dealer to sell the firearm(s) or to transfer ownership in accordance with state and federal law, to a qualified named individual who is not a member of the person's dwelling house, who is not related to the person by blood, marriage, or relationship as defined by § 15-15-1(7), and who is not prohibited from possessing firearms under state or federal law. The owner of any firearm(s) sold shall receive any financial value received from its sale, less the cost associated with taking possession of, storing, and transferring of the firearm(s).

(iii) Every individual to whom possession of a firearm(s) is transferred pursuant to this subsection shall be prohibited from transferring or returning any firearm(s) to the person restrained under this section while the protective order remains in effect and shall be informed of this prohibition. Any knowing violation of this subsection is a felony that shall be punishable by a fine of not more than one thousand dollars ($1,000), or by imprisonment for a term of not less than one year and not more than five (5) years, or both.

(iv) An individual to whom possession of a firearm(s) is transferred pursuant to this subsection shall return a firearm(s) to the person formerly restrained under this section only if the person formerly restrained under this section provides documentation issued by a court indicating that the restraining order issued pursuant to this section that prohibited the person from purchasing, carrying, transporting, or possessing firearms has expired and has not been extended.

(b) After notice to the respondent and after a hearing, which shall be held within fifteen (15) days of surrendering said firearms, the court, in addition to any other restrictions, may, for any protective order issued or renewed on or after July 1, 2017, continue the order of surrender, and shall further order a person restrained under this section not to purchase or receive, or attempt to purchase or receive, any firearms while the protective order is in effect.

(c) The district court shall provide a notice on all forms requesting a protective order that a person restrained under this section shall be ordered pursuant to § 11-47-5, to surrender possession or control of any firearms and not to purchase or receive, or attempt to purchase or receive, any firearms while the restraining order is in effect. The form shall further provide that any person who has surrendered their firearms shall be afforded a hearing within fifteen (15) days of surrendering their firearms.

(d) Any firearm surrendered in accordance with this section to the Rhode Island state police or local police department shall be returned to the person formerly restrained under this section upon their request when:

(1) The person formerly restrained under this section produces documentation issued by a court indicating, that the restraining order issued pursuant to this section that prohibited the person from purchasing, carrying, transporting, or possessing firearms has expired and has not been extended; and

(2) The law enforcement agency in possession of the firearms determines that the person formerly restrained under this section is not otherwise prohibited from possessing a firearm under state or federal law.

(3) The person required to surrender his or her firearms pursuant to this section shall not be responsible for any costs of storage of any firearms surrendered pursuant to this section.

(e) The Rhode Island state police are authorized to develop rules and procedures pertaining to the storage and return of firearms surrendered to the Rhode Island state police or local police departments pursuant to this section. The Rhode Island state police may consult with the Rhode Island Police Chiefs' Association in developing rules and procedures.

(f) Nothing in this section shall be construed to limit, expand, or in any way modify orders issued under §§ 12-29-4 or 15-5-19.

(g) Nothing in this section shall limit a defendant's right under existing law to petition the court at a later date for modification of the order.

(h) The court shall immediately notify the person suffering from domestic abuse whose complaint gave rise to the protective order and the law enforcement agency where the person restrained under this section resides of the hearing.

(i) The person suffering from domestic abuse, local law enforcement, and the person restrained under this section shall all have an opportunity to be present and to testify when the court considers the petition.

(j) At the hearing, the person restrained under this section shall have the burden of showing, by clear and convincing evidence, that, if his or her firearm rights were restored, he or she would not pose a danger to the person suffering from domestic abuse or to any other person.

(1) In determining whether to restore a person's firearm rights, the court shall examine all relevant evidence, including, but not limited to: the complaint seeking a protective order; the

criminal record of the person restrained under this section; the mental health history of the person restrained under this section; any evidence that the person restrained under this section has, since being served with the order, engaged in violent or threatening behavior against the person suffering from domestic abuse or any other person.

(2) If the court determines, after a review of all relevant evidence and after all parties have had an opportunity to be heard, that the person restrained under this section would not pose a danger to the person suffering from domestic abuse or to any other person if his or her firearm rights were restored, then the court may grant the petition and modify the protective order and lift the firearm prohibition.

(3) If the court lifts a person's firearms prohibition pursuant to this subsection, the court shall issue the person written notice that he or she is no longer prohibited under this section from purchasing or possessing firearms while the protective order is in effect.

(k) The prohibition against possessing a firearm(s) due solely to the existence of a domestic violence restraining order issued under this section shall not apply with respect to sworn peace officers as defined in § 12-7-21 and active members of military service, including members of the reserve components thereof, who are required by law or departmental policy to carry departmental firearms while on duty or any person who is required by his or her employment to carry a firearm in the performance of his or her duties. Any individual exempted pursuant to this exception may possess a firearm only during the course of his or her employment. Any firearm required for employment must be stored at the place of employment when not being possessed for employment use; all other firearm(s) must be surrendered in accordance with this section.

(l) Any violation of the aforementioned protective order shall subject the defendant to being found in contempt of court.

(m) No order shall issue under this section that would have the effect of compelling a defendant who has the sole legal interest in a residence to vacate that residence.

(n) The contempt order shall not be exclusive and shall not preclude any other available civil or criminal remedies. Any relief granted by the court shall be for a fixed period of time not to exceed three (3) years, at the expiration of which time the court may extend any order upon motion of the plaintiff for such additional time as it deems necessary to protect the plaintiff from abuse. The court may modify its order at any time upon motion of either party.

(o) Any violation of a protective order under this chapter of which the defendant has actual notice shall be a misdemeanor that shall be punished by a fine of no more than one thousand dollars ($1,000) or by imprisonment for not more than one year, or both.

(p) The penalties for violation of this section shall also include the penalties provided under

§ 12-29-5.

(q) "Actual notice" means that the defendant has received a copy of the order by service thereof or by being handed a copy of the order by a police officer pursuant to § 8-8.1-5(d).

(r) The district court shall have criminal jurisdiction over all violations of this chapter.

SECTION 2. This act shall take effect upon passage.

LC002192

EXPLANATION

BY THE LEGISLATIVE COUNCIL

OF

AN ACT

RELATING TO COURTS AND CIVIL PROCEDURE -- COURTS

***

1 This act would remove references to minors in certain sections relative to domestic assault
2 protective orders as the family court currently has jurisdiction over protective orders involving
3 minors.
4 This act would take effect upon passage.

LC002192

2021 -- S 0877 SUBSTITUTE A

LC002805/SUB A

STATE OF RHODE ISLAND

IN GENERAL ASSEMBLY

JANUARY SESSION, A.D. 2021

AN ACT

RELATING TO INSURANCE

Introduced By: Senators DiMario, Valverde, Sosnowski, Acosta, Lawson, Mendes, Anderson, and Kallman
Date Introduced: May 07, 2021

Referred To: Senate Health & Human Services

It is enacted by the General Assembly as follows:

1 SECTION 1. Chapter 27-18 of the General Laws entitled "Accident and Sickness Insurance
2 Policies" is hereby amended by adding thereto the following section:
3 **27-18-85. Health insurance contracts – copayments exemption for COVID-19**
4 **vaccinations.**
5 (a) Any individual or group health insurance plan or policy shall not impose any
6 copayment, coinsurance or charge any out-of-pocket deductible to the insured for COVID-19
7 related services, including, but not limited to, emergency services, inpatient services, provider
8 office visits, and inpatient hospital stays, as long as the COVID-19 state of emergency remains in
9 effect.
10 (b) Any individual or group health insurance plan or policy shall not impose any
11 copayment, coinsurance or charge any out-of-pocket deductible to the insured for the
12 administration of the COVID-19 vaccine or a COVID-19 test.
13 (c) The health insurance commissioner shall promulgate any rules and regulations as the
14 commissioner deems necessary for the efficient administration and enforcement of this section.
15 SECTION 2. Chapter 27-19 of the General Laws entitled "Nonprofit Hospital Service
16 Corporations" is hereby amended by adding thereto the following section:
17 **27-19-77. Health insurance contracts – copayments exemption for COVID-19**
18 **vaccinations.**
19 (a) Any individual or group health insurance plan or policy shall not impose any

copayment, coinsurance or charge any out-of-pocket deductible to the insured for COVID-19 related services, including, but not limited to, emergency services, inpatient services, provider office visits, and inpatient hospital stays, as long as the COVID-19 state of emergency remains in effect.

(b) Any individual or group health insurance plan or policy shall not impose any copayment, coinsurance or charge any out-of-pocket deductible to the insured for the administration of the COVID-19 vaccine or a COVID-19 test.

(c) The health insurance commissioner shall promulgate any rules and regulations as the commissioner deems necessary for the efficient administration and enforcement of this section.

SECTION 3. Chapter 27-20 of the General Laws entitled "Nonprofit Medical Service Corporations" is hereby amended by adding thereto the following section:

27-20-73. Health insurance contracts - copayments exemption for COVID-19 vaccinations.

(a) Any individual or group health insurance plan or policy shall not impose any copayment, coinsurance or charge any out-of-pocket deductible to the insured for COVID-19 related services, including, but not limited to, emergency services, inpatient services, provider office visits, and inpatient hospital stays, as long as the COVID-19 state of emergency remains in effect.

(b) Any individual or group health insurance plan or policy shall not impose any copayment, coinsurance or charge any out-of-pocket deductible to the insured for the administration of the COVID-19 vaccine or a COVID-19 test.

(c) The health insurance commissioner shall promulgate any rules and regulations as the commissioner deems necessary for the efficient administration and enforcement of this section.

SECTION 4. Chapter 27-41 of the General Laws entitled "Health Maintenance Organizations" is hereby amended by adding thereto the following section:

27-41-90. Health insurance contracts - copayments exemption for COVID-19 vaccinations.

(a) Any individual or group health insurance plan or policy shall not impose any copayment, coinsurance or charge any out-of-pocket deductible to the insured for COVID-19 related services, including, but not limited to, emergency services, inpatient services, provider office visits, and inpatient hospital stays, as long as the COVID-19 state of emergency remains in effect.

(b) Any individual or group health insurance plan or policy shall not impose any copayment, coinsurance or charge any out-of-pocket deductible to the insured for the

1 administration of the COVID-19 vaccine or a COVID-19 test.
2   (c) The health insurance commissioner shall promulgate any rules and regulations as the
3 commissioner deems necessary for the efficient administration and enforcement of this section.
4   SECTION 5. This act shall take effect upon passage.

EXPLANATION

BY THE LEGISLATIVE COUNCIL

OF

AN ACT

RELATING TO INSURANCE

***

1 This act would prohibit insurance carriers from charging any out-of-pocket expenses to the
2 insured for treatment related to the COVID-19 pandemic while the state of emergency order is in
3 effect. This act would further mandate that all COVID-19 testing or vaccination is free during and
4 upon the expiration of the state of emergency order.
5 This act would take effect upon passage.

LC002805/SUB A

Black & Brown Leadership 2020-2040

Latino Leadership 2020: Honoring Our Past, Our Present and Leading Our Future

Tomás Ávila

July 2, 2020

Black & Brown Leadership 2020-2040 The Future of Rhode Island Political Transformation

This year as I've done for the past 25 years, I've collected the names of candidates that have registered their intent to run for elected office during the September 8, 2020 Rhode Island Primary Elections, and as in the past it's telling me that in the next 20 years Rhode Island's State House and Municipal governments will be turning Black & Brown.

With approximately 80 candidates seeking elected office from United State Senator to district committees, and the expansion of the districts through thirteen of thirty nice cities and towns (Barrington, Central Falls, Cranston, East Providence, Johnston, Newport, Pawtucket, Portsmouth, Providence, Smithfield, Warwick, West Warwick, Woonsocket) across the state from the traditional urban core, change is definitely coming to the Rhode Island Political scene within the next twenty years.

Since I became involved in the socio political empowerment of the Latino community, I've kept my attention in the evolution of the state electoral cycles and been an active participant along with many Friends in the growth and expansion of Latino elected officials from one in 2000 to the election of forty, and 24 presently serving by 2020 and have published two books capturing such achievements and political success: Rhode Island Latino Political Empowerment: The Evolution of Latino Politics, 1996 - 2006 published in 2007, documenting what has been called the renaissance of Latino politics, and Growing Into Power, and Rhode Island Black and Brown Ethnic Succession 1984 – 1995 published in 2012, documenting the from African Americans elected officials in the Southside of Providence to the present Latino dominated scenario, that expanded to Central Falls, and Pawtucket, the election three Mayors (Providence, Central Falls) , and four City/Town Council Presidents (Providence 2, Luis Aponte and Sabina Matos, Central Falls 1, Maria Rivera, Smithfield 1, Suzy Alba, during the decade of 2010 - 2020.

In celebration of the political success of the Latino Community, I've been conducting a series of historical conversations I titled: "Latino Leadership 2020: Honoring Our Past, Transforming Our Present and Leading Our Future" about Latino Leadership evolution across Rhode Island during the past 20 years 2000-2020, and Latino Leadership Successful Transformational Leadership Evolution, and Rhode Island politics by empowering other communities seek elected offices and elevate their communities advocacy. Effective with this writing, I'm transitioning the Black & Brown Leadership 2020 - 2040, based on my research and the trends evolving with this elections, the diversity of Blacks seeking elected office, the ramifications of the Coronavirus (COVID-19) that brought to the forefront long-standing systemic inequities in our society against the Black and Brown Communities, exacerbated by the murdered of George Floyd by a Minneapolis Policeman on Memorial Day protest marches throughout the world and Rhode Island demanding social justice and economic equity, encouraging many more people of color to run for office.

The face of America is changing, and the population is rapidly diversifying. Already, more than half of all babies born in the United States are people of color. By 2030, the majority of young workers will be people of color. And by 2043, the United States will be a majority people-of color nation. Yet racial and income inequality is high and persistent. Over the past several decades, long standing inequities in income, wealth, health, and opportunity have reached unprecedented levels, and communities of color have felt the greatest pains as the economy has shifted and stagnated, Equity is an economic imperative as well as a moral one.

According to the report, An Equity Profile of Rhode Island by PolicyLink and PERE in 2013 for the planning department, "Rhode Island is moderately diverse and is experiencing rapid demographic change and its share of people of color increased from 7 to 24 percent between 1980 and 2010, and all of the state's recent population growth is attributable to people of color. Latinos, Asians, and African Americans are driving growth and change in the state and will continue to do so for the foreseeable future.

The people of color are growing quickly in the state's nine largest cities and in the state. By 2040, 41 percent of Rhode Islanders will be people of color, there is a significant and growing racial generation gap between the region's predominantly white senior population and its increasingly diverse youth population." Twenty-four percent of residents are people of color, including a diverse mix of racial and ethnic groups. Over the past decade, Rhode Island's Latino population grew 44 percent, adding almost 40,000 residents. The Asian and African American populations also grew by 28 and 23 percent, or 7,000 and 10,000 residents, respectively. The state's non-Hispanic white population shrank by six percent (55,000 residents). Much of the growth in the state's Latino and Asian populations over the past decade has not been due to immigration but to new births among U.S. residents.

The report continues that the rapid growth of people of color in Rhode Island is helping to stem population decline in many of the state's cities. Five of Rhode Island's nine largest cities (Warwick, Pawtucket, East Providence, Woonsocket, and Newport) experienced population losses of 2 to 7 percent over the past decade, and these losses would have been more severe were it not for the robust growth of their people-of color populations. Providence, Cranston, Central Falls, and Westerly all grew slightly (1 to 3 percent), and that growth was propelled by the growth of their people-of-color populations. Providence, home to 17 percent of the state's residents, had the fastest overall growth rate at 3 percent but its people-of-color population grew six times as fast, at 18 percent.

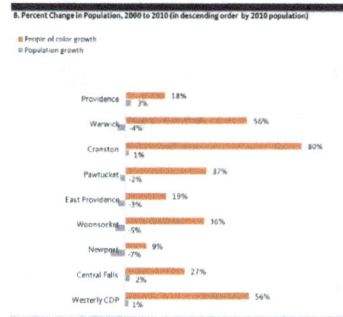

As attested by the research data, Rhode Island will continue to grow more diverse in the future, at a rate that is like that of the past few decades and slightly higher than the nation. Therefore, my conclusion is that the future of the state's Black and Brown elected officers will accelerate within the forthcoming 20 years of 2020 - 2040.

www.blackandbrowneconomicequity.com

www.blackandbrownLeadership.org

https://drive.google.com/file/d/1iCJU7D86Aet3G1NY8Foy1zTdsbIpGupj/view

http://www.planning.ri.gov/documents/LU/ri-equity-profile-executive-summary.pdf

https://open.spotify.com/episode/2McTbMp8CBqsxtV6fjoh91?si=olrGNeqIQMyX1ar_35rEQg

Liderazgo & Negro y Latino 2020-2040

Liderazgo latino 2020: honrando nuestro pasado, nuestro presente y liderando nuestro futuro

Tomás Ávila
2 de julio de 2020

Este año, como lo he hecho durante los últimos 25 años, he recopilado los nombres de los candidatos que han registrado su intención de postularse para un cargo electo durante las elecciones primarias de Rhode Island del 8 de septiembre de 2020, y como en el pasado me está diciendo que en los próximos 20 años, la Casa del Estado de Rhode Island y los gobiernos municipales se convertirán en Black & Brown.

Con aproximadamente 80 candidatos que buscan un cargo electo del Senador de los Estados Unidos a los comités de distrito, y la expansión de los distritos a través de trece de treinta ciudades y pueblos agradables (Barrington, Central Falls, Cranston, East Providence, Johnston, Newport, Pawtucket, Portsmouth, Providence, Smithfield, Warwick, West Warwick, Woonsocket) en todo el estado desde el núcleo urbano tradicional, el cambio definitivamente está llegando a la escena política de Rhode Island en los próximos veinte años.

Desde que me involucré en el empoderamiento sociopolítico de la comunidad latina, he mantenido mi atención en la evolución de los ciclos electorales estatales y he sido un participante activo junto con muchos amigos en el crecimiento y la expansión de funcionarios latinos elegidos de uno en 2000 a la elección de cuarenta y 24 que actualmente sirven para 2020 y han publicado dos libros que capturan tales logros y éxito político: Rhode Island Latino Political

Empowerment: The Evolution of Latino Politics, 1996 - 2006 publicado en 2007, documentando lo que se ha llamado el renacimiento de política latina, y Growing Into Power, y Rhode Island Black and Brown Ethnic Succession 1984 - 1995 publicado en 2012, documentando los funcionarios elegidos por afroamericanos en el sur de Providence para el escenario dominado por los latinos, que se expandió a Central Falls, y Pawtucket, la elección de tres alcaldes (Providence, Central Falls) y cuatro presidentes del Ayuntamiento / Ciudad (Providence 2, Luis Apo nte y Sabina Matos, Central Falls 1, Maria Rivera, Smithfield 1, Suzy Alba, durante la década de 2010-2020.

Para celebrar el éxito político de la comunidad latina, he estado llevando a cabo una serie de conversaciones históricas que titulé: "Liderazgo latino 2020: honrando nuestro pasado, transformando nuestro presente y liderando nuestro futuro" sobre la evolución del liderazgo latino en Rhode Island durante en los últimos 20 años, 2000-2020, y Liderazgo latino Evolución exitosa del liderazgo transformacional, y la política de Rhode Island al empoderar a otras comunidades buscan cargos elegidos y elevan la defensa de sus comunidades. Efectivo con este escrito, estoy haciendo la transición del Black & Brown Leadership 2020 - 2040, basado en mi investigación y las tendencias que evolucionan con estas elecciones, la diversidad de negros que buscan cargos electos, las ramificaciones del Coronavirus (COVID-19) que trajo consigo a la vanguardia de las desigualdades sistémicas de larga data en nuestra sociedad contra las comunidades negras y marrones, exacerbadas por el asesinato de George Floyd por un policía de Minneapolis en las marchas de protesta en todo el mundo y Rhode Island exigiendo justicia social y equidad económica, alentando a muchos más personas de color para postularse para un cargo.

La faz de los Estados Unidos está cambiando y la población se está diversificando rápidamente. Ya, más de la mitad de todos los bebés nacidos en los Estados Unidos son personas de color. Para 2030, la mayoría de los trabajadores jóvenes serán personas de color. Y para 2043, Estados Unidos será una nación mayoritaria de personas de color. Sin embargo, la desigualdad racial y de ingresos es alta y persistente. En las últimas décadas, las desigualdades de larga data en ingresos, riqueza, salud y oportunidades han alcanzado niveles sin precedentes, y las comunidades de color han sentido los mayores dolores a medida que la economía ha cambiado y se estancó. La equidad es un imperativo económico y moral uno.

Según el informe, Un perfil de equidad de Rhode Island por PolicyLink y PERE en 2013 para el departamento de planificación, "Rhode Island es moderadamente diversa y está experimentando un rápido cambio demográfico y su participación de personas de color aumentó del 7 al 24 por ciento entre 1980 y 2010, y todo el crecimiento demográfico reciente del estado es atribuible a las personas de color. Los latinos, asiáticos y afroamericanos están impulsando el crecimiento y el cambio en el estado y continuarán haciéndolo en el futuro previsible. La gente de color está creciendo rápidamente en las nueve ciudades más grandes del estado y en el estado.

Para 2040, el 41 por ciento de los habitantes de Rhode Island serán personas de color, existe una brecha de generación racial significativa y creciente entre la población predominantemente blanca de la región y su población juvenil cada vez más diversa ". El veinticuatro por ciento de los residentes son personas de color, incluida una mezcla diversa de grupos raciales y étnicos. Durante la última década, la población latina de Rhode Island creció un 44 por ciento, sumando casi 40,000 residentes. Las poblaciones asiáticas y afroamericanas también crecieron en un 28 y 23 por ciento, o 7,000 a nd 10,000 residentes, respectivamente. La población blanca no hispana del estado se redujo en un seis por ciento (55,000 residentes).

Gran parte del crecimiento en las poblaciones latinas y asiáticas del estado durante la última década no se ha debido a la inmigración, sino a nuevos nacimientos entre los residentes de EE. UU.

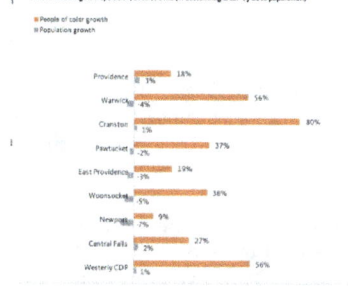

El informe continúa que el rápido crecimiento de las personas de color en Rhode Island está ayudando a frenar el declive de la población en muchas de las ciudades del estado. Cinco de las nueve ciudades más grandes de Rhode Island (Warwick, Pawtucket, East Providence, Woonsocket y Newport) experimentaron pérdidas de población del 2 al 7 por ciento en la última década, y estas pérdidas habrían sido más graves si no hubiera sido por el sólido crecimiento de sus poblaciones de personas de color. Providence, Cranston, Central Falls y Westerly crecieron ligeramente (1 a 3 por ciento), y ese crecimiento fue impulsado por el crecimiento de sus poblaciones de personas de color. Providence, hogar del 17 por ciento de los residentes del estado, tuvo la tasa de crecimiento general más rápida con un 3 por ciento, pero su población de personas de color creció seis veces más rápido, con un 18 por ciento.

Como lo atestiguan los datos de la investigación, Rhode Island continuará creciendo en diversidad en el futuro, a un ritmo similar al de las últimas décadas y un poco más alto que la nación. Por lo tanto, mi conclusión es que el futuro de los funcionarios electos negros y marrones del estado se acelerará en los próximos 20 años de 2020 a 2040.

Latino Leadership 2020: Honoring Our Past, Our Present and Leading Our Future

Black & Brown Leadership 2020-2040

Tomás Ávila
July 2, 2020

This year as I've done for the past 25 years, I've collected the names of candidates that have registered their intent to run for elected office during the September 8, 2020 Rhode Island Primary Elections, and as in the past it's telling me that in the next 20 years Rhode Island's State House and Municipal governments will be turning Black & Brown.

With approximately 80 candidates seeking elected office from United State Senator to district committees, and the expansion of the districts through thirteen of thirty nice cities and towns (Barrington, Central Falls, Cranston, East Providence, Johnston, Newport, Pawtucket, Portsmouth, Providence, Smithfield, Warwick, West Warwick, Woonsocket) across the state from the traditional urban core, change is definitely coming to the Rhode Island Political scene within the next twenty years.

Since I became involved in the socio political empowerment of the Latino community, I've kept my attention in the evolution of the state electoral cycles and been an active participant along with many Friends in the growth and expansion of Latino elected officials from one in 2000 to the election of forty, and 24 presently serving by 2020 and have published two books capturing such achievements and political success: Rhode Island Latino Political Empowerment: The Evolution of Latino Politics, 1996 - 2006 published in 2007, documenting what has been called the renaissance of Latino politics, and Growing Into Power, and Rhode Island Black and Brown Ethnic Succession 1984 – 1995 published in 2012, documenting the from African Americans elected officials in the Southside of Providence to the present Latino dominated scenario, that expanded to Central Falls, and Pawtucket, the election three Mayors (Providence, Central Falls) , and four City/Town Council Presidents (Providence 2, Luis Aponte and Sabina Matos, Central Falls 1, Maria Rivera, Smithfield 1, Suzy Alba, during the decade of 2010 - 2020.

In celebration of the political success of the Latino Community, I've been conducting a series of historical conversations I titled: "Latino Leadership 2020: Honoring Our Past, Transforming Our Present and Leading Our Future" about Latino Leadership evolution across Rhode Island during the past 20 years 2000-2020, and Latino Leadership Successful Transformational Leadership Evolution, and Rhode Island politics by empowering other communities seek elected offices and elevate their communities advocacy. Effective with this writing, I'm transitioning the Black & Brown Leadership 2020 - 2040, based on my research and the trends evolving with this elections, the diversity of Blacks seeking elected office, the ramifications of the Coronavirus (COVID-19) that brought to the forefront long-standing systemic inequities in our society

against the Black and Brown Communities, exacerbated by the murdered of George Floyd by a Minneapolis Policeman on Memorial Day protest marches throughout the world and Rhode Island demanding social justice and economic equity, encouraging many more people of color to run for office.

The face of America is changing, and the population is rapidly diversifying. Already, more than half of all babies born in the United States are people of color. By 2030, the majority of young workers will be people of color. And by 2043, the United States will be a majority people-of color nation. Yet racial and income inequality is high and persistent. Over the past several decades, long standing inequities in income, wealth, health, and opportunity have reached unprecedented levels, and communities of color have felt the greatest pains as the economy has shifted and stagnated, Equity is an economic imperative as well as a moral one.

According to the report, An Equity Profile of Rhode Island by PolicyLink and PERE in 2013 for the planning department, "Rhode Island is moderately diverse and is experiencing rapid demographic change and its share of people of color increased from 7 to 24 percent between 1980 and 2010, and all of the state's recent population growth is attributable to people of color. Latinos, Asians, and African Americans are driving growth and change in the state and will continue to do so for the foreseeable future.

The people of color are growing quickly in the state's nine largest cities and in the state. By 2040, 41 percent of Rhode Islanders will be people of color, there is a significant and growing racial generation gap between the region's predominantly white senior population and its increasingly diverse youth population." Twenty-four percent of residents are people of color, including a diverse mix of racial and ethnic groups. Over the past decade, Rhode Island's Latino population grew 44 percent, adding almost 40,000 residents. The Asian and African American populations also grew by 28 and 23 percent, or 7,000 and 10,000 residents, respectively. The state's non-Hispanic white population shrank by six percent (55,000 residents). Much of the growth in the state's Latino and Asian populations over the past decade has not been due to immigration but to new births among U.S. residents.

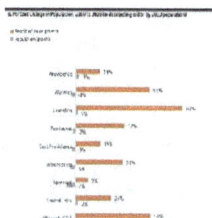

The report continues that the rapid growth of people of color in Rhode Island is helping to stem population decline in many of the state's cities. Five of Rhode Island's nine largest cities (Warwick, Pawtucket, East Providence, Woonsocket, and Newport) experienced population losses of 2 to 7 percent over the past decade, and these losses would have been more severe were it not for the robust growth of their people-of color populations. Providence, Cranston, Central Falls, and Westerly all grew slightly (1 to 3 percent), and that growth was propelled by the growth of their people-of-color populations. Providence, home to 17 percent of the state's residents, had the fastest overall growth rate at 3 percent but its people-of-color population grew six times as fast, at 18 percent.

As attested by the research data, Rhode Island will continue to grow more diverse in the future, at a rate that is like that of the past few decades and slightly higher than the nation. Therefore, my conclusion is that the future of the state's Black and Brown elected officers will accelerate within the forthcoming 20 years of 2020 - 2040.

Liderazgo latino 2020: honrando nuestro pasado, nuestro presente y liderando nuestro futuro

Liderazgo Negro y Marrón 2020-2040
Tomás Ávila
2 de julio de 2020

Este año, como lo he hecho durante los últimos 25 años, he recopilado los nombres de los candidatos que han registrado su intención de postularse para un cargo electo durante las elecciones primarias de Rhode Island del 8 de septiembre de 2020, y como en el pasado me está diciendo que en los próximos 20 años, la Casa del Estado de Rhode Island y los gobiernos municipales se convertirán en Black & Brown.

Con aproximadamente 80 candidatos que buscan un cargo electo del Senador de los Estados Unidos a los comités de distrito, y la expansión de los distritos a través de trece de treinta ciudades y pueblos agradables (Barrington, Central Falls, Cranston, East Providence, Johnston, Newport, Pawtucket, Portsmouth, Providence, Smithfield, Warwick, West Warwick, Woonsocket) en todo el estado desde el núcleo urbano tradicional, el cambio definitivamente está llegando a la escena política de Rhode Island en los próximos veinte años.

Desde que me involucré en el empoderamiento sociopolítico de la comunidad latina, he mantenido mi atención en la evolución de los ciclos electorales estatales y he sido un participante activo junto con muchos amigos en el crecimiento y la expansión de funcionarios latinos elegidos de uno en 2000 a la elección de cuarenta y 24 que actualmente sirven para 2020 y han publicado dos libros que capturan tales logros y éxito político: Rhode Island Latino Political Empowerment: The Evolution of Latino Politics, 1996 - 2006 publicado en 2007, documentando lo que se ha llamado el renacimiento de política latina, y Growing Into Power, y Rhode Island Black and Brown Ethnic Succession 1984 - 1995 publicado en 2012, documentando los funcionarios elegidos por afroamericanos en el sur de Providence para el escenario dominado por los latinos, que se expandió a Central Falls, y Pawtucket, la elección de tres alcaldes (Providence, Central Falls) y cuatro presidentes del Ayuntamiento / Ciudad (Providence 2, Luis Aponte y Sabina Matos, Central Falls 1, Maria Rivera, Smithfield 1, Suzy Alba, durante la década de 2010-2020.

Para celebrar el éxito político de la comunidad latina, he estado llevando a cabo una serie de conversaciones históricas que titulé: "Liderazgo latino 2020: honrando nuestro pasado, transformando nuestro presente y liderando nuestro futuro" sobre la evolución del liderazgo latino en Rhode Island durante en los últimos 20 años, 2000-2020, y Liderazgo latino Evolución exitosa del liderazgo transformacional, y la política de Rhode Island al empoderar a otras comunidades buscan cargos elegidos y elevan la defensa de sus comunidades. Efectivo con este escrito, estoy haciendo la transición del Black & Brown Leadership 2020 - 2040, basado en mi investigación y las tendencias que evolucionan con estas elecciones, la diversidad de negros que buscan cargos electos, las ramificaciones del Coronavirus (COVID-19) que trajo consigo a la vanguardia de las desigualdades sistémicas de larga data en nuestra sociedad contra las comunidades negras y marrones, exacerbadas por el asesinato de George Floyd por un policía de Minneapolis en las marchas de protesta en todo el mundo y Rhode Island exigiendo justicia social y equidad económica, alentando a muchos más personas de color para postularse para un cargo.

La faz de los Estados Unidos está cambiando y la población se está diversificando rápidamente. Ya, más de la mitad de todos los bebés nacidos en los Estados Unidos son personas de color. Para 2030, la mayoría de los trabajadores jóvenes serán personas de color. Y para 2043, Estados Unidos será una nación mayoritaria de personas de color. Sin embargo, la desigualdad racial y de ingresos es alta y persistente. En las últimas décadas, las desigualdades de larga data en ingresos, riqueza, salud y oportunidades han alcanzado niveles sin precedentes, y las comunidades de color han sentido los mayores dolores a medida que la economía ha cambiado y se estancó. La equidad es un imperativo económico y moral uno.

Según el informe, Un perfil de equidad de Rhode Island por PolicyLink y PERE en 2013 para el departamento de planificación, "Rhode Island es moderadamente diversa y está experimentando un rápido cambio demográfico y su participación de personas de color aumentó del 7 al 24 por ciento entre 1980 y 2010, y todo el crecimiento demográfico reciente del estado es atribuible a las personas de color. Los latinos, asiáticos y afroamericanos están impulsando el crecimiento y el cambio en el estado y continuarán haciéndolo en el futuro previsible. La gente de color está creciendo rápidamente en las nueve ciudades más grandes del estado y en  el estado. Para 2040, el 41 por ciento de los habitantes de Rhode Island serán personas de color, existe una brecha de generación racial significativa y creciente entre la población predominantemente blanca de la región y su población juvenil cada vez más diversa ". El veinticuatro por ciento de los residentes son personas de color, incluida una mezcla diversa de grupos raciales y étnicos. Durante la última década, la población latina de Rhode Island creció un 44 por ciento, sumando casi 40,000 residentes. Las poblaciones asiáticas y afroamericanas también crecieron en un 28 y 23 por ciento, o 7,000 a nd 10,000 residentes, respectivamente. La población blanca no hispana del estado se redujo en un seis por ciento (55,000 residentes). Gran parte del crecimiento en las poblaciones latinas y asiáticas del estado durante la última década no se ha debido a la inmigración, sino a nuevos nacimientos entre los residentes de EE. UU.

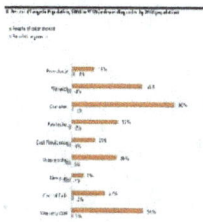 El informe continúa que el rápido crecimiento de las personas de color en Rhode Island está ayudando a frenar el declive de la población en muchas de las ciudades del estado. Cinco de las nueve ciudades más grandes de Rhode Island (Warwick, Pawtucket, East Providence, Woonsocket y Newport) experimentaron pérdidas de población del 2 al 7 por ciento en la última década, y estas pérdidas habrían sido más graves si no hubiera sido por el sólido crecimiento de sus poblaciones de personas de color. Providence, Cranston, Central Falls y Westerly crecieron ligeramente (1 a 3 por ciento), y ese crecimiento fue impulsado por el crecimiento de sus poblaciones de personas de color. Providence, hogar del 17 por ciento de los residentes del estado, tuvo la tasa de crecimiento general más rápida con un 3 por ciento, pero su población de personas de color creció seis veces más rápido, con un 18 por ciento.

Como lo atestiguan los datos de la investigación, Rhode Island continuará creciendo en diversidad en el futuro, a un ritmo similar al de las últimas décadas y un poco más alto que la nación. Por lo tanto, mi conclusión es que el futuro de los funcionarios electos negros y marrones del estado se acelerará en los próximos 20 años de 2020 a 2040.

Candidates in Upcoming Elections 09/08/2020 STATEWIDE PRIMARY
Source: https://vote.sos.ri.gov/Candidates/CandidateSearch?CityTown=00027lection=17018

Name	Party	Office Name	District	CITY/TOWN
ALLEN R WATERS	Republican	SENATOR IN CONGRESS	CON 1,CON 2	
WILLIAM LEBRON JR	Republican	REPRESENTATIVE IN GENERAL ASSEMBLY	REP 02	PROVIDENCE
MARCIA P RANGLIN VASSELL	Democrat	REPRESENTATIVE IN GENERAL ASSEMBLY	REP 05	PROVIDENCE
RAYMOND A HULL	Democrat	REPRESENTATIVE IN GENERAL ASSEMBLY	REP 06	PROVIDENCE
JORGE PORRAS	Independent	REPRESENTATIVE IN GENERAL ASSEMBLY	PROVIDENCE	PROVIDENCE
ANGEL SUBERVI	Democrat	REPRESENTATIVE IN GENERAL ASSEMBLY	REP 07	PROVIDENCE
DAVID MORALES	Democrat	REPRESENTATIVE IN GENERAL ASSEMBLY	REP 07	PROVIDENCE
JESSENIA A GRIJALVA	Democrat	REPRESENTATIVE IN GENERAL ASSEMBLY	REP 07	PROVIDENCE
DARWIN CASTRO	Democrat	REPRESENTATIVE IN GENERAL ASSEMBLY	REP 08	PROVIDENCE
ANASTASIA P WILLIAMS	Democrat	REPRESENTATIVE IN GENERAL ASSEMBLY	REP 09	PROVIDENCE
ROSA MARIE HILL	Independent	REPRESENTATIVE IN GENERAL ASSEMBLY	REP 09	PROVIDENCE
GRACE DIAZ	Democrat	REPRESENTATIVE IN GENERAL ASSEMBLY	REP 11	PROVIDENCE
LAURA PEREZ	Democrat	REPRESENTATIVE IN GENERAL ASSEMBLY	REP 11	PROVIDENCE
EMMANUEL C NYEMA	Independent	REPRESENTATIVE IN GENERAL ASSEMBLY	REP 11	PROVIDENCE
CARLOS CEDENO	Democrat	REPRESENTATIVE IN GENERAL ASSEMBLY	REP 12	PROVIDENCE
JOSE F BATISTA	Democrat	REPRESENTATIVE IN GENERAL ASSEMBLY	REP 12	PROVIDENCE
JOSEPH S ALMEIDA	Democrat	REPRESENTATIVE IN GENERAL ASSEMBLY	REP 12	PROVIDENCE
MARIO F MENDEZ	Democrat	REPRESENTATIVE IN GENERAL ASSEMBLY	REP 13	PROVIDENCE
RAMON A PEREZ	Democrat	REPRESENTATIVE IN GENERAL ASSEMBLY	REP 13	PROVIDENCE
JANICE A FALCONER	Democrat	REPRESENTATIVE IN GENERAL ASSEMBLY	REP 13	PROVIDENCE
MELINDA LOPEZ	Democrat	REPRESENTATIVE IN GENERAL ASSEMBLY	REP 43	JOHNSTON
JOSHUA J GIRALDO	Democrat	REPRESENTATIVE IN GENERAL ASSEMBLY	REP 56	CENTRAL FALLS
CARLOS EDUARDO TOBON	Democrat	REPRESENTATIVE IN GENERAL ASSEMBLY	REP 58	PAWTUCKET
JEAN P BARROS	Democrat	REPRESENTATIVE IN GENERAL ASSEMBLY	REP 59	PAWTUCKET

Tomás Ávila   Rev 3.1   July 1, 2020

Candidates in Upcoming Elections 09/08/2020 STATEWIDE PRIMARY
Source: https://vote.sos.ri.gov/Candidates/CandidateSearch?CityTown=00027lection=17018

Name	Party	Office Name	District	CITY/TOWN
KAREN ALZATE	Democrat	REPRESENTATIVE IN GENERAL ASSEMBLY	REP 60	PAWTUCKET
LEONELA FELIX	Democrat	REPRESENTATIVE IN GENERAL ASSEMBLY	REP 61	PAWTUCKET
BRIANNA E HENRIES	Democrat	REPRESENTATIVE IN GENERAL ASSEMBLY	REP 64	EAST PROVIDENCE
LIANA M CASSAR	Democrat	REPRESENTATIVE IN GENERAL ASSEMBLY	REP 66	BARRINGTON
MARVIN L ABNEY	Democrat	REPRESENTATIVE IN GENERAL ASSEMBLY	REP 73	NEWPORT
ANA B QUEZADA	Democrat	SENATOR IN GENERAL ASSEMBLY	SEN 02	PROVIDENCE
HAROLD M METTS	Democrat	SENATOR IN GENERAL ASSEMBLY	SEN 06	PROVIDENCE
TIARA T MACK	Democrat	SENATOR IN GENERAL ASSEMBLY	SEN 06	PROVIDENCE
SANDRA C CANO	Democrat	SENATOR IN GENERAL ASSEMBLY	SEN 08	PAWTUCKET
JONATHON ACOSTA	Democrat	SENATOR IN GENERAL ASSEMBLY	SEN 16	CENTRAL FALLS
LESLIE ESTRADA	Democrat	SENATOR IN GENERAL ASSEMBLY	SEN 16	CENTRAL FALLS
JENNIFER T ROURKE	Democrat	SENATOR IN GENERAL ASSEMBLY	SEN 29	WARWICK
JOSE L BENITEZ	Republican	SENATOR IN GENERAL ASSEMBLY	SEN 33	COVENTRY
L MARIA RIVERA	Non-Partisan Local Office	MAYOR	Townwide	CENTRAL FALLS
GLENDALIZ COLON	Non-Partisan Local Office	CITY COUNCIL - AT LARGE	Townwide	CENTRAL FALLS
TATIANA BAENA	Non-Partisan Local Office	CITY COUNCIL - AT LARGE	Townwide	CENTRAL FALLS
MEAGHAN LEVASSEUR	Non-Partisan Local Office	CITY COUNCIL	WAR 01	CENTRAL FALLS
ADAMARIS VILLAR	Non-Partisan Local Office	CITY COUNCIL	WAR 02	CENTRAL FALLS
HUGO A FIGUEROA	Non-Partisan Local Office	CITY COUNCIL	WAR 03	CENTRAL FALLS
FRANKLIN SOLANO	Non-Partisan Local Office	CITY COUNCIL	WAR 04	CENTRAL FALLS
JESSICA VEGA	Non-Partisan Local Office	CITY COUNCIL	WAR 05	CENTRAL FALLS
CARLENE P FONSECA	Non-Partisan Local Office	CITY COUNCIL - AT LARGE	Townwide	CENTRAL FALLS
LAMMIS J VARGAS	Democrat	COUNCIL	WAR 01	CRANSTON
DONALD J ROACH	Republican	COUNCIL - CITY WIDE	Townwide	CRANSTON
WILDA GUTIERREZ	Democrat	DEMOCRAT WARD COMMITTEE	WAR 01	CRANSTON

Tomás Ávila   Rev 3.1   July 1, 2020

314

Candidates in Upcoming Elections 09/08/2020 STATEWIDE PRIMARY
Source: https://vote.sos.ri.gov/Candidates/CandidateSearch?CityTown=00027lection=17018

Name	Party	Office	Ward	City
PAOLA N FERNANDEZ	Democrat	DEMOCRAT WARD COMMITTEE	WAR 01	CRANSTON
ANIECE GERMAIN	Democrat	COUNCIL	WAR 02	CRANSTON
NORLY GERMAIN	Democrat	DEMOCRAT WARD COMMITTEE	WAR 02	CRANSTON
ELIZABETH FUERTE	Non-Partisan Local Office	NON PARTISAN COUNCIL AT LARGE	Townwide	NEWPORT
ANGELA McCALLA	Democrat	DEMOCRAT CITY COMMITTEE	WAR 01	NEWPORT
NICOLE M VAZQUEZ	Democrat	DEMOCRAT CITY COMMITTEE	WAR 02	NEWPORT
CRISOLITA D FIGUEIREDO	Democrat	COUNCIL	WAR 01	PAWTUCKET
ALEXIS C SCHUETTE	Democrat	COUNCIL	WAR 04	PAWTUCKET
JANIE LEE SEGUI RODRIGUEZ	Democrat	COUNCIL	WAR 05	PAWTUCKET
AMA MENSAH AMPONSAH	Democrat	COUNCIL	WAR 05	PAWTUCKET
ELENA VASQUEZ	Democrat	COUNCIL-AT-LARGE		PAWTUCKET
TARSHIRE BATTLE	Democrat	COUNCIL-AT-LARGE		PAWTUCKET
MELISSA L DAROSA	Democrat	COUNCIL-AT-LARGE		PAWTUCKET
AGI F GAI-KAH	Democrat	COUNCIL-AT-LARGE		PAWTUCKET
ROBERTO H MORENO	Democrat	SCHOOL COMMITTEE	Townwide	PAWTUCKET
STEPHEN O LARBI	Democrat	SCHOOL COMMITTEE	Townwide	PAWTUCKET
STELLA CARRERA	Democrat	WARD COMMITTEE	WAR 04	PAWTUCKET
JUAN CARLOS PAYERO	Democrat	SCHOOL COMMITTEE	Townwide	PORTSMOUTH
SUZANNA L ALBA	Democrat	DEMOCRAT TOWN COMMITTEE	Townwide	SMITHFIELD
ANGEL V GARCIA	Democrat	DEMOCRAT WARD COMMITTEE	WAR 02	WARWICK
ZACHARY A COLON	Democrat	COUNCIL	WAR 09	WARWICK
LUIS R COLON JR	Democrat	DEMOCRAT TOWN COMMITTEE	CPR 3810	WEST WARWICK
VALERIE GONZALEZ	Non-Partisan Local Office	NON-PARTISAN CITY COUNCIL	Townwide	WOONSOCKET
DENISE D SIERRA	Non-Partisan Local Office	NON-PARTISAN CITY COUNCIL	Townwide	WOONSOCKET
CHARMAINE WEBSTER	Democrat	CITY COMMITTEE DEMOCRAT	Townwide	WOONSOCKET

Tomás Ávila   Rev 3.1   July 1, 2020

Representative Anastasia P. Williams, a Providence Democrat COURTESY OF REPRESENTATIVE ANASTASIA P. WILLIAMS

David Morales, Democratic candidate for state House of Representatives District 7 in Providence COURTESY OF DAVID MORALES

The Rev. Mahlon Van Horne, of Newport, who was the first Black person elected to the Rhode Island General Assembly. COURTESY OF KEITH STOKES

LATINO LEADERSHIP 2020: HONORING OUR PAST, TRANSFORMING OUR PRESENT & LEADING OUR FUTURE

A SERIES OF PRESENTATIONS ABOUT LATINO LEADERSHIP EVOLUTION

TOMÁS ÁVILA

GROWING INTO POWER IN RI

- Although present in the state since the 1980s, Rhode Island Latinos erupted into the consciousness of the region in the late 1990s with two critical facts. The first is that the growth of the Latino population in the state had been explosive. Since 1990, Latinos quadrupled their share of the population, and today, with 90,820 persons, they account for 8.7 percent of the total population and for 48 percent of the racial ethnic minority population of the state. Without the influx of Latinos, Rhode Island would have experienced negative population growth in the 1990s. In Providence and Central Falls, Latinos account for a significant percent of the populations of those cities, 30 percent and 47.6 percent, respectively. In those cities, the presence of Latinos can no longer be ignored.

GROWING INTO POWER IN RI

- 2000-2020. Latino leadership successful transformational leadership evolution:
- Rise to electoral success the swiftness of which was unparalleled in New England. (Latinos in New England)
- The way Latinos in Rhode Island have addressed the great diversity of its population in terms of national groups and immigration has been an important component of their political success.
- The strategies they devised in response to the social and political environment that greeted them.

Source: Latinos in New England: Growing into Power in Rhode Island, Miren Uriar, Chapter 5, pp 125-147

WHERE DO WE GO FROM HERE WITHIN THE NEXT 20 YEARS

- TWENTY YEARS AFTER "GROWING INTO POWER IN RHODE ISLAND" WE ARE CONFRONTED WITH THE CORONA VIRUS COVID-19 THAT DISPROPORTIONATELY HAS AFFECTED OUR COMMUNITY; AND THROWN INTO RELIEF THE STARK INEQUALITIES THAT CONTINUE TO AFFECT US DESPITE THE ADVANCEMENT ACHIEVED 2000-2020.
- PAST-PRESENT-FUTURE: HONORING OUR PAST, TRANSFORMING OUR PRESENT AND LEADING OUR FUTURE.
- WHERE DO WE GO FROM HERE WITHIN THE NEXT 20 YEARS: LATINO LEADERSHIP 2020.

LATINO LEADERSHIP 2040

- UNIFY, LEAD CHANGE IN EDUCATION, FINANCIAL EMPOWERMENT, IMAGE OF HISPANICS
- TURNING OPEN DOORS INTO A PLATFORM FOR EVERYONE ELSE ALONG US.
- MAKING SURE OUR STORIES ARE BEING TOLD, AND EDUCATING SOCIETY THAT HISPANIC STORIES ARE AMERICAN STORIES,"
- EVOLVING LATINO POLITICAL POWER INTO AMERICAN POLITICS.
- LEVERAGE THE U.S. DEMOGRAPHIC SHIFT EVOLVING IN FRONT OF US.

LATINO LEADERSHIP HISTORY

- JUNE 8, 2020
  - SECRETARY OF STATE NELLIE GORBEA
  - DR. PABLO RODRIGUEZ, MD
  - ALIDO BALDERA
  - TOMÁS ÁVILA

LATINO LEADERSHIP PARADIGM

- **JUNE 10 2020**
  - **JONATHON ACOSTA**
  - **TOMÁS ÁVILA**

LATINO LEADERSHIP THE COMMITMENT & SUPPORT OF JOURNALISTS

- **JUNE 17, 2020**
  - **M. CHARLES BAKST**
  - **ED FITZPATRICK**
  - **IAN DONNIS**
  - **SCOTT MCKAY**
  - **DR. PABLO RODRIGUEZ**
  - **TOMÁS ÁVILA**

LATINO LEADERSHIP GROWING INTO POWER

- **JUNE 22 2020**
  - **ANGEL TAVERAS**
  - **JUAN PICHARDO**
  - **TOMÁS ÁVILA**

LATINO LEADERSHIP GROWING INTO POWER

- **JUNE 29 2020**
  - VICTOR CAPELLA
  - TBD
  - TOMÁS ÁVILA

A NEW LATINO LEADERSHIP PARADIGM

- **PUBLISH JUNE 8 2000**
  - TOMAS ALBERTO AVILA
  - PROVIDENCE JOURNAL
  - TOMÁS ÁVILA

THANK YOU VERY MUCH & LOOK FORWARD TO JOINING US ON FACEBOOK LIVE

MILENIO LATINO INSTITUTE, INC.

TAVILA@MILENIOLATINOINSTITUTE.ORG

About Tomás Alberto Ávila

Tomás Ávila is a bilingual/bicultural, professional and community servant, with extensive experience in economic development, capacity building and Civic Engagement. He possesses strong organizational development, strategic planning/implementation, and demonstrated commitment to successful community building.

He spent over 40 years in the corporate, private, nonprofit and government sectors; most recently as Commissioner and Chairman of the City of Providence Board of Canvassers, appointed by Mayor Angel Taveras, becoming the first Latino Chairman in the city's 378 years history.

He was appointed to the City Government Equity Task Force by Mayor David N. Cicilline charged to review the City's affirmative action policy, minority contracting procedures, equal opportunity compliance, and other related issues, playing a significant role in the research, analysis and restructuring of the City's First Source Ordinance.

As a political activist, strategist, and consultant, he's been recognized as a political power broker and key player in the empowerment of the Latino/Hispanic community and involved in the election of many elected officials throughout Rhode Island and Northeast United States.

He is a founding member and past President of the Rhode Island Latino Political Action Committee (RILPAC), a nonpartisan organization that works "to influence the political process in the state of Rhode Island," to improve the quality of life in the Latino and urban communities. Cofounder of the New York Latina PAC, Delaware Latino PAC, New York Garifuna PAC. A founding member of the Rhode Island Redistricting Coalition (2000-2004), responsible for developing clear, legally defensible standards that were written into the enabling legislation and developed a highly public process for the 2002 redistricting of the Rhode Island political districts.

Ávila was appointed by Secretary of State Edward Inman to serve in the Commission to Study Rhode Island Election Procedures, that successfully prepared the state of Rhode Island for the Help America Vote Act (HAVA) of 2002, and most recently appointed by the Speaker of the Rhode Island House of Representatives Gordon Fox to serve in the Commission to study Rhode Island Election Process (2013).

He served the Governor's Commission on Hispanic Affairs as Policy Analyst with the responsibilities of identifying and tracking of legislative issues that impact the Latino community and was appointed by Mayor David Cicilline to the Mayor's City Government Equity Task Force charged to review the City's affirmative action policy, minority contracting procedures, equal opportunity compliance, and other related issues. He also served as executive director of Progreso Latino, in Central Falls, Deputy Director and Policy Analyst at the Center for Hispanic Policy & Advocacy (CHisPA), President of the Rhode Island Political Action Committee (RILPAC).

He is the founder and president of the Milenio Latino Institute, *a* tax-exempt, non-profit, non-partisan public policy analysis organization chartered in 2008 with the purpose to: conduct basic research aimed at improving the level of political and economic participation in Latino and other underrepresented communities.

Ávila is the editor of two books documenting the rise of Latino political power in Rhode Island; A Decade of Latino Political Empowerment (2006), Mayor Angel Taveras, An Administration of Political Will (2011), and Rhode Island Black & Brown Ethnic Succession: 1984 – 1994, 2012

Proactive in bringing business development services to the growing Latino community in the region; Avila assisted in meeting training and participation goals for entrepreneurs and existing businesses;

managed and facilitated the Primer Paso FastTrac feasibility planning program, that provided assistance the skills necessary to successfully establish a business; and has been vital in the growth of Latino-owned business across Rhode Island. For his guidance and knowledge, he was awarded the 2007 State Star Award by the Association of Small Business Development Centers (ASBDC) annually awarded to outstanding SBDC employees who are exemplary performers, make significant contributions to their state or region and show a strong commitment to small business.

He is a graduate of Leadership Rhode Island Upsilon class of 2000, AFL-CIO Leadership for a Future Class of 2000, the Pew Foundation Providence Civic Entrepreneurship Initiative class of 1998, the RISBDC Entrepreneurship Training Program (ETP) class of 1997. He's been involved with many community organizations, such as Quisqueya in Action, NCCJ, Common Cause Rhode Island, Adopt A Doctor, the Rhode Island Latino Political Action Committee, the Democracy Compact, the Southside/Broad Street, North End Housing Development Corporation, Board, Providence Civic Entrepreneur Initiative, CHisPA, Progreso Latino, to name a few.

During the 2020 John H. Chafee Lifetime Service Award presented to Ávila, by the United Way of Rhode Island, according to Mr. Zechariah Chaffee, a role that certainly would have appealed to his late father, US senator John H. Chafee, his many years, engaged in hands-on action in the election victories of Latino political candidates. and Ávila's understanding that "the path to power goes through the ballot box to ensure that the path is open to his people," and in recognition of his commitment to free and fair elections, former Providence Mayor Angel Taveras, appointed him a commissioner on and chairman of the Providence Board of canvassers, the first Latino to lead the board in the city's 378-year history. Tomas is a force for good in our state."

He pitched in the wellbeing of Latinos, as executive director of Progreso Latino, the largest and oldest Latino human services state nonprofit responsible for managing and implementing policies and programs that lead to the success of the agency's diverse clientele and stakeholders located in Central Falls, deputy director and Policy

Analyst at the Center for Hispanic policy and advocacy (CHisPA), responsible of identifying and tracking legislative issues that impact the Latino and minority communities. in Providence, Policy Analyst at the Governor's Advisory Commission on Hispanic Affairs, and cofounder and president of the Rhode Island Latino Political Action Committee (RILPAC), among many other positions.

Ávila played a key role in the 2002 redistricting as a member of both the Rhode Island Latino Political Action Committee, the Common Cause board, host of the founding meeting of the Fair Redistricting, responsible of developing clear, legally defensible standards those were written into the enabling legislation, developed a highly public process for 2002 redistricting, and successfully advocated to keep Providence districts entirely within the city to avoid diluting minority districts, and the Latino Voting Right Project, that promoted the participation of the Latino community in the 2002 redistricting process critical to determining the nature of Latino political representation at the Congressional, state and local levels of government for the next decade.

Ávila has been the recipient of multiple awards for his volunteer services such as: Center for Hispanic Policy & Advocacy (CHisPA) Outstanding Leadership (2002), Quisqueya In Action Outstanding Latino Professional (2003), Delaware PAC, Leadership Award (2003), Imagen Hispana Magazine Influential Hispanic of New England (2004), John Hope Settlement House Outstanding Community Leader (2004), ASBDC State Star Award (2007), Cesar Chavez Exceptional Leadership Award (2011), Quetzal Award (2013), NAACP Thurgood Marshall diversity empowerment Award (2014), HUDO Excellence in Civic Engagement Award (2015), RILPBN Exceptional Leadership in growth and development of Future Leaders (2015), Mujeres Emprendedoras Leadership Award (2015), Dominican Independence and Heritage Award (2016), RIPLA Outstanding Community Involvement Award (2016), Honduras General Consulate in New York, Outstanding Community Leadership Award (2016), Telemundo Providence Héroe de La Humanidad Award (2016), The Rhode Island Professional Latino Association (RIPLA) spotlight, (2020), Grand Marshal, The Dominican Festival and Parade of Rhode Island, in recognition of his dedication as a community servant, his commitment to economic development on all levels and helping to empower the :Latino community(2017), United Way of Rhode Island, John H. Chafee Lifetime Service Award (2020).

Published: Providence Journal, Providence American, Providence Business News, Pawtucket Times, Providence En Español, Siglo 21, Latino Express, Acontecer Latinot, Boston Globe.

www.ingramcontent.com/pod-product-compliance
Lightning Source LLC
Chambersburg PA
CBHW071956220426
43662CB00009B/1158